THE LIGHT OF WISDOM

Life and Works of Swami Pranvananda Saraswati

The 12th century AD Mahadev Temple near Patne.

THE LIGHT OF WISDOM
Life and Works of
Swami Pranvananda Saraswati

Brig. G.D. Bakshi, SM, VSM

SHARADA

Sharada Publishing House
Delhi-110 035
2003

First Published : 2003

ISBN : 81-85616-98-1

Published by :
SHARADA PUBLISHING HOUSE
(Publishers on India's Past and Present)
40, Anand Nagar, Inder Lok,
Delhi-110035
Ph. : 23657538

Laser Typesetting by :
Creative Graphics
Ph. 22195643

Printed at :
Santosh Offset, Delhi-110035

Dedicated to the sacred memory
of our Guru,
SWAMI PRANVANANDA SARASWATI
an engineer and a
sage par excellence.
He was a revivalist and
exemplar. His deep concern for
ecology was the liet motif
of that sacred life.
In more ways than one
he was an Atharvan,
a torch bearer of the
sacred tradition of
this most ancient civilisation

इतना दे गुरु

इतना दे गुरु
कि देने से कम न हो
इतना दे गुरु
कि देने से थम न हो
इतना दे गुरु कि
हम देते ही रहें
इतना दे गुरु
कि हम देते न थकें
इतना दे गुरु
कि सरस्वती का वास हो
इतना दे गुरु
कि उल्लास ही उल्लास हो
इतना दे गुरु
कि निहाल कर दे मुझे
इतना दे गुरु
कि बेमिसाल कर दे मुझे
इतना दे गुरु
कि तू गुरु महान है
इतना दे गुरु
कि तू मेरा भगवान है।

प्रभात शोभा लिडर

CONTENTS

या देवी सर्वभूतेषु शक्तिरूपेण संस्थिता ।
नमस्तस्यै नमस्तस्यै नमस्तस्यै नमो नमः ।।

या देवी सर्वभूतेषु विष्णूमायेति शद्बिता ।
नमस्तस्यै नमस्तस्यै नमस्तस्यै नमो नमः ।।

SWAMIJI AND THE MAHAMANDALESWAR

Preface

This is a book about a remarkable being, about a sage who lived for many years in a dense forest in the Ajanta-Ellora tract, absorbed in deep meditation. In the forest, he felt the peace that emanates from the plants. He experienced the tranquility that comes from the trees. Over the months and years this peace deepened and blossomed into euphoria. Extended episodes of euphoria led to experiences of intense ecstasy. He encountered the experiences of Soma- the sunlit tracts of a river of happiness that tinkles in the depths of our consciousness. The Vedas speak of the "Ritasyadharas" or the "Madhudharas"- the streams of Truth and Honey that descend on us from the great silence of the forest to make us joyful. He had experienced the ecological ecstasy of those streams of sunlit joy. He had tasted Soma. In his deep meditations he had touched that core of truth, aliveness and ecstasy that forms the basis of our immortal selves.

The Atharva Veda, the most mystic of all the Vedas, records a remarkable dialogue. The sage Shaunaka asked the great Sage Angira

"Lord, which is that Science having known which all else is known?"

"That", replied the sage Angira "is the Science of Brahman. Having known that all else is known".

The modern sage of Patne, Swami Pranvananda Saraswati was such a sage. He was an Atharvan. He was a knower of Brahman, the one having known which all else is known. He was an exemplar and a revivalist of our sacred traditions. He did not preach sermons. He taught us by his silence and his shining example. His actions spoke far louder than his words. He taught us to love the plants and trees. He exhorted us to cultivate an ecological outlook. Everything in the Universe, he said, is conscious. There is no such thing as "Jada" or "Chetan" as sentient or insentient, as "living" and "non-living". We have a kinship with the stars, comets and galaxies, with the rocks and minerals, with the oceans and seas, with the birds, beasts and trees, with all these life forms in the universe. All these myriads of things that we see around us, arise from that infinite ocean of consciousness-energy- that Chit Shakti. To experience that ocean in our hearts we have to be silent and still. Only then can we hear the murmur of that eternal river of happiness that courses in the depths of our being; only then can we rise on the waves of an immortal ecstasy – the wave of bliss that arises in the "Hridyat Samudrat" the ocean of our hearts. To be fearless is to be free. To be free is to be joyful. The greatest fetter is the fetter of time that conditions us to our reality. We have to unlearn this reality before we evolve to the next through the gateway of ecstasy and the portals of heavenly peace. This is the saga of a remarkable life. This is the saga of a remarkable sage – the sage of Patne. One was blessed to bask in his aura of healing and happiness. One was blessed in deed to learn from him the art of deep meditation. It is an art and an outlook that mankind needs most urgently to tide over its looming crises and the impending ecological catastrophes. These have made the present industrial civilisation wholly unsustainable. What we need is a revolution in our outlook – from the material to the mystical; from the economic to the ecological, from ennui to ecstasy. All this, the sage said, will come from a paradigm shift from the Western Darwinian metaphor of a struggle for survival, where the weak perish and only the strong survive, to the infinitely more harmonious paradigm of the Atharvan seers of the mystical Atharva Veda. The Atharva Veda enunciates this paradigm in its quintessential Madhu Vidya- or the "Wisdom of Honey". "All things on this earth are beneficial to one another and to this earth. The earth in turn is beneficial to all its creatures". The contrast with the Darwinian metaphor of ceaseless struggle and competition could not be more marked. Here is an outlook of harmony, of symbiosis, of a network of communities and supportive relationships as opposed to a fierce struggle for survival.

Swami Pranvananda Saraswati taught us to live in harmony with nature; he taught us to leverage upon the peace that the plants exude; he taught us to be still and silent. He taught us the lost art of deep meditation and in the bargain we learnt to go beyond the stressors of linear time that forever speeds from the past, to the present and into a future that we do not know. Months of meditation caused us to transit from a linear to a cyclic mode of time. In the bargain the peace blossomed into bliss, the bliss into euphoria and euphoria culminated in supreme ecstasy. We learnt to be joyful and free.

His was a remarkable life, remarkable for its gift of ecstasy and understanding. He lived as an exemplar of the ancient traditions of this land. His life taught us those ancient values, not by sermons and discourses but by personal example. Modernisation is not mere Westernisation. He taught us the validity of the ancient Indian meditative cultures in this day and age. He chose as his action field and domain a forest stretch near Ellora that breathed history. He built his retreat in the Forest stretches between the ancient Ajanta and Ellora caves – right beneath the Pitanglya Vihara of the Buddhist monks of the 2nd century before Christ. This tract was also the seat of the renowned Bhaskaracharya – the great Indian Mathematical genius who discovered the zero. It was in this historic forest region that he sat down to meditate, to transcend the barriers of space and time and link us with that ancient past of a deeply contemplative civilization. The Rajpath from the ancient city of Ujjaini to Prathisthan (Paithan) passed through this forest tract. At every one days march, there were Buddhist Chaityas and Viharas located along this route to inner peace and external plentitude. A rich and vibrant culture flourished here. He showed us the riches of our own heritage even as he showed us a new future that embraces all life forms, not just on this planet but everywhere in the vast reaches of inter stellar space. That Consciousness – Energy is the basal material of this cosmos. It is the same everywhere. All that we see and do not see, is fashioned from its joy. Pranvananda's life and experiences were remarkable in as much as they gave us a *Vedic perspective to the ancient phenomena of the Kundalini.*

Today, many years after he has gone, we invoke again that joyfulness and ecstasy that he taught us to experience in our own beings. That Chitshakti is beyond space and time. It is the cause of everything that we see in the universe. To know that is to know Brahman. To know that is to know the truth. That is the depth ecology of consciousness. He who has experienced it, will be known by the sparkle of a supreme ecstasy in his eyes and the tears of joy that bathe his being in beatitude.

G. D. Bakshi

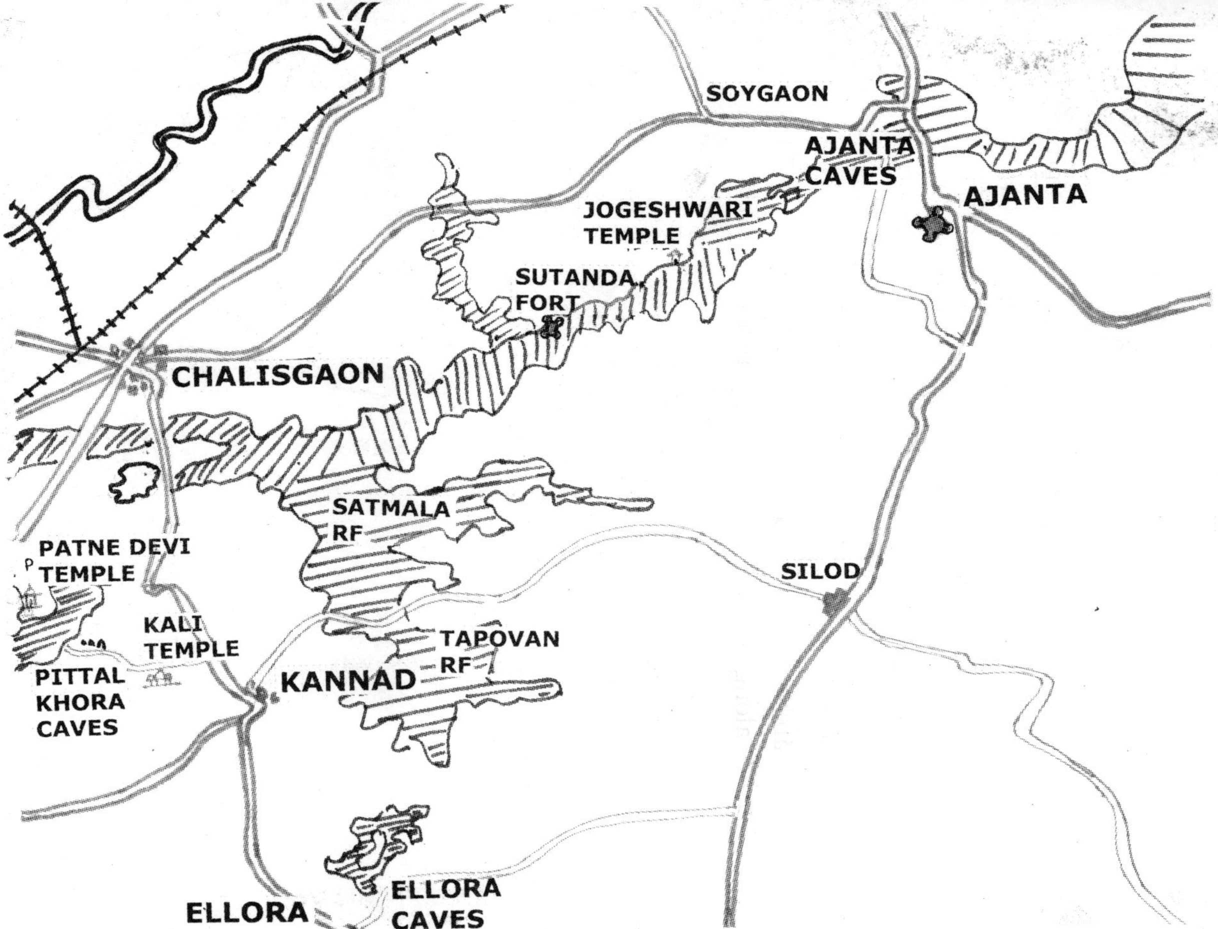

Map of Chalisgaon and surrounding cave complexes.

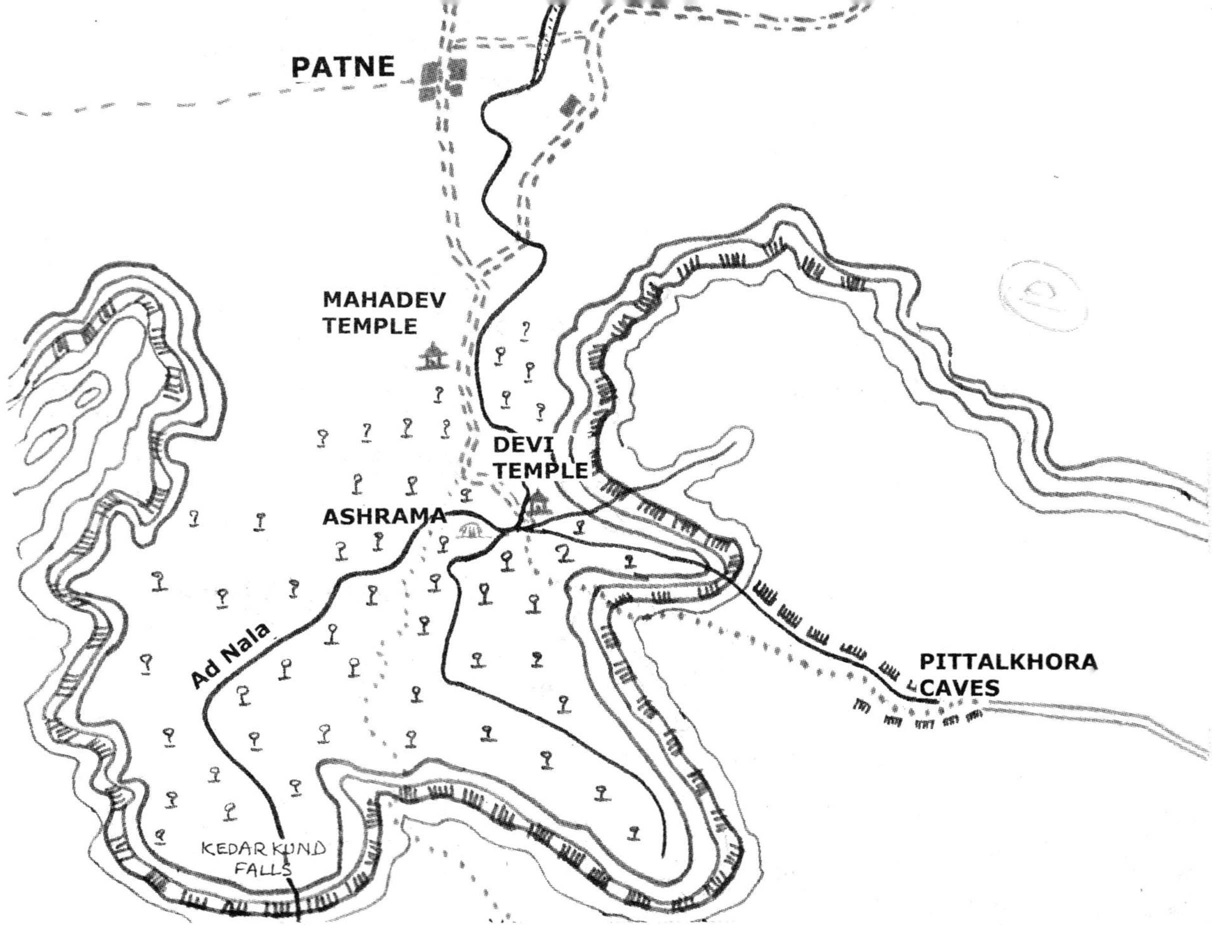

The Basalt cliffs that loom above the Patne Devi Temple.

"In a forest, in a cave, near a stream
In such a place the monks should dwell "

BOOK ONE
OF A SAGE AND A SHRINE

Not in the cities
But in the forests
are the fountain heads
of civilisation
In the sylvan hermitages
of the sages
the disciples build
a kinship with
the plants and trees
the rivers and mountains
all these, for ages.

(Rig. Veda 8.6.23)

Deepa Stambhas

1

A New Sage in an Ancient Shrine

The Shrine

On the main rail trunk route to the Indian metropolis of *Mumbai,* lies the milk-producing town of Chalisgaon. It used to be a small mofussil town but over the years, it has grown and prospered considerably. Some 10 Kilometers from this town, nestling at the foot of the Syhadri hill ranges, lies the village of Patne. Patne is a small village. Some years back, it was the last stop on the state bus service in this area. The dense forest tracts start just a little distance away from this village.

Hardly a Kilometer from this village, lie the ancient Mahadeva Temples. These were built by the Yadava dynasty in the 12th century AD and have some exquisite sculptures. Overlooking them are the Shringar Chawdi caves-reputedly the abode of the mythical Pandavas when they were hiding. If you proceed further into the forest, you suddenly cross a deep nala, and then step into a clearing in the forest. Here, right at the foot of the Syhadri ranges, lies the ancient Devi temple of Patne.

It is a breath-taking locale. The Syhadri hills rise abruptly in the form of sheer basalt cliffs over 1000 feet high. The cliffs form a huge amphitheater of gaunt rocks that form a semi circle some 8 to 10 kilometers in width. The floor of this natural amphitheatre is covered with dense forest. This forest teems with snakes, scorpions, peacocks, wild boar and deer. Some years back, it also had the occasional Cheetah and the dreaded Tiger. The Patne Devi Temple lies at the entrance of this forested amphitheatre.

Patne was once a flourishing town. The present village of that name bears no resemblance to the bygone glory of that ancient town-ship. When the ancient Satvahanas were in power (from the second century BC to the second century AD), Patne was a flourishing town that lay astride the national highway or "Rajapatha" that linked Ujjain with the major southern city of Prathisthan or Paithan.

This route passed via the famous caves of Ellora. (Patne incidentally is located just 23 miles as the crow flies from Ellora caves and 50 miles from the fabled Ajanta caves). The Patne Devi temple was built in the 12th century AD by the Yadava kings of Devagiri (Daultabad). A rock edict in the temple records the grant given by the ruler for the construction of this temple .It is made from Basalt rock.

A huge statue of the Mahishasur Mardini – the Goddess Durga, adorns the Garbha Griha of the temple. Its most imposing feature however is the two huge Deepa Stambhas that guard its entrance. These 60-feet high pillars were once used to light huge mashals that lit up the center of what once must have been a bustling market place. Today there is only the deep and eloquent silence of the forest. . The wild growth of shrubs and trees speaks of the ravages of time that have destroyed the once flourishing city of Patne.

The Pitangalya Vihara (Pittal Khora Caves)

From the Devi temple a foot track ascends steeply into the Sayadhri ranges. After climbing over 1500 feet, one

Patne Devi Temple—The Deepa Stambhas

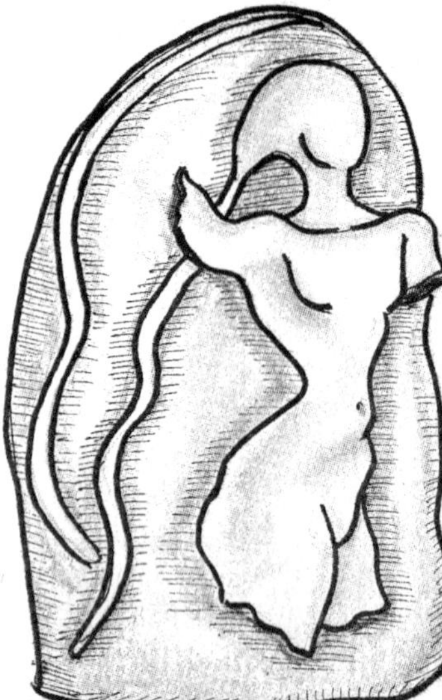

Statues Dug Up in the Vicinity of the Patne Devi Temple

Statue of the Ganga Ellora Caves

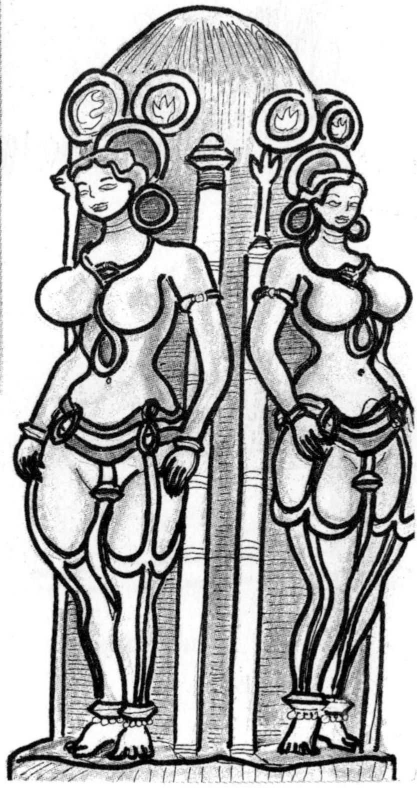

Yakshis (Statue in Patne Temple Courtyard)

The Pitangalya Vihar-Chaitya Caves

Patangala Vihar—Cave Entrance (Pittal Khora)

reaches the historic Buddhist caves of Pitangalya or Pittalkhora.The Satavahana rulers built these in the 2nd century BC. These are Chaitya caves – gaunt, imposing and majestic structures cut into the sheer rock faces. The ravages of time have left little trace of the Buddhist paintings and frescoes that once adorned these Chaitya walls. A fabulous collection of jewels was discovered in one of the stupas in this cave complex. A stream still flows through the center of these eleven caves. The setting is so incredibly peaceful and serene, it brings to mind the Upnashadic verse which says, " In a forest, near a stream, in a cave. In such a place the monks should dwell". John Wilson, who gave a detailed description of the Chaitya cave (cave 3) and the adjoining viharas, ,discovered these rock cut caves in 1863. A flourishing community of saffron clad monks once inhabited these rock cubicles and prayed and meditated in the silence of this imposing Chaitya. Their monastery lay along the ancient caravan route that ascended from Paithan –to-Ellora- on to Patne and then via these caves on to Ujjaini. From Patne this caravan route ascended steeply up the near precipitous cliffs of the Indyahadri hills. Today, over 2000 years later, the same gaunt, Basalt cliffs stand straight and tall. The water of the Monsoons of two millenniums has flown down these sheer rock faces and left its marks. But the Buddhist monks and the traders and the bejewelled temple dancers have all gone forever.

At the entrance of the Devi temple and in its courtyards are piled some sculptures and statues that were dug up in the vicinity of the Patne Devi temple- exquisite works of the Pallava sculptors-tall dwarpalas, the guardians of heaven and beautiful and voluptuous yakshis with ornate hairdos, earrings and ornaments. The umistakable impress of the Gandhara School of art is clearly discernible in these exquisitely sculptured statues. Looking at them, one is transported into an ancient era when Buddhism was at its peak. Saffron clad monks and bare breasted courtesans with elaborate hairdos and coiffeurs studded with precious stones, beads and gems roamed about this land. It is said that in those ancient times, there was a Buddhist Vihara or monastery at every 30-35 kms or one day's march. Thus the famous Buddhist caves of Ajanta, Ellora and Pittalkhora, lie in a large triangle – all more or less within a day's march of one another.

From the Vihara and Chaitya caves of Pittalkhora, which lie high in the Indyahadri cliffs above the Patne temple- you can see a long flight of stone steps leading right to the very top of these cliffs. It is said that from this elevated perch, the ancient Indian mathematician Bhasakaracharya used to make his astronomical observations.

- Bhaskaracharya Bhaskaracharya was a great sage and mathematical genius who flourished in the 12th century A.D. In 1130 A.D Bhaskaracharya had written a mathematical treatise called "Siddhant Shiromani". This magnum opus was in four parts. Part one was called "Leelawati". It was named after the beautiful daughter of Bhaskaracharya and dealt with Arithmetic, Algebra and Geometry. In Book II he dealt at length with Algebra (particularly Kuttavaya Prakruti and Chandrawala Paditi). Book III dealt with Arithmetic, Astrology and Palmistry (Khugol Shastra). Book IV dealt with Palmistry and Astrology.

In addition Bhaskaracharya wrote a score of other mathematical treatises (to include Savtovahdra Yantra, Vaishishta Tulya etc.). All his works are in Sanskrit, and in the form of exquisite poetry. Bhaskracharya, it is said discovered the zero. That ranks as a monumental intellectual feat of the Indian civilization. James Taylor translated his works into English in 1816. In 1817 Col. Brook translated his works on Algebra into English and this ancient mathematician was made known to the world. Bhaskaracharya was a Shandilya Brahmin by Gotra, and his native place is said to be at Vijjaylavid. A commentary on his book Lilawati (called Munishavara) has a shloka (stanza) which explains that Vijjayelavid was in Patne. It is said that Bhaskaracharya's Ashrama was located just next to the Patne Devi Temple. For his astronomical observations, Bhaskaracharya used to climb up the cliffs of the Indyahadri hills that loomed above the ancient city of Patne. The sage loved his daughter Leelavati. Legend has it that she was an intelligent and highly accomplished maiden. Today, just a few hundred meters from the Patne Devi Temple is a forest rest house. It has a unique tree trunk architecture that supports its roof. The rest house is most appropriately named – Leelavati.

Today the state transport buses come right up till the temple. Rest houses and rooms and a thriving shopping complex have come up where the pilgrims pick up their coconuts and joss sticks. Wayside eateries provide cheap meals for the peasants and pilgrims. The place fairly bustles with activity. The Reserved Forest has been declared a protected wild life sanctuary-an "Abhay Aranya".

Some 40 years back, in the 1960s it used to be absolutely deserted. Very few people dared to venture outside the Patne village after sunset. The forest teemed with reptiles and predators. The temple priest of Patne used to come well after sunrise, perform his prayers and leave nervously by midday. Except for the annual fair, he rarely waited till the evening. The Lad Vanjara tribals inhabited the villages of the forest. They were a fierce and quarrelsome lot. The place exuded history. But its ancient glory was buried deep under the earth. The teeming forest had overgrown and overlaid the last vistages of that once glorious and thriving civilisation. Its pulsating and sophisticated culture, its city states and learned assemblies, its beautiful and accomplished courtesans and wealthy merchants and its caravans laden with exotic goods, were all a vanished dream- overlaid by Hawthorn bushes and wild creepers.

Patne however remained a place of pilgrimage. It was a powerful spiritual center – a beacon that often attracted spiritual aspirants and monks. It was a "Tapovana", a forest of sages which was deemed most conducive for deep meditation. The famous sage Bhaskaracharya had done his deep meditation here and composed his poetical treatises on mathematics. Before him, the Buddhist monks had chanted their sonorous prayers in the chaityas and engaged in deep meditation in the rock-cut caves and viharas. The tinkling music of the forest streams had lulled them to sleep and the great white stars had shone impassively upon these gaunt basalt cliffs and forest canopies of the Tapovana of Patne .

In the late sixties and early seventies, however, it was a dangerous place. Very few sages in recent memory had been able to live in Patne in peace and tranquility. The fierce deity of the temple, it was rumoured, did not tolerate any but the purest ascetics. Early in the 1960s, it is said, an ascetic had come to the Patne Devi temple. He was thrilled by the deep spiritual ambience of the place and the eloquent silence of the forest. He decided to stay on in the temple to carry out his sadhana and deep meditation. He stayed for many months. One night however a group of Lad Banjara tribals reached the temple. They were in a totally drunken state. They caught hold of the ascetic. They were certain that fabulous treasures and jewels were stashed away somewhere in this historic temple or its environs. They were also sure that the ascetic knew where. Their surmise of hidden treasures was not entirely baseless. Many years later a large collection of precious stones and jewels was discovered from the caves nearby. The ascetic however was horrified and pleaded total ignorance. The drunk tribals beat him black and blue. They tortured the poor man *horribly* till dawn and then left him for dead. His screams echoed ineffectually in the forest gloom. The next morning the poor soul dragged himself painfully to the Patne village. He caught the first bullock cart that came his way and fled the scene. No one ever dared to spend a night in the Devi temple after that. It was an ancient monument and hundreds of bats had made it their permanent abode.

On the 12th of September 1968, a young Sanyasi came to Chalisgaon town. He looked every inch a Buddhist monk. A shaved pate, large expressive eyes, a radiant visage, broad shoulders and long arms that came to his knees. He wore a seamless, single-piece saffron robe dyed with natural herbal colours. A very small bundle contained all his belongings. (These, we learnt later were a painting of the Goddess Kali, and a copy of the Geeta)

He spoke Marathi only haltingly. From his speech he appeared to be from Bengal. The people in the bustling market place looked at him quizzically. He had a letter of introduction for one Sheokar Shastri, a local scholar and pious man. No one knew where this sanyasi had come from or who he was. Looks of intense surprise greeted him everywhere. Silently, people directed him to the Shastri's house and he was profuse in his gratitude. What struck every one was the warbling quality of his voice.

Sheokar Shastri was astounded to receive this visitor. He read through the letter of introduction from one of his acquaintances in the Saptashringgad Shrine high up in the Maharashtrian plateau. The letter beseeched him to help this young Swami go to the Patne Devi Temple . He intended to carry out his sadhna there. The Shastri was horrified. Patne Devi? Did he know that it was in the heart of a dangerous forest? There were snakes, scorpions, panthers and tigers there besides some rather temperamental tribals.

The young Swami nodded simply. Yes –he wanted to

go there. The Shastri looked at him pityingly. The Swami appeared so young and vulnerable. He appeared to be in his twenties. He shook his head doubtfully. Then he called his good friend Badri Kaka over. Badri Kaka was a very pious businessman of Chalisgaon. He was a saintly figure with a flowing white beard that gave him the look of a Biblical sage. The Shastri explained the situation to him. Badri Kaka was astounded. Perhaps the Swami had been wrongly informed. He told him the fate of the previous ascetic who had tried to stay at the Devi temple in Patne. Even leading spiritual lights of that age like Swami Muktananda, himself a man of deep meditation and spiritual accomplishment, had found it difficult to stay in Patne Devi for long. The young Sanyasi however remained adamant and beseeched them to take him to his destination- otherwise he would have to walk the distance alone. Badri Kaka then had his bullock cart readied. The Shastri and he accompanied the young Swami. The monsoons had gotten over and the first chill of winter was in the air. The sunshine was limpid and the skies washed cerulean Blue. The rich scent of hay came from the fields. The aroma of musk and spices assailed their nostrils as they wound their way through the crowded streets of the Bazaar. It was a long ride to Patne. The villagers greeted the Shastri and Badri Kaka effusively. They were surprised to see a saffron clad Sanyasi with them. How young and innocent he looked- remarked some of the village women.

"He wanted to do what?" "Stay in the Devi temple for his sadhna?"

A murmur of horror spread through the small-assembled throng of villagers.

Kashinath Sonavane, a tribal farmer who owned some land on the outskirts of the village pushed his way through the throng surrounding the bullock cart.

He looked at the young swami. There was something in his mien that impressed him deeply. It is good to get the blessings of the sages. It helps in the ripening of the grain and keeps it from pests and the evil eye. He cleared his throat and offered the Swami the use of his hut in his fields.

The young Swami shook his head and declined politely. He had to go to the temple. It was essential for his Sadhna he explained in broken Marathi.

There was a chorus of protest from the villagers. After what had happened to the last ascetic, they were not keen for any further trouble. It did not help to get the police in to the affairs of the village.

Staying alone in the Devi Temple needed some courage. The womenfolk of the village, especially the pious old maids were most alarmed and sympathetic.

The young Sanyasi remained adamant. So, after lunch with the Sonavane household, the Bullock cart trundled out of the village and into the forest path. Some boys from the village accompanied it till the temple. On their way, a huge brown snake slithered across the track and disappeared in to the bushes. The men looked apprehensively at the Swami. He showed no trace of emotion. He just sat their silently lost in thought.

They reached the clearance in the forest and crossed the nala on foot. "There, this is the Devi temple". The Swami looked at it, most intently. He washed his hands and feet in the stream and then prostrated himself before the deity of the temple. He lay motionless like that for a long time. The boys brought in his pathetic bundle of belongings. Badri Kaka's wife had added some rice, lentils and potatoes. The villagers had added packets of salt and tea and one cooking utensil. The sun was driving its broad golden spokes through the lower branches of the wild tamarind trees. An awed hush fell over the forest.

Shastriji and Badri Kaka asked the sanyasi one last time. Was he sure he wanted to stay? He silently nodded his head in assent. They looked at one another uncertainly. It would be dark soon and they had to go. The Sanyasi asked them to leave him there. With sturdy common sense he bade them to hurry, as it would be getting dark soon. Sheokar Shastri and Babdri Kaka nodded silently and left. They crossed the stream and got into the bullock cart. Badri Kaka looked back for one last time. The young Sanyasi was standing in the temple courtyard watching them depart. He looked so young, vulnerable and innocent. Recalled Badri Kaka "I felt so sorry for him. I honestly thought we were seeing him for the last time."

The 12th century AD Mahadev Temple near Patne.

2

The Test of Lonliness

Was that the end of the Sage? Was that the last they heard of him? How did that unknown sage fare in the desolate temple? Did he survive his exile in the heart of the forest? Did he survive his tryst with the snakes and scorpions and the panthers, with the tigers and other wild beasts of the forest? Did he come to grief at the hands of some temperamental tribals or some fortune hunters seeking fabulous jewels and precious ornaments amidst those ruins?

No he did not.

He survived his ordeal very well in that ancient monument. How did he cope with the utter loneliness? He hardly had to "cope".He had come looking for it. Well before he arrived in that ancient shrine, his sadhna, his meditation had apparently reached a stage of profundity in which he now needed the utter stillness and silence. He needed the solitude of the deep forest to match the deep silence that was engulfing his being from within. For years, this unknown sage had prepared himself for this retreat in the forest. To cope with the loneliness he had a powerful tool-deep meditation. He would just close his eyes and sink into a comforting darkness within. He recalled later that it was like a tortoise entering his shell. He just slunk within to a realm of profound peace and stillness. It was warm, living and comforting presence within. He sank deep into his ownself, and the self knew no fear, simply because it did not recognise another. Many months before he came to Patne he had been lengthening the duration of his meditation spells. He could go on meditating for hours. His posture now had the stability and fixity of a rock. His breathing would cease altogether. He sank within, deep, deep within to a warm and cloistered space – where there was no fear- simply because there was no other. The self rested in the self. Even before coming to Patne he had reached the stage when prolonged spells of meditation filled him with a vague sense of suffused happiness and contentment – with: Sukha". This turned to a deep peace- a green peace of the forest when his consciousness seemed to merge with the sunlit ecstasy of the plants and trees and lose itself in the filigree of leaves and creepers. As his meditation deepened, it had a strange and palpable effect upon the ancient shrine and its surrounding forests. A palpable curtain of peace and quiet descended. It was so palpable that you could feel that deep block of peace like a physical presence. He continued to meditate for hours on end. Fear? Loneliness? Far from it. The territory and the inner landscape that he slipped into were one of utter peace and profundity. A deep current of happiness welled up in his being. Like a river of happiness he could feel his consciousness tinkling and singing. Slowly he felt transported into states of incredible ecstasy. His eyes would feel glued together. It took a great effort to prise them open. His posture had become firm and immovable like a rock. It appeared as if he had become just another one of those exquisitely sculpted statues of the ancient shrine. Those deep tracts of happiness and ecstasy! So deep and thrilling was the experience that the coming of another human being was like a noisy intrusion into the personal oasis of his peace and happiness. When he heard the sounds of some villagers coming (they spoke loudly from afar to give themselves courage and frighten off any lurking beasts), very often he would get up and slink into the forest and wait for them to leave. Normal conversation with humans had become a painful digression from the joy of his meditations.

His meditations deepened with the months. He lost all sense of his body. He also lost all count of time. Life became a cyclic progression of daybreak dawn, noon and dusk. At night the deep, deep silence of the forest did not hold any dread for him. It was a familiar soothing, silken and comforting, darkness, and a primeval back to the womb experience of entering a cloistered space of joy and deep silence. He would meditate mostly at night now. For eight to ten hours at night he would sit in deep meditation undisturbed by man or beast. The deep primeval silence of the forest was a perfect backdrop for his deep dives into the depth of his consciousness. Through the window of his own limited awareness, he would gradually slip into the great ocean of a cosmic consciousness where *he experienced his deep connectivity with all living things. In the experience of this deep connectivity of all life forms is a source of great joy and serenity.* Only those who have experienced it can tell you of this incredible joy. The Vedic seers called this experience of depth ecology- the experience of the "Madhu Vidya" or the Honey wisdom. It was, in essence, the sweetness of this earth. The Atharva Veda says: The earth is Madhu (honey – beneficial) to all its creatures. All creatures are Honey to this earth. In the experience of this honey wisdom is a feeling of great ecstasy. That was the ancient wisdom of the Atharvan rishis- the sages who had composed the Atharva Veda. Unknown to the village folk they had in their midst an Atharvan sage of the ancient forest civilisation. .

The Great Sage Atharvan and Angirasa

He often meditated at night. In the darkness at night, occasionally the hoop of a frightened ape would echo over the silence. Then stillness again. There would be the faint rustle of bushes as a predator came close and gazed at the ancient ruins. Occasionally you could hear the snarl of a cheetah or the deep-throated roar of a tiger. But in the depths of his meditations he heard nothing. He just heard the tinkling of the waves of a sunlit river of perennial happiness. He heard the waves of a cosmic ocean of bliss and supreme connectivity; a deep cosmic connectivity that exuded love, care and compassion. He became deeply aware of how everything in the cosmos is connected to every thing else in an ecstatic celebration of life. No beasts of the forest would attack such a sage. They would come close, stop suddenly in their tracks and gaze with awe at the strange aura of peace that exuded from the place. Sometimes the beast would standstill like that for a long time. Then it would slink away quietly.

The diamond brightness of the dawn was a miracle of beauty that occurred each day over the forest. In the mornings the sounds of bird song would awaken the sage from his deep, deep meditations. Loneliness? Exile? A tryst with fear and terror? The only emotion he knew was profound happiness and ecstasy. The experience of that honey – the sweetness of the "Madhu Vidya" of the Vedic seers. His meditations deepened with the months. One day in his meditation he beheld flashes of light like lightening in a summer sky. The light converged to a Blue point of ecstasy. Before his eyes, he beheld a glittering Blue pearl. It was an intense sky Blue dot. It was a fascinating vision – an unearthly sight. The Blue dot had a hypnotic effect. It fascinated the observer. You lost all count of time – you just gazed and gazed at that spectacle and it filled you with the peace of the inexpressible. Many months later came the experience of the exteriorisation of consciousness or the so called "out of the body "experience. He felt himself detached from his bodily frame and free to roam the cosmos as it were. It was a deeply moving experience that seemed to take away all fear of death.

What about his creature needs? He slept on a stone

slab in the small cubicle in the temple that was meant for the priest. Many, many years later people learnt that he had practiced for this life of austerity by sleeping on the floor of his family mansion. He had toughened himself for his days in exile from the world of men. He performed Yogic Asanas with great dexterity and skill. His physique was perfect and leonine, unusually broad shoulders tapered down to a slim waist, long arms that came till his knees almost- a body as perfect as some of the exquisitely sculpted statues in that ancient shrine.

Cooking his meals was a problem at first. From his aristocratic demeanour it was evident that he came from a rich and prosperous background. He had never worked with his hands. Lighting a fire for cooking his meals was therefore a great ordeal. He would gather the wood and twigs from the forest nearby. Then came the difficult chore of setting them alight. He would blow on them till his eyes smarted and watered profusely. He would prepare a few rotis or roast some potatoes or local tubers to keep body and soul together.

The villagers used to come rarely in those days. They came well after daybreak and always in groups. They were awed by the subtle but deeply palpable change in the aura of the shrine. The sage seemed to have ensouled it. A deep and profound feeling of peace seemed to radiate out from him and soak into the rocks and trees and shrubs around. They felt awed by his presence. There was something deeply hypnotic about his large, expressive eyes. Silently they would touch his feet and sit down to soak in that peace which flowed from his being. They would bring humble offerings- a handful of rice, some lentils, salt and tea. Kashinath Sonavane was a more regular visitor. A pious man, he would come regularly every week to leave behind provisions. Once in a month Badri Kaka would drive down in his bullock cart. A relatively prosperous merchant, he would leave behind more generous offerings of food and occasional fruits.

Once, on a full moon night, one of the pious families of the village of Patne invited him for a meal. He was hungry. He accepted hesitatingly. He went over to the household and was treated like a guest of honour. Curiously he watched the lady of the house lighting the fire. She used a long bamboo blow pipe to fan the flames. It was a simple kitchen appliance but it fascinated the sage. Shyly he asked if he could have one of those. The villagers were hugely amused and complied at once.

The sage now became quite dexterous at lighting his fires and cooking his meals. The blow pipe was a godsend and saved him from the ordeal of smarting eyes. But a strange thing happened thereafter. Child-like, he used to recount this to his visitors in the later years. No sooner had he mastered the art of cooking than he was freed from these kitchen chores forever. The villagers at first decided to provide cooked meals for him at the temple. Families vied with one another for that honour. Months later, as the sage held on at the ancient shrine, the local people began to overcome their fear and diffidence. There was something about the sage, an indescribable sweetness that drew people to him like bees to honey. More and more people began to visit the shrine. People began to stay longer. He spoke very little but people were content just to be in his saintly presence. Then Kashinath took courage in his hands. His son Sudam was a wild tribal lad- very courageous and difficult to tame. He was awed by the Saint and had grown very attached to him. Sunvane prayed to the sage to let his son stay with him and cook his meals and serve him.

This freed the sage of all housekeeping chores. He was overjoyed and now increased the duration of his meditations. Soon other families from Patne vied with one another to send their sons to serve the sage in the forest and thus acquire merit. The depth and profoundity of his meditations deepened incomparably till it transformed the place. Slowly miracles of a sort began to unfold in Patne- simple miracles of transformation and change.

One day the village headman came to meet the Sage.He was a short statured, white haired man with a drooping mustache and a huge Magenta turban. 'Holy one', he intoned, this is an ancient temple and a great seat of spiritual power. Unfortunately, it has fallen upon bad times of neglect. Some years back in 1964 the government wanted to build a huge dam across the mouth of this valley. That would have drowned the temple in a deep reservoir forever. We protested but no one listened. Fortunately, the engineers took soundings but could not locate suitable rock strata underneath for the construction of the dam and so this temple was saved. But now I perceive a great danger looming again. For the past few years, the flash floods have been cutting away at the right wall of this temple. The huge pillar at its entrance fell last year .I fear that if we don't take urgent steps soon, we will lose this temple in the coming Monsoons.We in this village are poor folk and lack the resources. I have tried to mobilise the local *Samiti* but it can do precious little. I had despaired, but in your coming to this temple I see a ray of hope. I beseech you holy one to do some thing. 'You must save this shrine.'The old man bowed reverently before the Sage and left silently. The Sage said nothing. For a long time he kept looking at the retreating back of the grave old man.

3

The Sage Saves the Shrine

In the year 1970, a remarkable man was appointed as the Guide Archeologist in charge of the famous Ellora Caves. He had an arresting personality. Tall, swarthy, curly haired and handsome- Madhukrishna Joshi was a dynamo of energy. He was a native of the village of Ellora itself. From his earliest childhood, the caves had been a part and parcel of his life. As a boy he roamed through these caves. They fascinated him

After the crowds and tourists had gone – he used to slink quietly into these ancient caves. A shiver used to course down his spine, as he stood rooted to the spot- staring at those exquisitely sculpted statues. The Kailash Temple cave was his favourite. It is a remarkable piece of art- an archeological marvel par excellence. All Temples and buildings are built upwards from a foundation. This Rock temple has been carved into the solid Basalt rocks – from the top downwards. Kailash Temple is cave number 16 in the Ellora complex of 39 caves. This cave temple was built in 756 AD by Krishna Raja of the Rashtrakuta dynasty. Krishna Raja had married the Raja Kanya (princess) of Nepal. His beautiful wife once had a dream- in which she received the divine command to have a temple of Kailash constructed in the Kingdom. It is said that she took a vow that till the temple was completed she would not partake of any grain. To fulfill the vow of his Queen, Krishna Raja undertook the construction of the Kailash temple. The Sayhadri hill ranges with their Basalt rocks were selected and the work on the fabulous rock temple commenced. A collection of the finest sculptors and craftsmen in the kingdom set to work on that rock face. They started carving from the top down – chipping away at the solid rock with their chisels. It took a hundred and fifty years before this dream carved a rock into a stirringly beautiful temple. Six generations of the Rashtrakuta dynasty perished in the process- but at long last the grandiose rock temple took on the final form of an enormous rock chariot with many cupolas. It is a rock chariot drawn by huge sculpted elephants and tigers.

Today it stands gaunt and immovable – a stone chariot shaped structure 107 feet high, 276 feet in length and 160 feet in width. The statues of Ganesha – the Lord of the mind and auspiciousness, adorn its entrance gate. As soon as one enters there is a gigantic statue of the Gaja Lakshmi – the Regal Goddess of wealth being bathed and propitiated by huge white elephants. In side along the courtyard are sculpted some statues of outstanding grace and beauty, depicting scenes from Indian mythology- the marriage of Shiva and Parvati; Ravana shaking mount Kailash, Kama (the Indian Cupid – God of love) with his beautiful consort Rati, the statues of the Goddess of the rivers Ganga and Yamuna and the Goddess of learning – the beauteous Saraswati who rides a great white Swan. Of all the 39 caves in the Ellora complex – the young Madhu Krishna Joshi was somehow fascinated by the Kailash cave temple. Once he had an extra ordinary experience of Déjà vu. He was standing alone in the Kailash cave when he felt a strange sensation. The cave seemed to heave about him; he swayed giddily and clutched his head. Suddenly he felt detached and remote as if watching the scene from a great distance. It was as if he had entered a strange time warp. He saw the Kailash cave in an incomplete form. He saw several sculptors and artisans working feverishly on those exquisite statues. Amongst them he saw a tall swarthy man with *curly hair,* gold ear rings and a strange attire – working intently on the statue of the Ganga . A great shiver ran down his spine as he recognized that dark stranger as himself -another person, in another age. The experience left a deep impress on Madhu Krishna Joshi. It left him with a deep conviction. Almost a thousand and four hundred years ago – in a previous incarnation – he had been one of the sculptors who had worked on the Kailash temple caves of Ellora. The caves and these carvings had a fascination that went from life to life and so Madhu Krishna felt, had pulled him back to be reborn in Ellora village next to his beloved caves. The caves are indeed a fascinating complex that transports you into a wondrous realm of exquisite beauty. These caves were carved out of the basalt rock over a number of centuries. There are Hindu Caves (as typified by the Kailash Cave). There are the earlier Buddhist caves. Of these, cave number 10 is a cave temple – a Chaitya. This was constructed between the Fourth and Seventh century AD. This cave was carved from the front to the rear and is shaped like an Elephant. Its roof is ridged and shaped like the inside of a musical instrument. It has specifically been designed for acoustic effect. Any sound made here reverberates and acquires a strange musical timbre. One can still imagine the hypnotic effect of scores of Buddhist monks chanting their sonorous hymns here. It has a stupa of the austere Hinayana sect and an exquisite Mahayana statue of the Buddha in the "Vyakhyana Mudra" (the teaching pose). Further on are Buddhist viharas where the monks used to stay. A stream once used to flow through this vihara. It's gentle murmur transporting the monks into a tranquil state of consciousness beyond the linear view of time and space. Further on, in space and time are the Jaina caves. They have some of the most beautiful statues and sculptures. One sculpture depicts the Indrani seated beneath the mythical

Kalpa tree. Each strand of her hair, each ornament and bracelet on her body is beautifully sculpted. At the entrance of this cave is a huge statue of the Goddess Ganga – the soul of that sacred Indian River. The Ganga statue symbolises the quintessence of the Indian ideal of feminine beauty and grace. It is an incredibly beautiful statue-so beautiful that it can still cast a spell over the beholder. Its creator must have fallen in love with his own creation. The Ellora caves are located in a time warp that takes you back to the times of the Buddha and Mahavira and then the Rashtrakutas. The Indian civilization then had reached a pinnacle of cultural glory. It was a deeply meditative and contemplative culture. There were thousands of saffron robed monks who lived a quiet contemplative life in these caves. In the towns and cities below there was magnificent wealth and opulence. Women coiffured their hair in elaborate hairdos, bedecked themselves with jewels and gems and precious stones and there were the artists and sculptors who captured their sensuous beauty in the elegant frescoes and marvelous sculptures of these rock caves. Their beauty assails your senses and leaves you with a curious feeling of Déjà vu even today.

When you see these caves, it is easy to understand why Madhu Krishna Joshi felt drawn to them like a bee to honey. He was a strange man. The only son of his parents, he had a bizarre hobby. He kept snakes- black venomous Cobras as his pets! He used to catch them from the forest and keep them at home in little wicker baskets and feed them milk. His mother was naturally terrified. One day she caught hold of him and asked him to give her a solemn promise. He promised he would do whatever she said. She asked him to take all those snakes out and cast them back into the forest. Beside that he was to take a solemn vow that he would never touch a snake again all his life. Madhu Krishna was heart broken.

Nevertheless, like a good son he obeyed. He left all the snakes in the forest and they fled. All except one. A female Cobra that would not go away. Recalls Madhu Krishna Joshi that it drove him to tears. He would shoo it away. The female cobra would go a little distance then stop and stare at him imploringly. Life is stranger than fiction. Madhu Krishna had to actually throw stones at the cobra to drive her away. He came back a forlorn and heart-broken young man from the forest that day.

Madhu Krishna Joshi grew up and went on to qualify from the School of Archeology at Delhi. His joy knew no bounds therefore when in 1970 he was appointed the Guide lecturer of his beloved Ellora Caves. It was a love that transcended many lives. Later on, Joshi would refuse his promotions so that he could stay on next to these fascinating caves of Ellora. Joshi was a dynamic and conscientious young man. He energetically went about his task. His charter of duties included the care of three protected archeological monuments. Apart from the Ellora caves these included the Mahadev Temple and the Devi Temple near Patne.

In March 1971, barely a few months after assuming charge at Ellora; Joshi mounted his sturdy BSA motorcycle and went off to Patne. He wanted to personally see the other two monuments. In those days a "Madrasi -Baba " was staying at the Mahadev temple. He was an uncouth and foul, tongued man. People said, many years ago he had served in the Army as a cook. He was addicted to Ganja (Cannabis). The whole temple complex was filled with ash. The Madrasi Baba had been lighting fires to keep himself warm. He was seemingly a great hit with the more adventurous boys of the village whom he had initiated to the dubious joys of cannabis. Joshi was quite horrified at the state of the monument and he resolved that even if he had to get the police he would get this man evicted from the premises. Next he had to see the Patne Devi Temple. He had been informed at the village that another Sanyasi was ensconced there. Joshi kicked his motorcycle to life and sped off there muttering. He had his job cut out for him trying to save the monuments on his charge from these unauthorized occupants and vandals. He reached the Devi temple. Even in its dilapidated state- the monument was imposing and majestic. Its walls were crumbling. One of the Deepa Stambhas, the tall pillars of light at the entrance had fallen in the last monsoons. The temple was in an open clearing in the forest. Three Nalas descended from the Indrahyadri range on top and confluenced in this open space below. In the rains they were prone to flash floods and became raging torrents in a matter of hours. The entire temple complex used to be surrounded by water. The raging currents had begun to wear down the entire right wall of the temple. The flash floods had already knocked down one of the magnificent Deepa Stambhas- the pillars of light that formed the gateway of the temple. The monument was in a sad state of neglect and disrepair. Where was the Swami? He enquired of the village boys and cowherds who were grazing their cattle there. He had shifted to that hut nearby, the boys said. Joshi strode over to the hut indicated. The door was closed. He was about to knock – when he saw a small board in vernacular " Swami ji meets people only on Purnima (full moon days) kindly do not knock".

" Wonderful", thought Joshi to himself sardonically. "The last sadhu in the Mahadeva temple was a ganja addict. But at least he was accessible. This one was smarter; he had made himself unavailable. This state of affairs would have to be rectified", he thought to himself angrily. He was about to start his bike and ride off when he heard that voice,"Mr. Joshi"

The warbling sound of a bird- so sweet and musical. Someone had addressed him in English – right in the middle of this forest.

He whirled around to look.

Framed in the doorway was a saffron robed monk- with shaven head, large eyes and long powerful arms. Madhu Krishna Joshi gaped in astonishment. He recalled many years later. 'In the Ellora Buddhist caves there were some statues of the Buddha and his monks. As a student of Archeology, I have come across many images with the "Prabha mandala" or divine halos around their heads. When I first gazed at that monk I distinctly had the feeling of a "Prabha"- a light without a halo- The Prabha without the Mandala.' He kept gaping . *It was* as if one of the statues of the Buddhist monks of yore had suddenly come to life.

What are the five signs of the Bodhisattava, he recalled The Prabha valya (halo), the curly hair, long arms that come up till the knees". The monk in front of him had a regal mien and an aura of purity. He had powerful shoulders and long majestic arms that came to his knees. Madhu Krishna Joshi was sensitive to impressions. This monk had left an indelible impress upon his consciousness in just one glance. Some two thousand years earlier monks like this one used to walk over this land. It was that feeling of the time warp again and Joshi was astounded.

"You must be Mr. Joshi from the Archeological Dept". The monk said in clear Oxford accented English.

This was the last thing Joshi had been expecting in this forest. "Yes I am"He stammered in confusion.

"The village people have told me about you. In fact, I was waiting eagerly to meet you. Why don't you come in?" Joshi walked into the hut in a daze. They sat down on the mat. The smell of incense lay heavily over the atmosphere. They sat silently for some time. One of the boys brought in a cup of tea. " Mr Joshi, I was an engineer once" the monk continued. " I have been here for a few years now. The flash floods have been taking a heavy toll of this temple structure. Most of the right wall has been swept away. Last year the Deepa Stambha at the entrance had fallen".

"Yes, I noticed that", said Joshi.

The monk now pulled out a sheaf of blue prints.

"I am afraid this temple will not be able to survive the next monsoons. This valley is the catchment area for all the rains in the Indyahadri hills. The flash floods are particularly strong at the base of these cliffs. You will lose this monument in the next monsoons. His large eyes looked up with concern at Joshi's face. The monk continued , " I have drawn up these plans and drawings. You will have to construct a retaining wall here. It will have to be constructed at an angle so that it deflects the floodwaters. Some additional breakwaters will have to be constructed up stream. The pillar itself could be reconstructed. I have noted the dimensions of the existing pillar and worked out your requirement of cement and stones. Most of the stones would be locally available". He spread the charts in front of Mr. Joshi.

Madhu Krishna Joshi could only gape.

"You are the right man and it is lucky you have come before the monsoons. The next season you would not have seen this monument ". The monk then took him around the temple, showed him the crumbling Right wall and the water channel that used to break the banks and cut against it in the flash floods. Earnestly he explained his plans for the reconstruction of the pillar, and the restoration of the courtyard.

Not only did the monk have a powerful aura of purity and a deep spiritual radiance- he was a brilliant engineer.

Joshi could not forget that saffron clad monk. His visage had etched itself on his consciousness. His voice was his most remarkable feature. It had that warbling quality of the birds of the forest.

Quite obviously that saffron clad monk with barely a bundle of possessions was from a very well-to-do family. He was highly educated and technically qualified. He was quite apparently an engineer. Who was he? How had he come to Patne? Joshi gazed thoughtfully at the blue prints and drawings that the monk had given to him. What an extraordinary experience it had been.

He went many times to Patne there after. It was a joy to sit in the company of that young monk. He had that odd feeling that he had known him for years. You looked at him and your heart flowed with surge of affection- a Christ-like love. The monk was a treasure house of wisdom. He had a deep, penetrating intellect that cut straight through to the heart of the problem. He heard you quietly. When he spoke, he had touched the core of the issue – either with an apt Sanskrit Text or quotation or a simple parable. But the monk spoke little. He was most reticent about his previous life. The villagers said that he meditated for hours on end. The villagers held him in awe and reverence. The snakes and wild animals did nothing to him. He lived alone in that forest. It needed courage. One villager swore that he had once seen a snake glide harmlessly over swamiji's feet.

Baba (that is what the villagers used to call him) was deeply concerned about the shrine. Each time Madhu Krishna Joshi met him he inquired about the project to save the temple. Time was running out. Joshi had taken up the matter officially and in writing. He was getting exasperated with the bureaucratic delays. After one meeting with Baba he picked up his motor cycle and drove off to Aurangabad- the regional headquarters of the Archeological Survey of India.

In those days his boss was the famous Dr S R Rao who was then the Superintendent Archeologist at Aurangabad. Dr Rao was the famous Indian archeologist who had deciphered the Indus Valley script and discovered the Lothal harbour and dockyard. In later years, Dr Rao had moved up the ladder to retire ultimately as the head of the Archeological Survey of India. The man was a legend in his own lifetime.

The financial powers to get those repairs through at Patne were then vested in him.

Joshi met him personally and told him all about his encounter with that extraordinary monk and his plans to save the monument. He insisted that he come to Patne and meet the man and see the temple for himself. Archeological monuments in India are classified under four categories (A, B, C & D). Funds are easily forthcoming for the more prestigious A and B category protected monuments. It is difficult to get them released for the lower C and D categories. The Devi temple at Patne came under the D category.

Dr. Rao heard out the young and enthusiastic Joshi in silence. He liked this earnest and sincere young man who seemed so charged with energy and zeal. Finally, he agreed to visit this monument the next week.

On the appointed day Madhu Krishna Joshi led Dr. Rao to the site of the Patne Devi temple. An excited throng of villagers took them to their young Baba .

Dr. Rao was struck by the arresting personality of that young monk. Like Joshi before him, he could not help thinking, how much like a Buddhist monk that Swami looked. It was as if he had just stepped out of the pages of the history books or materialised in physical form from one of the frescoes of Ajanta. Dr. Rao looked at the straw roofed hut he was living in. The fresh aroma of the jungle assailed his nostrils. It was a beautiful clear day in early spring when the skies are washed clear. The villagers brought in tea and sweet meats. They sat cross-legged on the floor on the strawmats. The young Swami spread out his charts and Blue prints and earnestly explained his proposal to save the temple. He emphasised the urgency of the project. It had to be done before the coming monsoons. Otherwise, this ancient temple would be lost forever.

As he spoke, Dr. Rao looked at him intently. The keen student of history that he was, he could not help thinking that the spot where they sat may well have been the Ashram of that mathematical genius Bhaskaracharya. What must Bhaskaracharya have looked like, he wondered? Dr. Rao smiled as he stroked his chin vigorously.

"Just like the young monk in front of him", he thought. The young swami had finished his presentation. He offered to take them around the temple so that they could survey for themselves the damage. The whole forest was filled with an indescribable sense of peace and profundity. Dr. Rao felt a deep current of happiness well up within himself. The more he saw of the young Sanyasi, the more he liked him. Silently they trooped out of the hut behind the monk. He wore the classical wooden sandals and the seamless single robe of saffron. The monk' blue prints were excellent. He had apparently been a good engineer prior to his renunciation.

Dr. Rao looked back at the thatched hut where the Swami stayed. Wasn't this what the ancient Ashrams of the Vedic seers must have looked like? What a perfect and sylvan setting it was, so peaceful, so tranquil, so idyllic – the classical "Aranyak" where the ancient Upnashdic seers must have sat and composed their inspired verses of the Divine Richas.

The monk was absolutely right. This dilapidated temple structure was not likely to survive the next rains. They finished their tour of inspection and came back to the hut. Dr. Rao turned to Madhu Krishna Joshi "Take down a note", he said. Eagerly, Joshi whipped out his notebook and pen and began to take down the dictation. "This monument" began Dr. Rao", is in an extremely dilapidated condition. I am surprised as to why it has not been deleted from the Protected Monuments list. It should have been done much earlier". A great wave of disappointment passed over Joshi's face. He put down his pen. "I didn't bring you all this way just for this" he interjected bitterly. "Young man, you are impatient like all young men are. Write on you will see", Dr. Rao said with a twinkle of merriment in his eyes. "However, if the PWD Engineers and civil contractors can not restore/ save this monument, I recommend that the Archeological Survey of India Engineers take it up as a challenge and restore this monument to its pristine glory".

Joshi could scarcely suppress a whoop of joy. The monk had been listening anxiously. His face beamed in a radiant smile of happiness. Dr. Rao saw the concern and the transformation that came over the face of the monk. How deeply committed he was to the protection of that ancient temple.

Dr. Rao went back and sanctioned Rs. 1.5 lakhs for the renovation / restoration of that temple. Within the next two months the place was transformed. The young Swami ji himself assumed charge of the engineering operation. He guided the work force. Apparently he had spent a long time on that site, breathing and living with the problem of saving that ancient temple. The Archeological Survey engineers were deeply impressed by him. They went back and spoke to their colleagues in the town. The fame of that monk began to spread slowly like perfume.

The temple wall was repaired. An exact replica of the old Deepa Stambha, the pillar at the entrance, was reconstructed to replace the one that had broken down in the floods. Retaining walls were constructed to divert the fury of.the flash flood waters. The men worked feverishly.

The local villagers joined in enthusiastically. It was a race against time. The repair and renovation had to be completed before the next monsoons – if the temple was to be saved at all.

The local people of all the surrounding Talukas held the shrine in deep reverence. Stories of the rehabilitation of the shrine and of the monk who had caused it began to do the rounds. They had a cascading effect. Curious to see the educated engineer Swami who lived all alone in the forest, a number of other govt. officials dropped in. They were all equally charmed. The engineer from the electricity dept. took up the job of pushing an electricity line to the temple so as to light up the monument and its surroundings. The PWD agreed to do up the road and the state Transport Dept. agreed to extend a daily bus service to the shrine.

Slowly, the partially destroyed temple regained its original shape and form. The two huge Deepa Stambhas now proudly reared their heads against the azure sky – the most potent symbols of the restoration and rehabilitation of that ancient shrine. The priest now summoned the courage to stay till evening. Sometimes before the major festivals he even spent the whole night there. More villagers summoned the courage to stay over night at that temple of the Mother Goddess. The major festivals of the Devi were now celebrated with a rare gusto.

It was the year 1971. The ancient Devi temple of Patne had been saved and rehabilitated. The broken pillar and walls were repaired just in time. The monsoon clouds rumbled in all their fury. Great flashes of lightning lit up the sky and the rain poured in sheets. The flash floods erupted in all their fury but the new temple wall stood firm even as the floodwaters swirled angrily all around.

Baba came out of his hut. The Forest Department people had accepted his application. A small portion of raised ground near the temple was leased to him and the villagers had built him a traditional straw roofed hut. Electricity had been supplied there and the villagers had even dug up a well. Baba had pointed the spot where water could be struck. A small, sylvan Ashram came up in the wilderness. The Forest Department personnel planted blood red Bougainvillea creepers behind the temple. The monsoon of 1971 came and went. The temple stood out majestically like a rock. It had survived the floods. The sage had saved the shrine.

Madhukar Joshi

4

The Sage of Soma : The Ecology of Ecstasy

Those who have never lived in a forest have really not experienced the sweetness and sublimity of this earth. Those who have never seen a forest have really missed the real fragrance of the Vasundhara – the Gaia- the good earth – the mother of all living beings. All forms of life spring up from her bosom. Even as we trample her underfoot when we walk, we do not realise that she – the Gaia the Good Earth – the Bhoodevi is a living organism, the source and support of all life. "All creatures, says the Atharva Veda, "are honey to this earth. The Earth is honey to all her creatures". This is the world's earliest enunciation of Ecology.

If you wish to experience the real sweetness of the essence of this good earth, then you must retire to a forest. This is what the Rig Vedic Rishis and the sages and seers of the Upanishads had done so many centuries ago. They had turned their back on the primitive first wave agricultural civilisations of their time and retired to the forests to live a life of deep meditation and contemplation. The serenity and tranquility they found in the forests sensitized their minds to deeper levels of reality. They sensed glimmerings of the strange paradoxical nature of the universe and of its underlying essence – the undecaying and deathless "Brahman". In the forests (the Aranyaks) they opened their minds to the inspirations and promptings of the cosmic mind – the Golden Hiranyagarbha: the cosmic womb from which all this has sprung. Their minds immersed in deep meditation – they sank into tranquil states of consciousness, where their physical and psychological beings were inundated in an ecological ecstasy and the ego boundaries of a separate and painful existence, were effaced forever. The Gaia – the good earth, is an expression of infinite bounty and the joy of supreme creativity.

Their minds grew as quiet and silent as the Himalayan peaks on those rare cloudless days when not a breath of wind blows over the mountain scape. Everything is so silent and so still. From that harvest of silence they felt the imperceptible upsurge of the rhythm of an inspired speech. The Divine Richas (inspirations) of the Vedic verses flowed down to their minds from the infinitude of deep silence. The Vedic verses were not their compositions, they said. They were *Apaurusheya* – not born of human beings. They did not struggle with the archaic rhythms and rhymes of those wondrous poems. They were not their creations, they said. They came to them fully formed and complete from that deep silence. They arose from Brahman. The Divine Richas (the inspirations) are immortal. They exist per se in the cosmic mind. They are archetypal expressions of immortality. We do not create them. They come to us. They are restless. They are forever seeking the illumined minds through which they can be born; —awakened minds through which they can express themselves in the biosphere.

The Rig Vedic Rishis, the Aatharvan Forest sages opened their eyes from their deep meditation. They beheld dawn breaking out in the Eastern horizon – over the hills – painting the river and sky in flaming reds and golds, filling the forest with broad, golden spokes of light.........................

...........They cried out in ecstasy.

Wondrous verses, beautiful poems in praise of Usha, the divine maiden of dawn, burst forth from their lips. That is how the Vedas were born. Have you ever seen a forest? Have you seen its riotous confusion of teeming life? The thousands of trees and creepers and flowers that reach up from the good earth up into the sunlit sky? Have you seen the sun kissed earth exult in the pure joy of sunshine? The forest is the earth's creativity run riot. The growth seems wild and uncontrolled but underlying it is a deep harmony and order. The fine-tuned checks and balances of the biosphere, its deep underlying connectivity and order bespeak a wonderous intelligence beyond compare. Not entropy but the ecstasy of creation is the basis of this universe. In the forest we get a direct experience of this ecological ecstasy that underlies all creation. The rains come and drum their ageless song upon this earth. After the rains have soaked the parched earth, she exults in ecstasy and reaches out for the blue sky. She rises with the trees and creepers and layanas. She fills the air with the heady perfume of her flowers.

The Green Peace—those who have experienced the green peace of the forest are transformed for ever. The green "vanaspati' – the vegetation puts up a net of leaves to trap the sunshine and synthesise it into the sap of life. Chlorophyll nourishes this earth and makes it green. In the rains, the peacocks spread their gorgeous plumes and dance in the forests in sheer joy and ecstasy. Their frenzied dance is the dance of life.

The Indian civilisation is the civilisation of the teeming forests of the subcontinent. In the Vedic times, forests covered almost the whole of this fertile land. The Rig Vedic Aryans came armed with their divine ally – Agni – the God of Fire. With the aid of Agni they burnt the forests and cleared the spaces for their settlements, their pastoral villages and later even their towns and cities and city-states. The First Wave agricultural civilisation relied upon the renewable bounty of this good earth. They lived in harmony with its rhythmic cycles and seasons and its immutable laws. Two thousand years before the Buddha was born – the Vedic civilisation flourished in its pristine purity in the lap of the rivers and forests of the Indian subcontinent.

Even in that ancient civilisation that was wholly green and ecological in its outlook, there were sages who felt it was not green enough. So they left the villages, the settlements and towns and returned into the pristine purity of the forests to merge with the chlorophyll, to immerse themselves into the deep ecological ecstasy and tranquillity of the good earth. They lived in little huts that had thatched roofs of straw and Kusha Grass. The faint aroma of the forests filled their nostrils with the headiness of a divine lavender scent. These thatched hutments in the middle of the forests were called Ashrams. There, the teachers lived with their small community of disciples and students – chanting the Vedic verses, studying the Aranyakas (the books that must be studied only in the deep silence of the forest). They lived in the closest communion with nature. They experienced the ecstasy of her ecological delights of spontaneous creativity and limitless growth. Tranquility opened the gates of heavenly peace in their psyches. It gave them glimmerings of a paradoxical reality of Brahman – of cosmic wholeness and the implicate order, many thousands of years before the birth of Bhom and Quantum mechanics and the Copenhagen Convention. A verse from the Rig Veda says "*Not in the cities but in the forests are the fountain heads of civilisation. In the Sylvan hermitage of the sages, the desciples build a kinship with the plants and trees, the rivers and mountains – all these"*.... *(Rig-Veda 8.6.23).*

To be specific that was almost 5000 years ago. In 1971 the new sage at Patne had built for himself an Ashram of two straw roofed huts. The thatched roofs gave out a faint perfume that burst upon your nostrils every time it rained. In one hut he slept and stayed. In the other he gave audience to the peasants and tribals and the occasional Forest dept., or State govt. or Archeological dept. officer who chanced that way on a tour or out of sheer curiosity to see an educated monk, a modern day engineer, living alone in the forest as a saffron-clad recluse.

It was not the existence of the noble savage, however. The govt. officials who chanced to come that way were excited by the novelty of this ecological experiment; this synthesis of the ancient past with modernity. Why had he renounced the world? Why had he taken sanyasa? They asked the sage. "To prove that the ideal of renunciation is as relevant in this day and age as it was 5000 years ago. The institution of the Forest sage is equally relevant to the India of today" he replied. They were excited by his revivalist conception and they all helped him in small but meaningful ways.

The Forest department people had given him a 50 years lease for the plot of forestland he had built the Ashram on (The sage was insistent upon living within the bounds of the laws of the land).

The Archeological Survey of India Engineers gave him an electrical connection from the lights installed in the Patne Devi Temple. Some one from the town installed an electric pump to draw water from the well. The huts the engineer sage had designed himself. They would have been the envy of Laurie Baker. The walls were of bricks and cemented – for sturdiness and strength. The roof was classical woven from scented straw and sloped to withstand the monsoonal rains. The windows were built at floor level- for everyone sat on the floor on the mats – cross-legged in the classical yogic pose, Everyone in the local community tried to contribute towards this novel experiment. Badrikaka, the bearded Biblical looking patriarch who had first brought him to this forest in 1968, had become a devout follower. He presented kerosene stoves and cooking utensils so that meals could be cooked not only for the sage but for the occasional visitor to his hut, Families from Chalisgaon and the Patne village that went to visit him presented fruits and offered cooked meals. Krishanath Sonavane, the tribal farmer of Patne village sent his son to stay at the Ashram and help the sage to cook his meals.

Sudam, the farmer's son was a mischievous and impish tribal boy with a wild mop of hair and a roguish look. He was terribly naughty, full of pranks and most unruly. His mother despaired about him. He would not go to school. Swamiji (or "Baba" as they called him) was the only one who could discipline him. Sudam almost worshipped the sage and the sage was fond of this mischievous young lad. He took him in his charge. The sage loved little children. He was so much like them in his purity and unsullied innocence. When the elders were gone he would drop his mask of solemnity and rectitude and play with them like a small child. It was almost as if he had never outgrown his boyhood, had never experienced puberty, and had never grown beyond the stage of a little boy full of childish pranks and fun. He was always surrounded by a group of small boys. They confided in him and played with him, He reminded one of Alyosha- the young monk in Dostyevisky's immortal classic "The Brothers Karmazov". Alyosha was most friendly with the little boys for he understood them so well and was so like them. That is why he spent most of his time with them. In the children he found an echo of his own unsullied innocence and purity, Ever so often, some little boy would play truant from school and run off to Baba to stay with him at the Ashram- to ask him to repair his kite or mend his toy cart. He would oblige but gently chide the young man and send him to school the next day. He would even help him with his homework at times. He was such a wizard at Maths that the children were astonished.

The elders, however, saw a totally different sage. He was aloof and reticent and indrawn. He would meditate for hours at an end. The little boys reported that he did not sleep at night. Most nights he spent in deep meditation, He would rise early at 3.30 in the morning, bathe and go to the temple to prostrate himself before the deity. Then he would resume his meditation. He emerged dreamy and withdrawn, around eight o' clock or so, had his tea and simple morning meal. There-after he met the peasants and tribals who came to the temple, and then to his simple hermitage.

"Baba, my cow does not give milk any more".

A tribal woman would complain, her arms covered with thick ivory bangles " Amma you could try this herb. It helps, I am told. But best is you take her to the veterinary hospital", He would respond. "My son does not study " another would complain.

"Don't force him – let him learn to enjoy his studies. Learning is not a punishment. It should be a joy. You can send him to me".

"My daughter-in-law gets fits. I think an evil spirit has taken possession of her. Could he give a charm".

"The Devi there is the only charm, I know", he would laugh and brush it away. ' Just pray- it works wonders but do show her to the Doctor in the town. It could be something else".

He had become fluent in Marathi by now.

He had a sturdy common sense and tremendous diagnostic abilities. He could cut straight through to the heart of any problem. The villagers were awed by him. He was an educated man- an engineer. He could speak to the Sahibs and officials in such flawless English. He was so good at maths. Even the village school teachers quietly came to him for help. Kashinath Sunavne, the tribal farmer's wife was convinced that he was the reincarnation of the ancient sage Bhaskaracharya, the great mathematician. Who was he really? The people said that he had been ordained as a monk of the Dashnami order. The spiritual name given to him was Swami Pranvananda Saraswati. The word "Pranva" means the sound of the "Om mantra" the highest mystic word in the Vedas. "Ananda" mean joy or ecstasy. Pranavananda, therefore, means the ecstasy of the mystic sound. All monks in India have the suffix "Ananda" added to their names. It denotes the fraternity of joy-of divine ecstasy. He belonged to the Dashnami order of Sadhus- the order founded by the great Adi Shankracharya himself. He was a great devotee of the Goddess Kali. The only thing he had brought from his home and his most secret treasure, was a small picture of the Goddess Kali – which he kept in his own hut.

Mahakali is the goddess of war, death and destruction. Kala means time. Maha Kali is the terrifying destructive power of time. Time, which destroys everything- empires, kingdoms, palaces, monuments, monasteries, all, is buried by the ravages of Time. Kali is the mistress of Time. She signifies the cosmic impatience. She is the embodiment of Entropy. She sweeps aside all forms that are created so that fresh creation can take place anew. She is the Mistress of Maya-of cosmic illusion. She is the goddess of the Tantriks, Mantriks and magicians- fierce maguses who, the villagers believe, can cast terrible spells to kill people at a distance or drive them insane.

Even though the Swami was an embodiment of Ahimsa and non-violence, (he never hurt a fly, he never lost his temper and no one had ever heard him raise his voice even in faint annoyance), yet he was somehow feared by the villagers and tribals. Who else but a great magus could stay alone in a forest like this, in such a wild place teeming with snakes, scorpions, panthers and tigers and yet stay unharmed.? When gently pressed for confirmation he would vehemently deny any such magical powers or knowledge of charms and spells. But the villagers and tribals were not convinced. The real maguses never display their powers or reveal their dreaded skills. He was feared. He was greatly respected. Those who came to know him intimately, however, were charmed by his incredible and child-like sweetness.

Educated Govt. officials like Madhu Krishna Joshi (of the Archeological Dept.) were able to get closer to him. They were astonished to discover how intelligent and well-read he was- not just in the classical scriptures and philosophy but in the secular sciences and history and much else besides. The way he had drawn up the blueprints for the restoration of the temple confirmed the fact that he was an outstanding engineer. He had admitted as much. Beyond that he was most reticent about his previous life. His speech and accent confirmed that he hailed from Bengal but where in Bengal he never elaborated. His Guru or teacher was Muktananda Paramhansa of Ganeshpuri. Why had he left his Ashram? He never explained much. When pressed on this issue he said it was to practice his Sadhana – his meditation in this forest. His Guru had desired as much.

Those who got to know him more intimately reported that he was a stern disciplinarian. He was very strict with himself. He got up well before dawn, bathed and visited the temple. Then he meditated and then he did yoga. He taught the village boys the complex yogic asanas. Few could match his dexterity and suppleness. The boys said he had incredible strength. Very soon he became an icon of worship in that area. The villagers were awed and tongue-tied in his presence. The coming of a sage in their community was most auspicious. It was excellent for the rains and the ripening of the crops. The milk yield of the cows would increase and peace and prosperity and "satva" (purity) were spread by his tremendous meditation. It was as if he had ensouled the ancient shrine and brought it back to life. Most definitely it was he who had saved it from the floods and rehabilitated it. Once people were terrified of this place. He had started living there. And now the trickle of devotees had resumed again. It was increasing by the month. They were sure it would become a flood in the years to come and that is exactly what happened over the decade.

The coming of the pilgrims brought prosperity and affluence to the village. The tea stalls and eateries did brisk business when the buses came. But the people were still apprehensive. By noon, almost everyone left and the shrine was silent and still once more. The sage stayed there alone then. In fact he used to heave a sigh of relief when the crowds departed. This was an ancient Tapovana – a forest where many ancient sages had done deep meditation. The peace and profundity was palpable and living. The silence was so deep you could cut it with a knife. The huge rock faces of the cliffs behind the temple acted as gigantic magnets that seemed to suck in all sounds and absorbed them without a trace. They stood tall, gaunt and utterly still, the mute sentinels of time. When the Sun sank behind the rim of the rock amphitheatre formed by these cliffs of the Indrahydri range- it seemed to soak in all the sounds to itself like a vacuum cleaner. What followed was an indescribable experience, a powerful and utter,"Nihil", a total and profound silence- a stillness that was like the utter shunyata- the great void of the Buddhists- the utter and inexpressible zero. The void that was paradoxically the womb of all things. The suchness of things rested upon a state of absolute nothingness. The silence actually came from him and radiated in waves across the stillness of the forest, the stillness of the tall Deepa Stambhas and the utter frozen stillness of those thousand feet high cliffs.

At dawn and dusk, it was forbidden to talk in the

Ashram. One stayed quiet and opened oneself to the experience of the profound silence of Patne. There was no need to enforce this silence. You were robbed of the power of speech. You were awed into a deep inner hush. You were transported into a timeless feeling of tranquility, a time warp between dimensions where everything came to an utter standstill. The gaunt cliffs were the guardians of the Gates of Eternal Tranquility. The great Deepa Stambhas – the light pillars were the gateways of heavenly peace and bliss.

As the sage stayed on and deepened his meditation, even the leaves of the forest stopped their rustling. The rich living silence deepened, in tone and texture. To experience it was to be changed forever. That was the greatest gift of that sage. Not speeches but silence- an experience of a deep, all engulfing and all encompassing silence.

Kailash Temple, Ellora Cave No. 16

5
Ganeshpuri Interlude

The first Ashram, the sage of Patne had built, was situated on a little mound. It was on a small island some fifty meters from the ancient shrine of the Patne Devi temple. All around it are the dry sandy nala beds. In normal times a small stream of water flows through this patch. It is hardly a few inches deep. In the rains, however, flash floods thunder down this opening. The trickle becomes a raging torrent. The floodwaters surround the temple and the little island. On this island, the sage had built his first hermitage. Initially, it had just two huts-one in which he lived and the other in which he met the people. Later, when his old associates and friends from the Muktananda Ashram started coming there, he had a third hut built for the out-station guests and old devotees who used to come and spend a few weeks with him every now and then.

Today, these straw, roofed huts have caved in. The walls of the first Ashram are broken. Five trees spread their leaves over these broken huts. They provide a dense shade from the summer heat. There is a tamarind tree, and a wild berry tree. Dense creepers have grown over them; the well is to the rear of the bigger hut. There used to be a small kitchen there where the village boys cooked the meals for Baba.

This first Ashram had been completed in 1971 – the year of the Bangladesh war. A number of devotees of Swami

Muktananda heard of the forest ashram that his disciple had built in the jungles of Patne. Out of curiosity and affection for the young Swami, they started visiting him. And so the strangers from outside began to come to Chalisgaon. It was from them that the people of Patne got some glimpses of the earlier life of Swami Pranvananda Saraswati. The more the saga unfolded- the more impressive it became. Somewhere in 1967, they learnt that the young swami Pranvananda had left his home in Calcutta. It was said that he had gone first to Haridwar and sought refuge in Bholagiri Ashram, which is situated, on the banks of the Blue-Green Ganga. There was a venerable old sage from Garhwal in that Ashram. The locals called him Swami Virjananda or "Pahari" Baba. A tall gaunt officer who had retired from service, Virjananda was a true seeker. The Bholagiri Ashram is a very well-established and old ashram. The management was delighted to get an-educated, young sanyasi who was well read and eloquent. After a few months they offered him the position of the manager of the Ashram. They were certain he would do a good job of the administration. Prior to his renunciation he had been a manager with a multinational firm, and they could put his talents to good use.

But that was not to be. The young Swami Pranvananda was troubled by this offer. He had left home inspired by the Buddhist metaphor of being " free as bird clothed only in its own feathers". From one managerial niche, he found himself slipping into another groove that was not renunciation- it was a different kind of job that would keep him in bondage.

He sought the advice of the tall Pahari Baba. The old man looked him firmly in the eye.

"What did you take Sanyasa for?" He demanded.

" To do sadhna" was the reply.

"Then fly away from here, little bird. Here they will

enmesh you in administration and management. You won't be able to do any serious sadhna here".

" Where do I go?" asked the young monk with a troubled look on his face.

The old Swami thought long and hard. He closed his eyes and breathed deeply.

" There is only one monk whom I can say has done deep " tapas" or sadhana and meditation in our times. He is a man of great personal realization. He is Muktananda- the disciple of the great Avadhoot Swami Nitya Nanda. Muktananda is in Ganeshpuri these days, He can guide you in your sadhana, go to him. Not here in these plains". He waved his hand " not in these plains". The young monk bowed deeply. For the second time, in the space of a few months, he had fled the meshes of an ordinary existence. His heart was set upon doing deep sadhana. He had reached the Ashram of Muktananda. For eight months, he did intensive sadhna under the personal supervision of that stern sage. Without doubt, Muktananda Parmahansa was a man of deep personal realization and power. He had done intense sadhana for 40 years. He had roamed about in the wilderness of Maharashtra and Andhra Pradesh till he chanced upon the great Avadhuta Swami Nityananda. This had been a turning point in his life. With the great teacher's blessings he had a significant breakthrough in his meditation. He personally aroused the Kundalini Shakti in himself and became a being of great realization and power. This sage, however was very irascible and short-tempered. He was a stern disciplinarian. Very few could keep pace with his stern methods of instruction. He made his disciples get up at 3 O'clock in the morning. He led them in the performance of yogic asanas. He then made them meditate for three to four hours. They had their morning meal and then did japa. This was followed by more yoga and more meditation and japa in the evenings. A number of disciples left. They could not keep pace. Swami Pranvananda Saraswati stayed on and was ordained as a monk in that Ashram at Ganeshpuri. He was given his diksha on the auspicious day of Buddha Purnima in May 1968. Swami Akhandananda Saraswati, the Mandaleshwar of Nasik, performed the diksha ceremony. He continued his intense sadhna now as an ordained monk.

A Banyan tree however does not grow in the shadow of another Banyan. The Ganeshpuri Ashram began to grow and expand. The old huts gifted by Nityananda to Muktananda were demolished and in their place a grand palatial Ashram complex with a golden roof began to take shape. In grandeur and opulence, it was breathtaking.

Pranvananda saw this Ashram growing into a fine administrative unit with residential quarters, marble floors, vast community kitchens and meditation and prayer halls. Slowly, his Guru got busier and busier in the management of this vast enterprise. He had less and less time for supervising the individual sadhna of his initial batch of disciples. Something began to deeply trouble the young Pranvananda as he watched the place grow and expand. It reminded him of the opulence of the Bholagiri Ashram and the house that he had left even earlier. He was a deeply troubled man again. One day the young monk sought an audience with his teacher. Muktananda's face lit up when he saw his favourite disciple. He had great hopes for this young monk. One day, possibly, he would take his place at the head of this Ashram. The young monk touched his teacher's feet with his head and sat down on the floor. Muktananda was seated upon the bed. He was quick to note the troubled expression on his disciple's face.

"What is it?" he asked.

The younger swami looked at him uncertainly and diffidently. He opened his mouth to say something, then fell silent and looked down. "Come, what is troubling you. Tell me". Said the elder sage in consternation. Young Pranvananda looked up anxiously.

"Baba, I have come to seek your permission to leave the Ashram".

"What?' the sage of Ganeshpuri was astounded..

" You want to leave? But why?"

"Baba, these days I get little time to meditate. I.....I keep so preoccupied. It's causing me great anguish. I feel it is hindering my sadhana. I...I want to go to some place where it is quiet and lonely – so that I can pursue my meditation unhindered. That is why I had come to seek your blessings".

The teachers' face became a picture of astonishment.

"You really want to leave?" He could not believe his ears. The sage had an explosive temper. But he restrained himself. He fell silent for a while. Then he said gently "Look, I left home as a child. For 40 years I roamed the wilderness. Life was extremely harsh. My path was not easy. There were days when I didn't get a morsel to eat. Once I was so hungry that I ate mud to assuage the pangs of hunger. So far, life has been kind to you after your renunciation. You have not had to suffer like I did. Why do you want to invite trouble for yourself? I only wanted to spare you the problem of keeping body and soul together that I had encountered in my sadhana.

The young disciple looked down.

"I would not be true to myself if I said I was happy here. I do beseech you to let me go so that I can pursue my meditation unhindered". A look of shock flitted across the stern teacher's face. "Go then", he exploded angrily " Go where you want. But let me assure you, you wont find this to sleep on" (he angrily patted the Dunlop mattress he was seated on). " I have known what is want and privation.

I only wanted to save you a part of the way".

The young disciple was taken aback by the outburst. Like all quiet men he was determined and firm.

"Baba, in the house I left there were many such mattresses. I wanted to meditate then. I feel compelled to seek solitude now".

The teacher gazed at him mystified.

"Please give me your blessings." The young monk implored.

Slowly the stern teacher raised his hand in benediction.

"Ashirwad", I bless you", he said simply. The disciple bowed at his feet and left. The elder sage kept gazing at the empty doorway for what seemed an eternity. He was deeply hurt. He loved that young monk as his own son. He fondly looked upon him as his spiritual heir. All this had been too sudden and surprising.

"Where is Swami Parnvananda?" the other disciples asked him in consternation, later. " I do not know". The stern teacher said angrily. "He wanted to go to some forest to meditate. Why? What is wrong with Ganeshpuri? But he will be back. Life in the forests is not easy- it's not a joke".

But the young monk did not come back. In fact he simply vanished without a trace.

Swami Muktananda Parmahansa went on to establish a worldwide chain of Ashrams. The rich and affluent but sick at heart, flocked to him at Ganeshpuri. The Ashram grew and grew. Then the foreigners began to stream in- the Americans, Australians, Canadians and Britishers. With their dollars the Ashram became an ultra-modern complex with close-circuit television and well-run Siddhi courses. Swami Pranvananda Saraswati was one of Muktananda's most favourite disciples. Had he stayed on, he might possibly have become the heir to one of the richest chain of Ashrams in the whole world.

How many paths in our lives do we break off without knowing that in the stillness of our hearts, they will be continued forever? The thousand shocks of sentiments that we suffer, build a little cacoon of pain around our hearts. Sometimes, they tie us down to our station in life. They sap us of the will to freedom- the strength of will to take charge of our individual destinies and shape them according to our will. We lose the power to do what we really want to do in our lives.

For the third time, in the space of a few years, the young monk sighed deeply and steeled himself. It was time for yet one more act of renunciation- a breaking free of the bonds before they become too comfortable and too clinging. His steps did not falter. He left without a backward glance- even as he had left his ancestral home just a year before and even as he had left Haridwar. Ganeshpuri was now a brief interlude.

Saptasringad A high plateau in Maharashtra. It looms up like an enormous misa- something out of the Colorado national park as it were. Right on top, after a very steep climb of some three to four hours, is the shrine of the " Raja Rajeshweri" the queen of queens- the regal goddess of wealth and splendour. It is one of the Shakti Peethas where, as mythology has it, the various parts of the divine body of Sati (the consort of Shiva) had fallen. The Markandya Purana was composed here. There was a small, very modest Ashram here. Swami Prakashananda used to run this Ashram. A tall broad-faced and large-framed monk, he was a simple and devout human being. His sincerity was transparent. He taught by the classical method of recounting parables.

Swami Pranvananda came and stayed at this Ashram for a few months. It was in the midst of a crowded cluster of shops and huts. Then, his restless spirit was stirring once more. This was not the landscape that he had dreamed of. It was some place else- but where? He needed deep solitude. He did not want to be bogged down in administrative duties and chores. Some where out there, in the plateau country of Maharashtra was a forest and a shrine that was waiting for him. That would be the seat of his deepest and most profound meditations.

6

Patne : The Place of Power

On this blessed earth, there is a particular spot that is made specifically for us. It is our chosen spot of power. When you sit there, the earth focuses her life-giving energies on to you- to give you power. Don Juan, the Yaqui- Indian master of Carlos Castaneda, had given this advice to his anthropologist disciple. If there is such a personalised place of power in our lives – the place for Pranvananda was the ancient temple of Patne. As a child in Bengal, he had strange dreams of an unknown place – in a deep forest- overgrown with creepers and trees: there was a gaunt temple with huge pillars at its entrance that loomed up against the sky like some mute sentinels to the gateway of time. There were sheer cliffs that formed an amphitheatre of rocks. There was a forest where the peacocks spread their gorgeous plumes and danced in wild abandon. There was a persistent and recurrent dream landscape- flashes and visions of a strange unknown locale. They were persistent and overpowering – these feelings of Deja Vu.

How many paths the sage had broken off in his young life in the quest of this dream landscape. His home- a decaying but grandiose old mansion in Behala- Calcutta. It had the look of decadence and an opulence that was slowly oozing away. A rich and affluent family of scholarly, Bengali Brahmins. He was the last scion of this family, the last male heir to a fortune worth lakhs. One day he just left it all behind.

An educated engineer, a manager with a multinational firm, he just walked out of his job and out of his life.

His wanderings brought him to Ganeshpuri-small straw roofed huts, a stern-teacher who did not just speak of realization. He had experienced it in his own being. He had aroused the Kundalini Shakti and it had given him the remarkable gifts of ecstasy, insight and tremendous charisma. Time went on. The huts bequeathed by Nityanada were demolished. In their place came up a grand palatial Ashram with gold plated roof and marble floors. People and more people began to crowd in upon the personal space of the young sage. By now, he had been ordained as a monk of the Dashnami order. His long silken hair had been shaved. All he wore now was a single, seamless robe of saffron. This young disciple of Muktananda was bewildered. Within the space of a few months the entire landscape was transformed. Hordes of rich people from Bombay came in their flashy cars. They poured in their wealth and the Ashram grew grander by the day. Worst of all, his teacher was swept up by the work. He had little time now for his initial batch of acolytes and disciples.

The sage of Patne slept fitfully at night. The dreams of a strange forest landscape were persistent. Tall pillars, gaunt and impassive cliffs. .... "Baba I wish to go. Please give me your blessings". The request hung in the stillness of the Ashram at Ganeshpuri for what seemed an eternity.

He left once again – not a manager and administrator of an Ashram corporation but a sanyasi, in a seamless saffron robe and classical wooden sandals. He did not even own a shawl.

Saptashring gad. The mesa like plateau looms up a few thousand feet into the sky. The winds have carved these mesas into fantastic shapes and rock spires. The prayer flags on the peak snap, snap in the breeze. The lines and crowds of pilgrims throng the narrow lanes through the little village. A quiet new monk, months of peace and solitude but the inner restlessness and the longing remained. He loved the children. They were the manifestation of Godhood on this earth. The Saptashring gad Ashram ran a school for the Adivasi children. Pranvananda Saraswati taught them Maths and Science and the Bhagwad Gita. Education must not be drudgery. Why can't work be like play? He brought a volleyball and carromboard for the tribal boys. They simply loved him. He made school-life such fun.

One day he was playing carromboard with the children. Squeals of delight filled the air. Deep "Ahas 'as he pocketed a disc once again. "What is going on here?" A hush fell over the room. The senior monk of that monastery stood framed in the doorway. "What is all this commotion? Why aren't you boys studying? Get back to your books at once before I whack you, impudent tribal apes'. The boys trooped out quietly. The young sage said nothing. Only his face turned red and his eyes flashed angrily.

He slept alone that night and put his arm over his eyes. He slept fitfully. Dreams again- fragments of visions – of a forest- of an old shrine- huge pillars, massive cliffs". He tossed and turned fitfully. Then he got up and began to stare out of the window into the ink black sky. The stars were twinkling with remarkable intensity. Everything was so still. The wind was singing in the lower reaches of that wind-weathered landscape. Not in Saptashring Gad.

Where then?

He sighed and lay down to sleep but sleep eluded him. Mr. Sonar- one of the trustees of the Saptshringad Ashram had come to visit the monastery. A pleasant and soft-spoken old man, he was talking to the monks. Prakashnanda sat benignly at the head of this gathering, his white stubble showing. Behind him was the young, clean-shaven new monk with long arms that came to his knees. Sonar started talking of other Devi Shrines in Maharashtra. Then he spoke of a shrine that had impressed him deeply. He spoke of an ancient Devi temple at Patne- in the middle of a forest. It was a Tapovana- a forest for doing tapas or deep meditation. Many ancient sages had done their deep penance and meditation there. The whole place radiated spiritual power. It was an unforgettable site. The temple had huge Deepa Stambhas at its entrance. Behind them were huge cliffs.

The young monk sat up bolt upright. It was as if an electric shock had coursed through his body.

"Sonarjee where is this temple? How far from here" the monk heard himself articulating this question in a strangled voice as it were. " Just a day's journey really. It is one of the ancient Tapovanas, a dense forest but there is something deeply spiritual in the atmosphere. I have never experienced anything quite like it. Only, it is a lonely place now. No one lives there- not even the temple priest. The Place demands perfection of the highest order. It is said that Baba Muktananda had gone there for his sadhana many years back. But he faced many obstacles, many problems and inner difficulties and had to leave. "Does this Devi temple have huge pillars at the entrance?" Asked the monk hesitatingly. "Why, yes. Have you been there?" "No" The monk shook his head. The conversation drifted off into other grooves. The young sage sat oblivious of his surroundings. So the place actually existed. It was there- the dreams- the visions and those fragments of images – were true. " I have to go," he whispered to himself " I have to go". But the monsoon rains came thereafter. The clouds, the lightening flashed across the sky and the rain fell in sheets. He hesitated. His resolve seemed to weaken. The rains drummed on their monotonous litany for two months. He felt a great restlessness within. He could not sleep. The visions- the flashes, the fragmented images kept coming back to haunt him. An ancient temple with huge pillars- cliffs – forests- peacocks with gorgeous plumes. His personal space of power.

The rains were over at long last.

The skies were clear and blue and the sun shone with limpid golden warmth.

The Azure skies of autumn seemed to radiate peace. They strengthened his resolve. One morning he bowed before the abbot of the monastery. Swami Prakashnand looked at him in silent surprise "Where are you going?" "To Patne" was all that the sage said simply. In his bundle was a letter of introduction from Sonar Sahib for one Sheokar Shastri of Chalisgaon.

* * * *

The sage came back from a long, long way off. He sighed and looked out. The little hutments of the first Ashram had come up some two years ago. Two to three boys from the village now always stayed with Swami Pranvananda Saraswati. They swept the huts and the dead leaves that formed a thick carpet before the huts. They drew water from the well and cooked food for Baba. One of them was a small and shy young tribal boy called Shivaji. A simple and diffident young lad, he was devoted to his teacher. His whole life was saga of service – totally selfless service for the sage. The sage never forgot his sincerity and service. Many years later, before he took his Maha Nirvana, he bequeathed the responsibility of the New Ashram of Kalimath to this young man. But when we saw this little boy in the early Nineteen Seventies – we could never imagine that one-day he would inherit the mantle of this sage.

Another tribal boy had started living with the Swami in those days. He just came in one day – from nowhere as it were. He was from a distant village and had run away from his house. "Can I stay with you, please? He asked the sage.

The sage looked at him for long. Then he shrugged and nodded. This boy was a queer creature of the forest. He was strangely quiet and had a wild mane of hair. He served the sage devotedly

The sage got up from his meditation that day. He had been reminiscensing the past in his hut. He stood up. It was time to go to the temple. He called out to the boys and they trooped out after him. The sage heard a rustle in the bushes. He stopped in his tracks.

There, a few feet from him was coiled a huge King Cobra. It was golden yellow in colour. It had an enormous hood and hypnotic eyes and the sacred mark of Shiva. The sage gaped in wonder. "What an extraordinarily beautiful creature" he exclaimed. The boys looked up at him in fright. But he said nothing and calmly walked on to the temple past the snake. The King Cobra lowered its hood and slithered away. As they were coming out of the temple, Swamiji heard a commotion in the Ashram. The new tribal boy had returned from the village with a bagful of vegetables and provisions. He suddenly saw the King Cobra and screeched in alarm. He was a flurry of activity thereafter. He threw down the bag and began to hurl stones at the great snake.

"Samp! Samp! " (Snake! Snake) he screamed for all he was worth.

There was a commotion. Several villagers rushed up to look curiously and apprehensively.

The great snake hissed angrily. Slowly it uncoiled itself and disappeared in the bushes. The boy picked up a stick and began to thrash the bushes in a frenzy of excitement.

Baba came back

"For God's sake, what is going on here" he exclaimed. "Baba! Baba! There is a huge snake here – a king cobra. I saw it. It is dangerous. We must kill it". The boy spluttered. "Why?

What has it done to you? "Said the sage. "Why did you hit it? he asked.

The tribal boy was besides himself with excitement. He threw stones at the bush and danced about in a frenzy. But there was no sign of the snake anymore. It had gone. Baba's face turned grim " Look child, that was a King Cobra. Why did you hit it? It had done you no harm. I have heard these snakes return for revenge". He told the boy solemnly.

The tribal boy was nonchalant and dismissive "No Baba, he wont dare come here again," he said. The sage shrugged and returned to his hut. Dusk gathered swiftly at Patne. The place emptied as usual. All the villagers went away, only Baba and the boys were left at the Ashram. After sunset, Swamiji and the boys went to the temple for darshan as part of their daily ritual. As they were returning Baba looked up and saw dark black clouds gathering in the sky. They looked ominous. " Its going to rain," he said. The first drops began to fall as soon as they entered the Ashram. As they were having their meals, a regular thunderstorm broke out in all its fury. The gales howled through the forests and bent the trees like bows. The rain lashed down in torrents and huge flashes of lightening lit up the sky.

Baba loved these storms. There was something in their elemental fury that excited him. He opened an umbrella and came out to see. Soon the nalas all around were transformed into raging, frothing torrents. The flash floods had started suddenly and without warning. The whole island on which the Ashram stood was now surrounded by raging, brown floodwaters. No one could enter or leave the island. Baba gazed at the elemental fury of the storm for some time and then returned to his hut. The boys touched his feet and trooped out to the main hut where they slept. Shivaji was leading.

At the door of the hut was an old sack on which the

peasants wiped their feet before entering. There in the doorway, with his hood fully expanded was poised that huge King Cobra. It had deliberately slid its tail under the sack in a calculated gesture of defiance as it were. It wanted that tribal boy to step on it so that he could kill him in retaliation. Shivaji screamed and fell back in terror. The new tribal boy behind him, the one who had stoned the snake, gaped in abject horror. His eyes turned round with fear and flecks of froth appeared at the corners of his mouth. The island was just three hundred feet by three hundred feet. It was surrounded on all sides by raging floodwaters. There was no escape, and he was stuck on that little island with a huge King Cobra that he had offended. The snake saw him and rose to its full regal height - its hood almost four feet above the ground at level with the boy's eyes. The tribal boy started trembling violently. He could not take his eyes off from the snake and he could not move. He was rooted to the ground. Only violent shudders passed though his frame. The snake hissed in anger. The boys fled screaming to Baba's hut. He came out and saw the snake. The snake looked at him intently. Then, slowly it lowered its hood and coiled itself up innocuously in the doorway of the hut.

Baba took the shivering boys to his hut. They were trembling and babbling. The rains were lashing the island. They all sat huddled on Swamiji's bed. The boys clung to him like chick's cling to a hen. The clouds rumbled, flashes of lightning split the sky. It rained all night and they stayed like that – the boys shivering and clinging to the sage. The tribal boy broke out into a fever.

By dawn he was in a state of delirium.

At dawn the winds swept away the clouds. The sun emerged in all its glory and the flash floods subsided as quickly as they had started. Swamiji came out of his hut The boys nervously came out behind, clinging to his saffron robe

The King Cobra was gone.

It was too regal a creature to strike at that tribal boy. It had departed quietly after the thunderstorm. The tribal boy saw the floodwaters had receded. He just ran. He simply fled the scene. He ran panting all the way to the village. The bus had come in. He jumped on top and clambered to its roof and disappeared. No one has ever seen him since then. Baba often used to recount this episode to us. It was lucky that young and innocent Shivaji had been leading the procession of boys into the hut that day. Had it been the other lad ... there would have been a tragedy.

Such was life in the Forest.

7
Followers of the Sage

Where is Swami Pranvananda?

The young monk who had come to Ganeshpuri in 1967 had vanished without a trace. It was as if the earth had opened up and swallowed him. He was lost in the vast teeming multitudes of the Indian subcontinent. Was he alive or had he perished on his chosen path? Had some harm befallen him? Muktananda, his stern teacher, worried about him secretly. He was sure that like the prodigal son, he would return to Ganeshpuri Ashram. People from all corners of the globe were flocking to Ganeshpuri but from the earliest batch of acolytes, one of his most favourite desciples had gone. He seemed to have vanished without a trace. The irascible old sage kept a paternal eye on all his disciples. He therefore made discreet inquiries about Swami Pranvananda.

Then word came through that Pranvananda was at Saptashring Gad high up in the abode of the Sapta Sringdevi, the Raja Rajeshwari. He was now staying at the ashram of the simple and devout Prakashananda Swami. The elder sage relaxed, he was still baffled though by his disciple's sudden decision. In sheer opulence, grandeur and facilities where was the comparison between Ganeshpuri and the very very modest block houses of the Saptashringgad Ashram? Then some months later came the news – Pranvananda had left Saptashring Gad. He had now well and truly vanished without a trace. This second disappearance was bewildering.

Why had he left? Where had he gone? What was the cause of this young monk's restlessness? What ultimate place was he seeking? Perhaps, he had an inner vision and a dream picture and he was pursuing his dream. Was such a classical perfection possible in this day and age?

The months stretched into years. One year passed, then another and then another. There was simply no sign of the young Swami Pranvananda. Muktananda Maharaja had some of his disciples conduct discreet inquiries. He felt responsible for this idealistic young man who insisted on wearing the traditional cotton saffron robe dyed with the colour of the flowers of the Parijata tree (This was the herbal colour used by the Buddhist monks to dye their saffron robes). He wore the traditional wooden sandals. He insisted upon following the injunctions of the order of Sanyasa and austerity faithfully and to the last letter. But he had now vanished without a trace.

The other early disciples at Ganeshpuri often made inquiries about him. The idealistic young monk had made a deep impression in his very brief interlude at Ganeshpuri. Everybody had seen him as the successor and heir apparent to Muktananda. They were astonished by his sudden decision to leave the Ashram. They were baffled by his disappearance. Many hoped secretly that he would return. When he did not, some of the older disciples made an earnest effort to trace him out.

The first one to locate him at Patne was one Koregaonkar Kaka. Kaka was a tall, gaunt and slim bachelor. For years he and his family had been disciples of the great Avadhoota Nitya Nanda. Then they had become followers of his famous disciple- Muktananda Baba of Ganeshpuri. Koregaonkar Kaka was genuinely fond of the young Swami Pranvananda. The increasing crush of humanity at Ganeshpuri had robbed the place of its personalised contact with the great master. The rich people of Bombay and the foreigners were coming in droves now and the earlier disciples were getting marginalised. Kaka knew all the initial disciples of the Avadhoota Nitya Nanda. He came to Sapta Shringad and made inquiries about Swami Pranvananda. Prakashananda was reticent. The young sage had sought a promise from him that he would not disclose his where-abouts. The story came out from the tribal boys – who greatly missed their teacher who had tried to make their curriculum more interesting and lively. Kaka learnt of the episode of the rebuke for letting the children play the Carom board. In a flash, he understood what had happened. The tribal boys did not know where the young sage had gone. Prakahananda would not tell. Ultimately, he learnt of the young monks' destination from Sonar Sahib, the trustee of the Ashram at Saptashringad himself.

Patne! An ancient Devi temple in a tapovan- a forest of deep meditation. Koregaonkar Kaka was fascinated. He had to see this for himself. So, without telling anyone, he came down from the Sapta Shringad Ashram. He caught the bus for Chalisgaon. In the town, he took the bus for Patne village. When he got down at the village the people looked up at him curiously. Pranvananda Saraswati? How did he know their Baba? Was he related? Was he from his family? Had he come to take their sage back? The villagers were worried and curious. The coming of the sage had transformed the shrine and their village. The various departments of the Govt. had woken up to the existence of this region. Light and electricity had come here. The bus service had become more regular. The temple itself had been saved from the floods, reconstructed and transformed. The harvests had been good and bountiful. If the sage went, these benedictions would go with him and hence they were deeply alarmed. They swarmed about the surprised Koregaonkar Kaka, anxious and worried.

"Was he a relative?"

"Yes and no", he smiled

What did that imply?

"He was his Guru Bhai- they were disciples of the same master".

"Oh"!

The effect was electrifying. The news was whispered from one to the other. The whole village assembled in a trite. Some boys picked up his small suitcase. Others offered him water, tea and sweetmeats. A big procession accompanied him to Baba's small, sylvan Ashram. They met like long lost brothers and Kaka stayed with Baba for a few days. He found his forest Ashram the most perfect retreat for meditation. What it lacked in grandeur and opulence, it more than made up by its classical simplicity and traditional purity. In more ways than one, Kaka felt this simple traditional Ashram was far superior in essence to the palatial structures at Ganeshpuri. It was as if time itself had stood still and he had entered the Ashrams of the classical Vedic Rishis and Atharvans of the forests of some 5000 years ago. What a revivalist conception it was. The Upanishdic seers and sages who composed the Aranyaks (the forest books) must have lived in straw roofed huts just like these. So would the Atharvan and Angiras seers have stayed in such retreats. He looked at his old friend. The young man seemed transformed by the depths and profundity of his meditations in the forest. He could feel his spiritual power and ojas. The young man was a perfectionist and idealist. Life has a strange way. If you will settle for nothing but the best, you often end up, by getting it. The little forest Ashram of Pranvananda was perfection itself. True, it was not grand and opulent like Ganeshpuri, but nor was it squalid and crowded like the more modest rooms of Saptashringad. This was just perfection itself. It was revivalist- it sought to recreate the traditional forest retreat of the Vedic and Upanishadic sages. In essence, it was the traditional forest retreat of the Atharvans.

Koregaonkar Kaka went back to Ganeshpuri and gave glowing reports to his guru. Even though Muktananda showed outward annoyance, he was greatly pleased. His disciple had kept photographs of the Avadhoota Nitya Nanda and the sage of Ganeshpuri in his Ashram. And so it was that the word spread, Pranvananda had created a perfect and classical Ashram in the forests of Patne. Slowly a trickle of visitors began from Ganeshpuri. Later, it became a regular stream. It was from them that the people of Patne were able to reconstruct the story of Pranvananda piece by piece and anecdote by anecdote. The more they came to know, the more awed they felt. Was such a sage for real? Did such a one truly live in our imperfect times? The leitmotif of his life and teachings was this emphasis on revivalism; on the validity of the ancient and the classical even in this modern day and age. This was his theme song as it were, right from the reason for his renunciation (I took Sanyasa to prove the validity of this life style in this modern day and age) to the way he lived and the nature of the Ashram that he built.

Koregaonkar Kaka passed the good word around. Swami Pranvananda had established a remarkable Ashram near the ancient shrine of the Patne Devi. The spiritual atmosphere and meditative ambience of that Tapovan (the forest of meditation) had to be seen and savoured. The Ganeshpuri Ashram inmates were curious to see this revivalist phenomenon and a number of them followed in the footsteps of Koregaonkar Kaka. Kaka himself kept coming every year till the very end of his days. The next to come was young Rahoul. Rahoul was a slim built, intense and a very sincere young man. Right from his birth he had been deeply inclined towards spirituality. His parents had sent him to the Ashram of Swami Muktananda at Ganeshpuri to fulfill his spiritual hunger.

Rahoul's father was an accomplished Architect from Gujarat. His mother, Didi Contractor, was a brilliant American lady who was herself an architect and designer of repute. Rahoul was a deeply spiritual young lad. He had started staying at Muktananda's Ashram in its early years. That was where he had met the young Pranvananda. He fascinated him and later he became one of his most ardent disciples. He and his mother used to come there very often. His mother (who later took sanyasa and became Ma Dayananda) was an accomplished artist. She did a beautiful oil painting of the Patne Devi that used to adorn the audience hut of Swami Pranvananda's austere but simple Ashram at Patne. It lent such grace and charm to the hut, and was one of its most attractive features. (This painting is still installed at Kalimath.) Ma Dayananda was a lady of deep learning. She had an encyclopedic knowledge of the texts and all her children inherited from her this hunger for things spiritual. There was Wing Commander Yadav, a crusty old bachelor from the Indian Air Force with silver white hair and heavy rimmed spectacles. I remember this benign old man with particular gratitude and reverence. He passed away almost a decade back. A great disciple of Swami Muktananda Parmahansa- he was captivated by the spell of this courageous young monk and visited him often (It was he, who in later year, had led me to my Guru.) There was also Oza Amma – a pious old Gujrati lady, another disciple of Muktananda. She used to come every year to the forest Ashram at Patne along with her daughter, a senior Revenue official (Dolly Bhen). And then there was the tall and frail but intense Mr. Trivedi- a devout Brahmin and a follower of Muktananda – who had become an ardent admirer of the young monk of Patne.

When these old disciples started coming, the legend of the sage of Patne was fleshed out by their accounts. He however, continued to remain quiet, aloof and withdrawn. He was always extremely reticent about his earlier life before Sanyasa.

" You do not trace the origin of two things" says a Sanskrit shloka- " the origin of a river and the origin of a Sage. These are both best left alone".

The occasional guests would come and go. The whole town of Chalisgaon and the village of Patne treated them as their own guests. Right from the railway station onwards, some local disciple would pitch in to help them with their luggage, put them on the bus to Patne or take them from the village to the Ashram in their bullock carts. It was like an extended family. The Christ-like love radiated from this young sage and seemed to tie us all together like some cosmic glue of connectivity. You never felt like a stranger in Chalisgaon or Patne. You were Baba's guest. You were a guest ipso facto of all the people of Chalisgaon and Patne who were so proud and so possessive about their sage.

Pay? It was unthinkable. No one would charge a paisa from Baba's guests. Such bonds of love and affection must have radiated from the divine cowherd in Vrindavan. That feeling of intrinsic spiritual kinship must have coursed through the veins of the drwellers of the Brajbhoomi- the comely milkmaids and the devout Yadava clansmen of Mathura. Chalisgaon was a milk-producing town too. And all those who came to this destination from different and faraway places – felt the Vridavana-like ambience of love and positivity that overflowed with the milk of this small dairy town. In its lush forests, the peacocks still spread their gorgeous plumes and danced in joy. Ecstasy exuded from this earth. In the little mofussil towns of India, the traders and petty businessmen are always on the look out for a sage. With his blessings, they are certain, they can gain prosperity.

Their business will bloom. Such is the deeply entrenched Indian belief. Hence, in almost each and every shop and grocery store you will find paintings and photographs of obscure local sages and little known saints. What is all important is that one must strike a personal equation with such a sage – strike an individual chord, ensure that he holds you in his thoughts, wait upon him patiently and devotedly, till one day he utters the divine benediction. Pleased by your devotion, he gives the much-sought for blessing. These blessings transform your life and your business. Wealth and positivity flow in your life and you flourish. Such is the belief of these simple people. One is not certain how far it is true or how much it is based on harmless autosuggestion and pure coincidence. Strangely, however, in my own lifetime, I have seen such things happen.

Anil Deshmukh was the scion of a rich landlord family of Chalisgaon. They owned vast tracts of land where sugar cane was grown. Later, this family set up sugar factories and became even more prosperous. I have seen this sleepy little mofussil town transformed over the years and wealth and prosperity flowed in. Anil Dada grew up to join politics and became a leader of consequence in that region. An intelligent and levelheaded young man, he says the sage of Patne cast a spell on him, as it were. He changed and transformed his whole life. It was Anil who realised the significance of that great spiritual experiment in Patne. Anil Dada (that is what the locals call him) first drew my attention to this marvellous aspect of the sage's life. In an age, reeking with Godmen and conmen of all hues and descriptions, here at last we had encountered something so classical and revivalist. We had seen the revival of the ecological lifestyle of the forest sages of the Rig Vedic and Buddhist times. This sage ruthlessly shunned miracles and psychic demonstrations. His life was a shining example of his method- solitude and deep silence- communion with ones deeper and innermost self.

There was Shebu Chaudhary, a stocky, well-built and muscular old wrestler in his late fifties. A man who knew no fear- Shebu Kaka was a born leader. He had started driving auto-rickshaw taxis after his wrestling days got over. Soon he became a union leader and then a town councilor in the grass roots democracy of the Chalisgaon town council. He was devoted to Baba. He worshipped the sage and took it upon himself to protect him and save him from all harm. There were the Mathurs, a devout couple who ran a milk dairy. Mathur used to go in his van, collecting milk from the villages. That is how he met the sage of Patne. On weekends the family would go to Patne with fruits and cooked food for the sage. Such were his disciples. They came from all walks of life- the high and low, the rich and poor, officers and administrators, townsmen and tribals. His doors were open to all and sundry. Caste, creed, community and even religion were no bar.

Kashinath Sonavane, the tribal farmer of Patne, one of the first devotees of Baba, died in his late fifties. He left behind his widow and four young children. Shambaji, the eldest son, had still to settle down to a job. Sudam was yet a child. The daughters had to be married. It was a catastrophe for the family. The sage heard that unscrupulous neighbours and relations were planning to usurp the widows' lands and drive them out of their fields. The sage's eyes flashed. Till this day the people of Patne tremble when they recall the one and only instance in which anger had overtaken the sage. He heard a village meeting was on to decide about the land dispute. Without a word he rushed off there in a towering rage. His eyes were flashing fire. A hush fell over the village council when they saw him. " Kashinath Sonavane was a pious man" he thundered "He lived an exemplary life. I have never in my life cursed anyone or wished him ill. But should anyone dare harm a hair on the head of his widow and the children of this family- then may the curse of the Goddess of

Patne fall on his accursed head. I do not wish to stay here anymore". His eyes were literally blazing like coals. A commotion spread through the village. The old maids were terrified. The village headmen and council of elders fell at his feet. There was a babble of voices. "We will never let this happen, forgive us Baba - these people are unworthy fools- quiet all of you". The claimants to the fields of Sonanwane fell at his feet. The whole village roundly berated them. The sage was pacified at last. A bullock cart was drawn up for him and he returned to his Ashram at Patne Devi- with half the village behind him beseeching and imploring " Please do not leave, O sage, your coming has been auspicious for this community". And so the sage stayed on at Patne.

Sharad Bhai was a Jain merchant of Chalisgaon. He had a small little shop where he sold unpackaged tea from the tea gardens- fresh tea leaves of Orange Peko, powdered tea and herbal tea concoctions and many other brands. It was a small non-descript shop. He and his wife, became ardent disciples of the sage of Patne. Rarely have I seen such devotion. Over the years, a strange thing happened. Sharad's business actually boomed. It flourished to an extent that it astonished the businessman himself. In stupification he once told me, "I never thought there would be so much wealth in this nondescript business". His little shop became a plush and aesthetically maintained modern store. Baba in fact taught him modern business practices.

Some years later, he constructed an opulent and modern home. For all of Baba's devotees who came from far off places, his house became a transit camp, as it was.

There was Mohan Seth- the swarthy young Sindhi businessman – with a kirana (general provision store) close to Sharads. As a young lad he had become an ardent disciple of the young Swami. His business, he said, bloomed with the blessings of the sage. And then there were the deeply pious Tekwanis, devout Sindhe merchants who came all the way from Jalgaon to serve the sage. I have heard many such expressions of this ancient sentiment. Even in the times of the Buddha himself, the traders and merchants formed the bulk of his disciples. It was this community of devout traders that supported the Buddhist Sangha and the Jain orders in ancient India. They came initially to seek his blessings and benediction so that their business would flourish. They stayed on to slip into contemplative and meditative moods in the presence of the inmost one. Later, some of them renounced life and became monks. The contemplative life style was not just the prerogative of the Brahmins but equally of the other communities and classes as well. The kshatriyas or the warrior princes led the way and the traders and artisans followed. The movement was from materialism to spiritualism- to the divinisation of even trade and those fields of endeavour that are traditionally said to be steeped in the materialistic ethos. In mofussil India, you can still see the close symbiosis between spiritual and material striving.

The spontaneous upsurge of devotion amongst the traders and tribals of that district was awe-inspiring to watch. Over the years, a strange but palpable influence of positivity and peace radiated out from the forest hermitage in to the villages and the town nearby and devinised it in a strange and inexplicable way. To a visitor from outside, the milk-producing town of Chalisgaon seemed to bear the imprint of the legendary Vrindavana of yore where a divine cowherd used to play upon his flute so many thousands of years from today.

In Chalisga, on we saw another God in human form tread upon this earth and radiate Satwa from his being. He divinised the life of a whole community by the sheer depth and profundity of his meditation. He spread Satwa by the very act of his being. What was so striking was the positive impact of the presence of a mystic in the evolution of the life of a whole community. He divinised the whole district with an unmistakable aura of positivity and bliss. Peace and prosperity spread across that entire swathe of villages and Mofussil township.

The Vishnu Shaligram One day, an old couple came to meet the Sage.They both had a look of great learning and piety about them. They had come from a distant town. They just came and sat down quietly in Baba's audience hut. They did not say a word but quietly and appraisingly they took in everything. They left in the evening but were back the next day. Baba looked up at them curiously but they said nothing. They just sat quietly, intently observing everything. They came back on the third day and sought a private audience with Baba.They came from a highly learned family of Brahmins.Many generations ago, their ancestor had faithfully served a Sage. Before dying, he gave to him a strange stone of power. It was a Vishnu Shaligram, a mystic stone of great spiritual power. It had been handed down from father to son for generations. He warned them that they should guard it with their lives and ensure that it never fell into the wrong hands. It had been with them for over three centuries. But now, the old couple had no issue. They felt that their time upon this earth had come to an end. They were anxious that before dying they should hand this mystic object over to some worthy person who could keep it safe and prevent its misuse after they were gone. They had heard of Baba and had come to see him. They now implored the sage to accept the Vishnu Shaligram and keep it in his custody. That they felt was their life's final mission. Baba was intensely surprised but accepted their gift. The old couple were overjoyed and fell at his feet. Then, they left as mysteriously as they had come. No one ever saw them again.

This Atman, this Agnim, is the warrior
of the light, the traveller to the truth.

BOOK TWO
ENCOUNTERS WITH THE SAGE

Yoked to the melodies
of the music of the spheres
Soma flows swiftly
like the waves
of a river of joy

(Rig. Veda 9.3.2)

Ellora Caves, Pitangalya Vihara (Pittalkhora Caves)

8

The Search for the Sage

Sweet Auburn, parent of the blissful hour
Thy glades forlorn, confess the tyrants power
Where many a year elapsed have returned to view
Once where the cottage stood
The Hawthorn grew
Remembrance with all her busy train
Swells at my breast and turns the past to pain".

The lines of that nostalgic poem course through my head today as I gaze at the dilapidated and broken huts of the first Ashram that the sage had built on that little island near the temple in the year 1971. The roofs have caved in and the walls are broken. Grass and thickets have grown wild all over the place. My eyes take it in slowly. These three huts- that dense grove of five trees with creepers and lianas growing in wild profusion. The wicker gate in front and the wide concrete parapet wall that was built to keep out the flood waters. Each of these places is replete with a thousand memories. I sit down at a distance and gaze at that old and deserted Ashram. I can not stop the flow of pain. Memories crowd upon my consciousness. Sacred memories of blessedness, memories of the time when he actually walked this earth, he sat with us, he meditated and taught us to experience the ecstasy of this earth. The Buddhic being of our age, the reincarnation of Bhaskaracharya. ......

My heart aches with a monotonous languor *"Remembrance with all her busy train- swells at my breast and turns the past to pain"*.

How many diverse strands of synchronicity weave the intricate webs of our lives together. That old Ashram is gone "The thought of the goodness that was but did not remain, troubles you. Is that it? You recalled the advice to the Buddhist monk.

"Then do not think of the past. Do not fret about the future, live only in the present".

Then present! You come back from a long, long way off. He is no more with us today on this earth – in the present. We have lost our Buddhic being- the last of our great ones. Your eyes mist over and the scene blurs. It was in the year 1971 that he had built this forest hermitage.

1971! A shiver runs down my being. The year of the war with Pakistan and the birth of Bangladesh. The Indian Military Academy, Dehradun. 14th November 1971. Our batch slow marched into the Chetwoode hall to the haunting strains of ' Auld lang Syne'. We took the fateful "first step" that proclaimed us as commissioned officers of the Indian Army- young, avid Second Lieutenants with a single pip on our shoulders- and starry eyed visions of the future. The 48th regular Course was commissioned a month ahead of schedule. The war clouds had been gathering ominously on the horizon. Young men were needed to fill the gaps in the ranks. Young men were urgently needed as cannon fodder. And so it was, we passed out on the 14th November 1971.

Most of us got off the trains and went straight into battle. Just in time to join the war. Many of my comrades were killed, shot up, mutilated and wounded. Many of us walk today on plastic limbs. Almost all of us then were below 21 years of age. I remember that cold, dismal winter morning as the train steamed out of Dehradun station into the mist and fog. I stood in the door of the railway carriage, waving out to my parents- straining to catch, what could well have been, a last glimpse.

For some strange reason, I remembered us waving out to my elder brother some six years earlier. He had similarly left on a train in 1965- for the Second Indo –Pakistan War. He did not return. We received a pink telegram from the Army Headquarters, informing my father that his eldest son had been killed in action. A few days later, we received a copper urn containing his ashes, his last mortal remains that we consigned to the Narmada River.

Six years later, another train steamed out of another station. I thought of the copper urn and the green waves of the Narmada. I asked myself how prepared was I to die at 21. I saw my father's worried face and I could not overcome a sense of guilt.

I had joined the Army in total defiance of his wishes. He had lost his eldest son in September 1965. In 1966 I had applied to join the National Defence Academy.

There had been a storm in the family. The loss of his eldest son had been a severe blow indeed for my father. Hadn't he had enough ? "Why did I wish to join the Army? he had demanded angrily. "Because"... I had spluttered defiantly and then had been at a loss for words.

Why do we do the things that we do? Where do the deepest well springs of our intention lie? Not in the body, nor in the etheric, emotional or mental planes. They lie at the deeper basic levels- at the cores of our psyches. They contain the reasons why we chose to be born. They also contain the reasons when and why we will choose our death. Sometimes we become aware of our own deep underlying spiritual intentions only when we come to a deep existential crisis.

Only when we face death.

It is only that deep crisis that brings us face to face with our true selves- that shows us a perfect and flawless mirror that reflects our true selves, our real intentions. A Tibetan proverb says- *" Mirrored in Takpos magic lake, I saw myself as I was and shall be. Both pictures were the same"*. Death is that magic lake – that spiritual prism- that flawless mirror that helps us to see our true selves. The greatest personal trauma and crisis generates the paradox of the highest tranquility. The gates of heavenly peace lie beyond the realm of our greatest individual terrors. Why do we do the thing that we do? The things that hurt our nearest and dearest ones.

My decision to join the Army had come as the biggest shock and surprise to the whole family. I was so different from my elder brother. He was an extrovert, fond of sports and games. I spent most of my time immersed in library books. He was smart and well turned out. I was most indifferent about my appearance. He was worldly wise. I was deeply interested in philosophy and Buddhism. The 'Vajrayana' or Tibetan school of Buddhism had left a profound impression on me. I had a deep interest in yoga, philosophy and poetry – patent disqualifications for a military career. So why did I want to join the Army? The question hung unanswered on the family dinner table. My decision was incomprehensible. "I feel a military career will take me to the mountains- to the high Himalayas – where I will, I am certain, be able to meet some great sage, a monk, a Lama, some one who has realized in his own being what is written in the scriptures- a great teacher, a sage I can follow". I had tried to explain.

"These are romantic illusions. Soldiering has little to do with the search for sages. You are not suited for the Army. You will be a square peg in a round hole," said Father.

"All the same I wish to go".

"What if I forbid you to?" He said.

" I will go nevertheless".

The silence that followed is something that has seared itself in my memory for aeons. There was a lump in my throat and tightness in my chest. I found it difficult to swallow my food. I Had never disobeyed my father till then.

' There is a very devout and learned Jain scholar in this town. He is a great disciple of Ramakrishna. I had shown him your horoscope and told him of your desire to join the Army. He says he would like to meet you", father told me the next day.

"I don't believe in astrology. Besides, my mind is already made up".

"I am sending you to him, not so much because he is an astrologer or soothsayer, but because he is a very learned man who practices deep meditation himself. His views may be of some use to you", Father said.

So I went and met the Jain scholar. He lived in a non-descript by lane in a crowded market place, in Jabalpur. His room was neat and clean and lined with books on Yoga and Philosophy. Despite the bustle of the market place there was a palpable atmosphere of peace in that room. In that din, it was an oasis of silence. Peace exuded from that man. He was nearly bald. He had a round child like face. His benign eyes gazed at you from behind round, very high-powered spectacles. He spoke softly and had a slight stammer. "I had gone through your natal chart and was intrigued. That is why I wanted to meet you. Possibly there is some mistake in the timings of your birth". The Jain scholar said. I told him the time. It was correct. He rubbed the white stubble on his chin." As per this chart you should be seriously interested in yoga and philosophy. But I am told that you are keen to join the Army. He said. " I do not see the contradiction" I said gently. His eyebrows shot up. "You don't? The armed forces are associated with glamour and glory, the Rajsic or extroverted kind of life style- not really with Yoga and spiritualism" He retorted. I was exasperated.

"Look, if I had been born a few centuries earlier, I would have become a monk. But today, where are the monasteries? Where are the great sages, guides and teachers? Wasn't Ramakrishna the last of our really great ones? I can't become a monk today, for people would laugh at me and call me a drop out. But if I join the Army, I open a path to the mountains, to the sacred Himalayas. While I serve out tenures in the forward areas, I can practice my meditation in the mountains". I said excitedly. He gaped at me in astonishment. He took off his spectacles and polished them vigorously." I never thought of a military career in that light," He said softly. He remained silent for sometime. Then he resumed "But may be you are right. Ramakrishna was possibly, the last of our great ones. There hasn't been another quite like him. For Sadhana, we need a living guru – a guide. Not one who has merely read the scriptures and memorised the verses. He can only be an Acharya – a teacher. A guru is a spiritual guide – a person who has experienced the spiritual truths in his own being, who has realised them for himself. Then and only then, do his words spring up from the truth of self-realization". He put on his spectacles and studied my chart. Your natal chart has four rulers, he said "Jupiter, Guru is in the ascendant. It trines with the source of unusual upsets and inspiration. Uranus is in the Fourth house – unusual psychic experiences towards the end of your life.... Moon in the mid heaven and Pisces rising.... Mars, Lord of energy and war is conjunct with your part of fortune – that is why this impulse towards soldiering..."

He intoned almost to himself.

I knit my brows and tried to concentrate on what he was saying. For some strange reason, I felt I had to hang on to every word of his -- not because he was a sooth sayer, but as father had said, a man of deep meditation and learning.

"Liberation comes only with the grace of a guru. There is little hope unless you get a guru – a living guide – one who has travelled the path and therefore can show it to you himself. Not the web of words but a living experience of that reality makes a man such a guide". He gazed at me intently. "You are young, full of energy – so clear and firm in your resolve. You will be going to the Himalayas, to those great mountains, the home of the eternal snows. You may be lucky – you may get such a guide – such a man of experience as your guru. I envy you really".

"Don't you have a guru?" I asked.

"Unfortunately, no. May be you are right. Rama Krishna was really the last of our great ones. I have tried to search for such a one today but I have met with little success. There are only the books. They can guide your footsteps but they can not replace a living guide – one who has experienced the deep truths in his own being. Possibly, you are right. There is no peace here in these crowded cities". He sighed intensely.

He fell silent for a long time. When he spoke again, it was almost as if he was talking to himself. "I have been meditating for over 20 years now. But I have not seen the light. I have not been able to experience the great truths for myself. I am well past my middle age. Worldly cares and worries weigh me down. My responsibilities bind me hopelessly. I have searched in vain all these years for a living guide. I have been to various Ashrams and holy ones but I have not really been able to meet such a one. And so, I flounder on alone. Sometimes I lose courage and hope. Why haven't I found the truth? Has the inner longing and aspiration not been intense enough?"

He looked at me, sadly.

"Have I been broken like a reed? Am I drifting on the surface currents of life? Why do I lack the power to assert my will and dive into the deeper sources of my being? I have striven so sincerely for over two decades. Why then have I not been able to achieve liberation from this bondage"? The question hung unanswered between us.

"It is because I do not have a guru – a spiritual guide. That is why I have been floundering perhaps. But you are young. You have energy and will. The responsibilities and cares of life as a householder do not burden you. Above all you are heading for the Himalayas – those lofty mountains of our inner landscape. Who knows? You may well meet some great spiritual master there. A sage – a living guide who can take you across the ocean of sansara. "He used the classical Sanskrit expression. "He tapped my horoscope. Suddenly large tears sprang up in his eyes.

"I envy you really", he whispered almost as if to himself "I have been meditating without much success. May be it is because I have not found a true guide – a guru. But you – if in the mountains you find such a one and attain salvation, will you come back and help me? "The man spoke with his entire being as it were. His sincerity was so transparent. I was deeply shaken. I could only nod. I folded my hands and I bowed low before him and took my leave.

Outside it was dark.

Many years later, I wondered to myself – would I be like this man, tired and spent and unsuccessful in my spiritual striving? With nothing to show for my efforts but a leaden tiredness and despair?

I joined the Army. The processes whereby a square peg is made to fit a round hole are not conducive to any extremes of joy. Those who are sensitive are cursed to suffer a thousand shocks of the sentiment. But I had consciously chosen this path for myself. At least my will was untrammeled and free. I felt I could mould my own destiny and lead the life I chose for myself. And so I set off in the search of that mystic being

– the great sage, the living guide, and the guru whose words would spring from the depths of personal experience. I searched long and in vain. My military career took me to the remotest corners of the Himalayas. I have been to North and East Sikkim, to Arunachal Pradesh, Ladakh, Kargil and Kashmir and to the Central Kedar Himalayas. I was one of the first officers to climb on to the southern Saichen Glacier in 1976. I have spent long years in desolate border out posts. But I did not meet such a man.

As a child, I had been greatly impressed by the image of the Enlightened one- the serene and tranquil features of the Buddha fascinated me. But Buddhism was a vanished creed in the land of its own birth. When I was 10 years old, I remember, I had gone for a holiday to Pachmarhi with my parents. There I had met a Burmese Buddhist monk. Shaved pate, large alpine face, saffron robes – he really fascinated me. I had run up to him and followed him around as if he was the Pied Piper of Hamlin. Many years later, when I met the sage of Patne – I was struck by the deep resemblance. But that was many years in the future. In between, were long years of bitterness: of fruitless searching and inner discord. The words of the Jain scholar often dinned in my ears.

"There is no salvation without a guru" You have to get a living guide". And so, I would get up and search again. Volunteer for patrols to the remotest mountain hamlets- visit monasteries and Gompas perched on rocky crags, where the Darchens, the prayer flags snap, snapped in the mountain breeze. In my quest, I did meet Lama Thin Le Dorji, a Lama of the Ying Ma Pa (the Red Hat Sect). He was my teacher of Tibetan at the National Defense Academy. A tall, warm and gentle human being – he and his wife were like my foster parents at the Academy. They were delighted at my interest in Buddhism and in meditation. They were devout and pious Buddhists and I often joined them for prayers at Logsar and Mon Lam and other Tibetan festivals. The Lama taught me the Tibetan school of meditation. He taught me to concentrate on the image of the Avaloketswara Buddha with a four-petalled lotus at His heart center bearing the sacred Buddhist mantra (Om Mane Padme Hum). I practised this for many months. He said I would get a symbol in my dreams. This I was to tell him so that he could give me the next meditation symbol. I tried very sincerely. But life in the Academy was hard. We fell on our beds dead tired and slipped into oblivion. All men dream, but most of us do not remember even a fragment. I was one of those unfortunate ones. For two years I tried sincerely Then my training at Pune came to an end and it was time to move on to the final stage at Dehradun.

I called on my Tibetan teacher for the last time. The Ying Ma Pa Lama and his wife were saddened. They had grown as fond of me as I of them. " Each one of us has his own path – his particular spiritual destiny. That path alone brings him release. In the years ahead, you will certainly get that. Do not lose heart. You have our blessings", said the Lama. I touched the feet of the tall Khampa Lama and his gentle wife and left.

I did reach the high Himalayan peaks but realized with a shock that inner peace and tranquility arise not from a place or geographic locale but from within the depths of our own beings. The restlessness and inner turmoil did not leave me. One has to prepare oneself for the final withdrawal to those peaks and lofty heights. A premature withdrawal can only bring disillusionment. The first bunker I moved into had a large lewd pin up left behind by the previous occupant. Instead of bliss and tranquility, the images of the world and the surges of the lower vital troubled me. One was 21 then, and a part of me yearned to live a normal life. I had reached the mountains but I had come without adequate spiritual preparation to deal with stark loneliness and exile. Above all, I did not have the benefit of guidance from a living guru- a guide who had personally travelled that route and could show me the path himself. The result was deep disillusionment and sadness. I came back home to Jabalpur on my annual leave in 1972. A new neighbour had moved into our locality- a tall, gaunt Ayyar Brahmin from our Civil Services. Mr. Iyyengar was a very learned man with a thorough knowledge of the Sanskrit texts. He was a disciple of Sri Aurobindo. A simple and austere person, his house was an oasis of peace and silence. Large photographs of Sri Aurobindo and the Mother adorned his drawing room and the shelves were lined with the works of Sri Aurobindo. Weekly meditation sessions and prayer meetings were held at his house. He introduced me to the works of Sri Aurobindo. I was fascinated by the concept of the descent of the Super mind as opposed to a classical ascent of the Kundalini and devoured all the available books of that great master. I regularly began to attend the meditation sessions. I used to experience a heavy pressure on my head and eyelids. Mr. Iyyengar was delighted at my progress in meditation. He urged me to visit the Ashram at Pondicherry and seek personal guidance from the "Mother".

Here at last, I felt, was just the intellectual kind of school of meditation that I was looking for- the answer to my prayers- the ideal system- that had a living guide who would lead you along the path of inner spiritual unfoldment- of Aspiration, Rejection and surrender to the Divine; a guide who would oversee the inner evolution of one's consciousness. My leave got over and I had to report back to Sikkim for duty. I met Mr. Iyyenger before going.

The Silver haired man had a wistful look in his eyes as I spoke to him of my Himalayan assignment.

" I envy you. How I wish I could go to the mountains at this stage of my personal evolution. I need it so desperately". I looked at him in surprise. Frankly, I had experienced more peace and tranquility in his drawing room- than I had in the bitter cold of my Himalayan bunker. There the urge to live, to survive the blizzards, howling gales and crevasses was so strong, that it left you little time or energy for any other enterprise. The extreme cold was miserable. Your teeth chattered uncontrollably and you wore layers, upon layers of clothing to survive. Yet, once in a while, when the weather cleared up- the views that you got from the Himalayan watershed was grand and awe-inspiring. I went back to my unit and the mountains, and the months passed. I came out one bright moon-lit night when it had stopped snowing. Far down on both sides of the Himalayan watershed, I saw a vast carpet of clouds, shining like masses of silver in the moonlight. The mighty snow spires of the Khang Chen Dzonga soared above the clouds on one side. On the other side, across the plateau of Tibet, one could see the incredibly beautiful and aesthetic peak of the Chomolohari. The Himalayas are awe-inspiring. No one ever returns the same from the snows. For many months, I was the sole officer in that remote outpost in the Himalayas. The avalanches and blizzards cut us off. I got no mail or newspapers for weeks. The radio set was the only real link with the outside world (for telephones had to be disconnected the moment lightening started). At night you crept into your sleeping bag and watched as the wind pushed powdery snow through the gaps between the stones of your bunker. The battle at these dizzy heights was for sheer survival-survival against the bitter cold and the dizzy altitude that made you breathless. The slightest carelessness could cause chill blains or frost bite and worse. We lost men to the lightening, snow blizzards and the avalanches. After months of this isolation, I was called down to the Battalion Headquarters. Gratefully, I sat down in the officers' mess and read through my mail. I devoured the newspapers and magazine. It was the year 1973. I picked up a copy of the Time Magazine and flipped through its pages.

My heart missed a beat as I read the news item "The

Mother", the head of the Sri Aurobindo Ashram at Pondicherry, had passed away. The great experiment to bring down the Super-mind into the physical plane had apparently failed. The Ashram was in disarray and feeling orphaned. It hit me like a bucket of ice cold water in the face. I felt like a man lost in a desert, who opens his water bottle and finds it full of petrol.

I had been so anxiously planning to go to the Aurobindo Ashram in Pondicherry to meet the Mother. Here at last, I felt, was just the kind of intellectual and spiritual guide that one was seeking. And suddenly, that hope had been dashed rudely to the ground. I was so shocked that the Mess NCO came up to me, and asked me if something was wrong. I quickly closed the magazine and walked out into the cold to steady myself. I just wanted to be alone. It was terrible. "Too late" the words kept dinning through my head. "Too late".

It was only after a few more months that I could go on leave again. I met Mr. Iyyenger at Jabalpur. He was equally distraught at the loss of the Mother. Had the great experiment to bring the "Super mind" down to the level of the physical plane failed? If both the spiritual giants- Sri Aurobindo and the Mother had failed-where was the hope that we lesser mortals could ever succeed?" Mr. Iyyenger tried to console me but I could see that he was shaken himself.

So books were our sole guides now. There was no great teacher anymore whose words would spring up from the depths of personal experience and truth. No "Lamp" that could light other lamps any more as per the classical spiritual metaphor. For some reason, I slipped into a mood of deep spiritual anguish and despair. Hopelessness seemed to overcome me and I often remembered that Jain scholar and his despair. 20 years down the line, would I resemble him, adrift, hopeless and rudderless? My spiritual strivings of decades gone waste. Was there no hope in these times? I sat for meditation but it was more an inner struggle. Personal and job-related problems tore at my peace of mind. One could only snuggle down with the books and slink deeper into oneself. One grew more and more silent and indrawn; the despair was palpable and overpowering. Your initial enthusiasm and avidness paled over the years.

It was in this somber mood, that I left home for my unit in the fall of 1973 "*And what of him, O many Armed, who having striven so sincerely fails. Having lost this world, not found the next, is he not lost like a cloud torn by the raging winds? Is he not lost for ever?*"

I remembered the despairing question of Arjun, the great Archer to the Divine Charioteer in the sixth chapter of the Geeta. At times the only hope that one clung to so tenaciously was that offered by the Divine Charioteer himself in reply to Arjuna's anguished query "There is no fall for him, O Mighty Arjun, neither here, nor in the hereafter. For none who strives for self redemption ever meets with an evil destiny". You sighed intensely as you sat in the train and gazed listlessly out of the window. At times that stanza seemed to be your only hope. It was a forlorn hope at best.

* * * *

Brauni Railway Junction. In those days the broad gauge Assam Mail used to end here and we changed into the slow moving, meandering and languid-paced meter gauge Assam Mail. It was a long and tiresome rail journey. I had to go till Siliguri from where one went by bus to Gangtok and then on into the gloomy, sunless and cloudy realm of Karponang for acclimatization. Final move up was by road and foot tracks to the Himalayan watershed some 16000 feet up in the rarified air. Before me right then, however, was an intensely tedious and tiring train journey. I threw in my baggage into the first class compartment and sat down next to the window. At least you could gaze out into the green landscape and let your thoughts drift idly with the interminable miles. "And what of him 'O' many Armed?" Sitting opposite me, was a young European in Kurta and jeans. He looked intelligent and cultured but aloof and withdrawn. I took a deep breath and started staring out of the window. On the platform, I noticed a middle aged man with streaks of silver in his hair and large horn rimmed spectacles. He had a placid look on his face.

He walked up to the Conductor.

"I am Wing commander Yadav. In which compartment am I booked?"

The Conductor studied his chart.

"You are in C. Sir."

The Wing Commander hesitated." Could you kindly shift me to E?"

The conductor agreed. Later the Wing Commander told me he was himself surprised as to why he had made that request. He had a curious feeling, he said (a hunch) that he would meet someone spiritually inclined. He walked up, looked into the compartment and saw a young European Hippie and an equally young Army Captain. He was acutely disappointed and sat down wearily for a long and boring journey. Possibly, his "hunch" had been wrong. The train steamed out of the station. The European pulled out a book and began to read. I could not help noticing the title. It was a translation of the "Tibetan Book of the Dead" by Dr Evans Wentz. I looked at him with renewed interest. The wheels of the train started clacking monotonously over the rails— "Clack! Clack" in a soothing litany. "Are you interested in Tibetan Buddhism?" I heard myself asking the European. "Well, yes" the young man said "As a matter of fact, I am going to meet the Gewa Karmapa Lama in Rumtek Monastery" . I looked at him with surprise. " And where are you coming from presently?" "Well I have spent two months at Puri in an Ashram". "That's interesting. Did you find something there? I mean did you get some peace of mind?" "Well, something certainly. It was very nice". The serene expression in his eyes. I looked at him quizzically as the train rocked along.

I had been born and brought up in this land. I had spent years striving, searching for its lost traditions. Looking for a living guide who would give it a renewed meaning for me. But I had found nothing. And yet, here was this foreigner, who had come straight and touched the heart of the matter. The peace and serenity in his eyes. How I wished I had that.

"Are you interested in Tibetan Buddhism?" I heard him asking me.

"Deeply. I studied under a Ying Mapa Lama for two years".

"Have you read the Bordo Thodol ?" He asked.

"Yes, but I prefer to read it in the original", I replied.

"And did you find something?" he asked me gently after sometime.

For some reason his question disturbed me. "Frankly, I haven't found the peace I sought. Yes, I have read the books, but unfortunately books are not quite the same things as a living guide- as one that has personally experienced these things and can communicate them to you. Yes, I have read Tibetan texts and the Upanishads, and know about the "Aham Brahmasmi" and "Tat twamasi" part, but they are for me only words, not a living experience or personal realisation.

That's very interesting", chimed in the silver-haired old man. "Are you really interested in all these things". The Wing Commander was addressing me. For a minute, I felt I detected a tone of raillery in his voice. He was a fairly senior officer, and next I thought he would berate me for wasting my time on such matters and exhort me to study the profession instead".

"Well, yes I am" I replied as curtly and briefly as I could.

"Don't get me wrong", he said defensively. "I am sorry I could not help over-hearing and so I butted in. Frankly, I do have more than a passing interest in the matter myself. But whom do you really follow?"

I put down my ego barriers. "Well, I have been deeply influenced by Sri Aurobindo's writings" I said guardedly.

"Have you been to the Ashram at Pondicherry?" This one really disturbed me. "No"– I very much wanted to but it just could not materialize...

He had touched a raw nerve and I passed my hand over my eyes.

He fell silent for some time. Then he renewed gently. "I have been to the Sri Aurobindo Ashram at Pondicherry", he said " in fact I spent two weeks there. It is very peaceful and the atmosphere is deeply spiritual, especially near Sri Aurobindo Samadhi. But there is an ancient Sanskrit proverb that says that you must change your guru or spiritual guide under these three circumstances: -

"First, when he dies and you are not advanced enough to be in contact with him"

"Second, if he goes mad"

"Third, if he violates the scriptures by his conduct".

Sri Aurobindo was a great Sage. But unfortunately, he is no more. Even his great disciple, the Mother has passed away. "Are you spiritually advanced enough to be in contact with them beyond their deaths?"

" I must confess that is far from the case. Infact that is my personal tragedy. I couldn't even meet these great beings before they passed away. Perhaps, I have been born too late.

Possibly, we have seen the last of our great ones. Perhaps, it is impossible to find a true guru or spiritual guide in these times". He looked at me intently, but said nothing. He fell silent and all one could hear was the monotonous clack-clack of the wheels of the train as they rattled interminably over the rails. The railway carriage swayed rhythmically. "The beat goes on. Life goes on," I thought to myself. I thought of the despair in the eyes of the Jain monk. Today, I could understand it much better.

"Have you ever been to Ganesh puri ?"

I heard the wing commander asking me gently.

"No, where is that?" I asked.

"It is in Maharashtra. Swami Muktananda Parmhamsa lives there. In modern day India, he is a sage of great personal realization. He is a disciple of Swami Nityananda - who was a great Avadhoota himself. You could go there and experience the spiritual atmosphere of the Ashram. You can then decide for yourself".

He had a magazine from the Ashram. I leafed through it. Baba's magnificent Ashram, Baba with the elephant, Baba after his triumphant tour of the West- the long suffering West. There was something in the eyes of that red robed sage that was arresting- but somehow it was not the image that I had unconsciously been searching for all these years.

"Have you been there?" I asked

"Yes, I go there every year. Scores of people visit the Ashram. It is very neat and clean. Many film stars from Bombay also come there.

"Film stars?" The word hung between us like a profanity. Film stars were hardly my idea of spiritual co-aspirants.

"I am sorry. But aren't there any Ashrams anymore which are far from the madding crowd as it were, more classical- more traditional, more in the archetypal image of the ancient Ashrams and Viharas?" I asked impulsively.

He looked at me quizzically but fell silent. The train swayed on drunkenly. I felt a little regretful. Possibly I had hurt his feelings. But he said nothing. I looked out of the window. We were passing a lotus pool, with scores of pink lotuses in full bloom. "Some years ago- a monk had come to Ganeshpuri" said the old Wing Commander almost in a whisper "He was, as you put it, very classical. He found the new opulence and grandeur of the Ashram not to his liking. He was keen on doing deep meditation. He was a man of deep realization. He looked like a Buddhist monk. But he left"

For some reason I sat bolt upright.

"Where did he go to?"

"To Patne. That is near Chalisgaon- a milk-producing town on the main rail route to Bombay. But he lives quite far from the town in a deep forest. He has simple Ashram- just two huts. He does deep meditation in that forest. But it is a little difficult to get there. You have to walk. There are no hotels close by so you have to sleep on the ground in the Ashram. The place has so many snakes, even tigers. Most people avoid going there because of these difficulties". For some reasons- the image of a classical Ashram deeply excited me.

"I am a soldier Sir, I don't mind walking and I am quite used to sleeping on the ground. Tell me more about him".

He smiled happily "I thought as much. I have been to his Ashram. This monk is surprisingly young. He was an engineer before he took sanyasa. So, you can relate to him better at the intellectual as well as the spiritual level. He has done deep meditation and aroused the Kundalini. In fact, he was a favourite disciple of Swami Muktananda. He may just be the sage you have been looking for".

I was fascinated by what I heard.

The Wing Commander had a photograph of Swami Pranvananda with him. He showed it to me. A shaved pate, large hypnotic eyes, powerful shoulders and long arms, a seamless saffron robe. He looked so much like a classical Buddhist monk. The image left a deep impression on me. There was something so classical and stern about that image and those eyes. Each one of us has an inherited storehouse of archetypal images. These are the denizens of the racial unconscious. They contain the figures of the Anima and the Animus (our archetypal male and female images) and the classical image of the wise old man- or the traditional sage. Ever since my childhood, I had such an image buried in my mind. The photograph of that sage fitted that image so perfectly that it was a bit astonishing. I felt a vague feeling of happiness steal over my being, an inexplicable excitement. I had seen the face of the promised one as it were and for some strange reason, he reminded me of that pleasant-faced Burmese Buddhist monk I had seen as a child.

I took down the address and the directions about the trains and buses involved, and thanked the Wing Commander profusely. A sage in a forest, an Ashram that looked exactly like the Ashram of the Vedic seers some 5000 years ago. An engineer and an educated person you could relate to. I felt excited. Was he for real?

"Why don't you go and find out for yourself" said the silver hared old man.

I felt a surge of happiness. I thanked him profusely and pumped his hand. "I certainly will. Thank you so much for telling me".

Siliguri junction in North Bengal. The Himalayas arise suddenly and abruptly like a blue wall from the billiard top flatness of the plains of Bengal. When you look out of the train window, you see what looks like a line of clouds on the horizon. These are the mighty Himalayas. I got down. The Wing Commander was going on further to the East. He came to the door to see me off. I thanked him profusely and sincerely, once again. "Each one of us has his own path to salvation" he said "But a guru, a living guide is a must for any real progress on this path, that has been my experience. You do need the grace of a living sage. Go and see if he is the man you were searching for all this while. You will know it in your being instantly if he is the one. You can't mistake that inner feeling. My blessings to you for your search. May God be with you," he said. The train began to steam out. I waved out to him gratefully. He waved back. The train disappeared into the dusk. I never saw him again in my life- but to this date- I remember this silver haired old man with deep gratitude.

9

The Sage of Synchronity

It was through a strange coincidence that I came to know about the sage of Patne. An even more remarkable series of coincidences or synchronous events forced me ultimately to go and meet him in the year that followed.

Carl Gustav Jung outlined the concepts of the collective unconscious and the Archetype. Archetypes are quintessential ideas, symbols and representations. They are core images buried deep in our collective unconscious. Jung in fact uses the notion of Archetype in two senses

As idea forms that could become actual events.

As predisposition to have certain experiences.

The archetypal predisposition is a form of psychic energy that is inclined to manifest in a corresponding empirical object. Thus, a man predisposed to search for a guru is then fated to meet the guru ultimately.

The hologramic core of our consciousness is a seething magma of such primal images or archetypes. In fact the word "imagination" comes from the formation of such "images". These core images or archetypes are organised in our psychic depths as hierarchies. One's father image, mother image, shadow, Anima (ideal woman image) and Animus (ideal male image) and the image of the wise old man. Also one's self image, world image etc. are all fundamental archetypal pre-dispositions. These archetypal images arise from the depths of our psyches, or collective unconscious. They float up to the surface of the psychic ocean- into our stream of consciousness. In so doing they impel us, in fact predispose us to undergo a corresponding set of real life experiences.

The underlying image of a saffron clad guru, a teacher of great purity; wisdom and spiritual experience had always been a part of my deeper spiritual heritage. It was a clear and distinct image. As a child, I had seen a Burmese Buddhist monk and recognized him instinctively. I had projected the archetypal image on to him. Even later, in 1973, when in a chance encounter, Wing Commander Yadav showed me the photograph of the sage of Patne, I was struck, as if by a bolt of lightning. A deeply buried image had surfaced from the depths of my psychic ocean into my stream of consciousness. I often thought about the chance encounter. I resolved to go to Patne in my next annual leave or at the first available opportunity. However, I had then to go back to my unit in Sikkim. There I got deeply involved in my military duties. I underwent strange experiences. I travelled to North Sikkim and for some time served on a remote border outpost at Tang kar La , a pass 16000 feet up on the Himalayan watershed.

From there, I was invited to witness a Lama Dance at the monastery of Lachung. Set amidst a backdrop of copper and magenta-coloured mountains, the monastery is imposing and picturesque. The experience of that strange dance ceremony to propitiate the Mahakala was an unforgettable experience. The huge Gelung trumpets hooted balefully. The cymbals clashed and the thigh bone trumpets set up eerie wails. The Lamas dressed in heavy brocade robes with colorful animal masks danced with a hypnotic cadence. They whirled and leapt and pirouetted, they bobbed their animal heads and lived the role of the animal archetype they were representing. The entire village of Lachung was out in its Sunday best finery, seated on the emerald green grass behind ornate picnic tables piled high with Mo Mos (meat dumplings), chow-chow (noodles) and chang (rice beer). In the East, religion is a celebration of life. That Lama dance is one of my most colourful and indelible impressions of Sikkim. The bright colourful images are still vivid in my mind to this day.

From Sikkim the unit moved out in Mar 1974 to Udhampur, across the breadth of India to the state of Jammu and Kashmir. I was now the Adjutant of the unit and up to my neck in work. In all this move and flurry of activity, I totally forgot about my chance encounter in the train. It was only in Aug 1974, a full one year later that I got my annual leave again and went home to Jabalpur.

I was tired and badly in need of rest. A two months annual leave is a wonderful feature of military life. It enables you to live out your other persona that can not find expression in the course of your professional career. I had frankly forgotten all about the sage of Patne and my resolve to meet him. My parents were happy to see me and I was happy to laze around the house- reading my books and enjoying my leisure. I was too tired to travel. I settled down to a highly introverted routine. I would read the whole day and then in the evenings stroll out to the hills behind my house. There I would climb up to an isolated hill and spend one or two hours in quiet contemplation and meditation. I sank deeper and deeper into myself as it were. On Wednesdays I used to attend the Aurobindo circle meeting at Mr. Iyyengar's house. They would put on the beautiful Sri Aurobindo centenary music, dim the lights and do collective meditation.

I found these sessions wonderful. One would sink deep into oneself, into a deeply personalised ego space- warm, dark and comforting. One's eyelids would feel heavy and almost as if glued together. I had to make an effort to prise them open. Sometimes, I began to feel strange pressures on top of my head, on my temples, on the bridge of my nose. In fact so palpable was the pressure that it made me uncomfortable and apprehensive.

Something strange was occurring in the depths of my psyche. I could feel something crystallizing as it were, swirling and forming deep in the magma of my unconscious-surging, pushing outwards to seek expression. Something that was vague and indefinable. I could sense that I was steadily approaching an important inner milestone.

It was then that I encountered a deep personal crisis. I was happy at the quiet and contemplative lifestyle that I was leading. Uninterrupted leisure put me into a cyclic mode of experiencing time in rhythm with dawn and dusk. It was a peaceful and serene monk-like existence. All of a sudden, I was alarmed to experience deep surges from the lower vital-the animal and instinctual level of existence. I had eagerly been looking forward to some spiritual experience. Instead I was alarmed to encounter these libidinal upsurges almost as a revolt of the lower vital. At this point it is difficult to describe my alarm, the sheer horror and panic I felt at this development. It rudely shook the even tenor of my peaceful existence. I was so alarmed that I stopped my meditational practices. Where was I going wrong? I had picked up these techniques from the various books on Yoga and Mahayana Buddhism that I had read. I experimented with various methods. Was I making a serious error somewhere? Was I straying from the path of inner purity? Were my meditational techniques flawed and leading me into error?

I went to the Jain scholar in Jabalpur. His words gave me peace. But once more he returned to the primal theme. In matters spiritual there is no salvation without the guidance of a living guru, a guide who has himself traversed the path. Books can not be a substitute for a guru. No student of Sadhana can make any meaningful progress without the personal guidance of a guru.

It is an inner economy of effort. Our basic instincts lead us to adopt the lifestyle of a householder. Our energies are then directed in the normal, time-worn channels. To achieve a spiritual break-through, however, these self-same creative energies must be sublimated and redirected. But such control and redirection goes against nature. It does not come easily. The cerebro-spinal axis is the axis of our consciousness. It has two centers for experiencing pleasure and ecstasy at both its terminal ends- deep in our brains and lower down in our vital organs. Millenniums of evolutionary experience have genetically predisposed us towards the tactile rewards of reproduction that are centered on the terminal end of our spine. We have to struggle against nature and redirect the energy flow upwards- to our brains- to the summits of our cerebro-spinal axons. This is not an easy task. It can not be accomplished without the grace and guidance of a living guru.

I had felt confident I could do it alone. I had felt so close to a breakthrough, an inner experience. I felt greatly disheartened. The conflict and struggle in the young psyche can be extremely painful. A strange man used to come and meet my father those days. He was Murthi, a tall thin and emaciated looking man with deep-set eyes and an unruly shock of hair. He used to practice deep meditation and was very learned in the scriptures. He was very taciturn, moody and temperamental like a Zen master. Sometimes, he would spend hours in animated, philosophical discussion. Then abruptly he would stop in the middle of a sentence and leave. His eyes had a strange, serene and mocking expression. He challenged everything you said. Father enjoyed engaging him in long metaphysical discussions on the nature of Brahman and the Atman. One day, I returned home from the hill in the evening to find Murthi engaged in deep philosophical disputation with my father.

"Brahman is the only reality", Murthy was saying. "There is no other. Brahman is truth- the world is Mithya. It is not true, it is not real or substantial". Father was a dualist and vehemently opposed the notion of the world as non-real. Murthy gave another analogy "You go to a cinema. You see the images on the screen and are deeply involved. You laugh and cry with the actors, you experience love, fear, terror and suffering. But then, if you move your head, you turn back and see the projector- the spell breaks. You realize that these images are not real. They are a phantasmagoria- they are merely being projected on the screen by the light. The *Bahir mukh vrittri*, the tendency of externalising our consciousness must similarly be switched off. It must be made *Antar mukha* or inward-looking. We must turn around. We must direct the searchlight, the beam of consciousness deep within ourselves if we wish to realise Brahman".

My father turned to me "Well, what do you say?" I was a little tired and dispirited by my inner struggles and lack of a breakthrough. I sighed deeply. "Well I think all these are mere words, arguments and analogies. They are not in themselves an experience of Brahman. This is all a 'shabda jala' a web of words. I have read the same scriptures too. But is that an experience of Brahman? The scriptures say 'Aham Brahmasmi'- I am Brahman. But is that the reality of our experience? It is just an aphorism for me". I turned to Murthy "Have you experienced Brahman yourself? Can you transmit that experience to me? I am tired of reading books. What I want is a real, a genuine experience of that reality". Murthy's eyebrows shot up in surprise. He stared at me intently. Then suddenly he got up, abruptly.

"Its late – I must be going", he said and left. My father was astonished. Later he remonstrated with me "You should not have been rude. We must have the maturity to listen to the view point of others". "I am sorry, father. But it is just

The Jain Scholar of Jabalpur

Murthi—The Vedantin

that is what I sincerely feel. We have to progress beyond mere words and written texts to a direct experience of that reality. The only problem is how? Arguments and philosophical disputation do not seem to resolve this problem".

Many days passed. I had gone for a walk in the hills. I was sitting alone and watching the Sunset when a servant rushed up to me. "Your father wants you to come back immediately. Someone has come to meet you". I came back and found Murthy in the drawing room. He was strangely excited and agitated.

"Ah there you are. So you want a direct experience of reality, is it? What prevents you from having it". I was surprised and mystified.

"My question really is, how? How does one get it?" I replied patiently.

"How? It is so simple. Don't you see?" Here, give me paper and a pencil. Here – *Shabda, Sparsha, Roopa, Rasa* and *Gandha* (Sound, Touch, Sight, Taste, and Smell). These are the five senses. They correspond to the five elements- to *Akasha* (the Ether), to *Vayu* (the Air), the *Agni* (the Fire), to *Prithvi* (the Earth) and *Jala* (the Liquids). Here Shabda- the Sound is the closest to the Ether- to Akasha. Do you understand?" he spluttered in tremendous excitement. I was baffled. Yet there was something in his air of excitement that was arresting and infectious. All my senses awakened as it were and strove to follow what he was saying. He seemed to have solved a great conundrum. He almost danced with impatience. "Oh, it is so simple. The Shabda- the Sound can give you a direct experience of reality. Just try it. Try it now. In seven days you will have an experience. You will experience reality".

"Shabda? Sound? What Sound? Which Sound will give me an experience of reality?" I asked mystified.

"Take any sound. Take 'OM'. It is the highest sound vibration. A-U M, it represents the alpha and omega of existence, the three states of consciousness and the fourth state that lies beyond. 'Ah' is the basic, the most primal sound- the first sound that we make. 'U' is the bridge and 'M' is the other end of the sound continuum. A-U-M represents the entire gamut of human sound. Close your eyes and start the chant of "Aum" inwardly. Do it. Do it for just seven days and you will have an experience. You are very close to it. Just do it".

With that Murthy got up and left. He had a look of triumph in his eyes. It was all so sudden and yet so strangely exciting. Just seven days? I could get an experience in just seven days? I was delighted. I had stopped meditation as a result of my inner problems. Now I resumed them with redoubled vigour. I closed my eyes and began the chant of Om- inwardly. I rapidly went through the same experiences. The fixty of posture. The deep interiorisation of awareness. The acuity of sensation in the space between my eyebrows. The loss of all sense of time. The pressures upon my head, temples and nape of the neck. The intrusion of the sound of my own breathing. I seemed to be flooded by the sound of my own breath. And then the libidinal upsurges and emotional peaks of excitement. I was horrified and gave up in alarm once more. What in Gods name was going on within me? Murthy was no where to be seen. I was panic stricken. Was the experience of mere libidinal upsurges to be the final experience? Could I transcend no deeper than that? I felt heart broken. All my efforts were coming to naught. I was deeply distressed and floundering. I needed guidance badly. I felt strong upsurges of emotions. Images of the many-Armed Goddess Kali, fierce entropic and impatient. A great force and power- the primal Shakti sweeping aside all our comfortable logical construct in a male storm; an energic expression of emotions, feelings and creative impulses;

upsurges of our vital emotions and imperial instinctual drives. At times, I felt that I was losing my reason, being relentlessly pushed by nameless forces beyond my control. It was so hopeless that I wept. Suddenly through the mist of tears and that onrushing depression, one day I heard a clear voice within.

"Om is the Pranva Mantra. Go to Pranvananda if you wish to experience the ecstasy of the Pranva sound".

I sat up bolt upright. It was like a bolt of lightning from the blue.

But of course! I had almost forgotten. It came rushing back all at once.

"Pranvananda, Patne. I had to go there. It was now so urgent and pressing. I had wasted my whole leave. The holidays were almost coming to an end. No, I could not afford to put it off by another year. I had to go right then and there.

I came out of my room all excited and determined to go.

What seems so certain at dawn, pales by noon and by dusk you are again beset by doubts and apprehensions.

Pranvananda?

Who was he? Was he really the master you were seeking? What, if he was a mere hoax? A Chimera? A charlatan or worse? I spoke to my father.

"Pranvananda? Who is he? I never heard of him? Where does he stay? Where is this Patne? Look son. Why do you want to go off now to some strange place? How can you be certain that he can help you? You are being irrational and impulsive. You are chasing a mirage. Don't waste your time".

What he said sounded perfectly rational. In fact he was voicing the misgivings of the more rational part of myself. I felt exasperated and confused. I decided to meet the Jain scholar. As usual, his room seemed an oasis of peace. "I am confused. I have come for guidance". He looked up in mild surprise. "For some days now I have been obsessed by an inner feeling or intuition- I don't know what to call it. It keeps impelling me to go to Patne- to meet a Swami Pranvananda Saraswati. Somehow, I feel he could be the guru I have been seeking all my life".

"Pranvananda Saraswati? I have not heard of him", said the Jain scholar gently. "He is a disciple of Muktananda Paramhamsa. He has been doing deep Sadhana alone in a forest for some years now". I said.

"Muktananda?" the Jain scholar's eyebrows shot up. "Of him I have certainly heard. He is a man of deep realisation. He has aroused the Kundalini in his own being. But he stays in Ganeshpuri".

Some how I feel, this sage at Patne is my guru. Only I am confused. Sometimes I feel I should go to him right away. Then I feel I may be mistaken. I am torn by doubt. I can not make up my mind. Is it a genuine intuition or a false mimicry of the mind" I said. The Jain monk looked at me intently. He remained silent for a long time. I strained to catch his every word- for some how I felt the answer would come from him. "We are rational beings. Doubt comes to us often and we despair. Is our rationality itself an obstacle or is it an aid?" He looked at me questioningly. Then he continued, "We are mere mortals. Even the great Ramakrishna was beset by doubts sometimes. He felt that the visions and intuitions that he had were hoaxes- tricks of the mind. He used to be greatly distressed then".

"How did he resolve his doubts?" I asked hesitatingly.

"He would ask for a sign. A clear sign to indicate that the inner voice of intuition was right. He would ask the Goddess to give him a clear sign, an indication that confirms the truth of your inner intuition? Why don't you ask for a sign?"

"Me?" I was astonished "But I am not Ramakrishna. He could speak to the void and get an answer- what about us? We are mere mortals. Will God speak to us if we try?"

The Jain scholar looked at me thoughtfully. "How will we ever know if we don't even try? Is there really a difference between a saint and one who is still striving? I think it is only a question of degrees. And perfection is the ultimate degree. We have to go step by step to the inner summits of our own beings. You must try."

I bowed before him and left. For some reason, I felt strangely at peace after many days. I came back home. It was around 10'0 clock in the morning. It was a serene and peaceful day. The birds cooed in the dense vegetation of the mango trees. I went up to our family prayer room and sat down before the altar. You must ask for an indication. What kind of an indication? What kind of sign? I pondered deeply for sometime. Suddenly it struck me. I had exhausted the money I had brought with me. I had no money left. Father did not want me to go to Patne and was not willing to pay for the trip. That would be a good test.

"I have no money with me now. If I am really required to go to Patne, let some money come to me of its own accord". I thought this to myself. Yes, that would be a clear test. I felt immensely pleased and bowed before the altar.

"Postman",

I had hardly raised my head when I heard the call outside. Now there is nothing earth shaking about a postman announcing his arrival but at that precise point in time- at that juncture, the sound of the postman's call left me speechless. It took my breath away. I suddenly felt frightened. I had spoken to the void. Was this the answer? I walked slowly to the door. My heart pounding against my ribs. My mother met the postman.

"Son there is a money order for you", she said.

Ramakrishna—Paramahansa
The Last of our great ones.

"Money order?" It was like a virtual bolt of lightning. Money order from where? From whom? I looked at the pay slip. My mother looked at the expression of astonishment and awe on my face and was alarmed. "Why? What is the matter son?" "Nothing", I said as I stared at the money order.

A few years ago I had lent some money to a fellow officer. He was a drunkard and in dire financial straits. He could not clear his mess bills while attending a course of instruction. One cheque had bounced and he was asked to clear his account to cash or face a court martial. He had implored me to help him. My friends advised me against it. I would never get back my money. Nevertheless I felt sorry for him and loaned him some 800 rupees. He was very grateful and promised to return it the next month. That was the last I saw of him. Months passed. I wrote to him. He gave more promises and assurances but no money. Ultimately I had only one option left. To report against him officially. I did not have the heart to do so. So I decided to forget about the whole episode.

I had forgotten about it. For some strange reason he remembered it. After almost a year and a half, on his own accord he sent me back half the amount (I am still waiting for the balance). That the sum should have reached me at that precise point in space and time after that aside the avoid a clear question made this synchronous event in to a crystal clear answer. The silent reply was deafening in its impact. It was this strange synchronity of events that led me finally to the sage of Patne.

10
The Seventh Day

"Just seven days and you will have an experience- just try it". The words of Murthy came back to me as I stood on the platform waiting for the train. It was exactly six days after he had come to our house. My father had come to see me off. He was unhappy about my going. "Some times we are too subjective in our perception of things. We tend to see them not as they are but as we would like them to be".

"Yes, father".

"We look for perfection but we don't find it. We are then acutely disappointed. Don't be too disappointed if this sage is not really what you imagine him to be".

"I won't be, father", I said mechanically.

"And what-ever happens- please, do come back" said father.

I looked at him in surprise, and then averted my gaze. I felt guilty over causing him so many heartaches and worries. But I had no option. I just had to go. There was simply no choice now. Not after I had spoken to the void and received a clear answer. I had gone excitedly to the Jain scholar after that experience and told him about it. He was equally excited. He sat up and polished his spectacles vigorously. Then he was a classical disputing scholar once more. "But when you meet him- how will you know that he is the Guru that you seek? How will you recognize him?"

"I don't know. I will just feel it within me I suppose?" I had said hesitatingly.

"But we must not abandon our reason. A Sanskrit text says "Drink water only after you have purified it with a cloth. Accept a man as a guru only after you have known him fully". What matters is what happens within you when you are in his presence. It is an intensely personal equation."

Today the doubts were all behind me. With each hour, I felt more positive and certain. I felt happy and euphoric. I was off on a joyous adventure into the unknown. I was excited. What would I see? Whom would I meet? What would he be like, the saffron-clad guru?

There is a joy sometimes in abandoning the shackles of your reason, your doubts, fears and apprehensions. There is a joy in acting out of non-reason – from a faith that springs from a far-deeper level of your own existence. When the actions are not focussed upon the narrow and personalized ego, they give us an experience of joy and happiness. "Do the lilies of the pond store for the morrow? Do the trees store their own fruit? They do not. They trust their maker and he provides."

We have to learn to trust the voidness –the that which is, the universal consciousness that pervades the cosmos. It is only when we dive to that inner level that we experience a cosmic connectivity that automatically plugs in our spiritual needs and desires to the sources of their fulfillment. It is a joyous consciousness born of faith and trust in our trans-personal destiny. More than one of us decides with intelligence. But true intelligence does not lie here – in the head. It resides in the heart. And who so ever follows the prompting of his heart acts from a level of joyfulness and trust. The way to happiness is not an arid path. It is a path with a heart. The train was yet to stream in. I decided to go over to the stall and pick up some book to read during the journey. It was a slim volume – a Ramakrishna Mission Publication. I hardly even glanced at the title.

The train steamed in. a flurry of movement. People rushing and pushing. I was ensconced in my seat by the window.

"Have you taken the water bottle?"

"Yes, father"

"And the packed dinner?"

"Yes, father".

The old man sighed "Very well, then". He was at a loss for words. I touched his feet. The train started. For a long time, he stood waving on the platform as it receded from view. I sighed deeply. Then I sat down and opened the book. I had almost 12 hours journey ahead of me. The title of the book was interesting "Spiritual Practice: Its Conditions and Preliminaries". The book spoke about the need for a guru for success in Sadhana. It spoke about renunciation. When are we ready to renounce? Should we retire to the forests or continue as householders? What should be our relationship with our guru? What are the signs of a true guru? How do we recognise him? What will he do for us and what should be our duty to him?" I now read with avid interest. The questions raised by the Jain scholar were being answered of their own accord. I, eagerly, raced through the book. I came to the last page. It had a simple invocation.

"We have accompanied the reader at last to the sacred feet of the guru. The guru will instruct him about the actual practices that lead to the ultimate truth. At that point his actual spiritual practice will begin."

I sat bolt upright. Another coincidence? Another synchronous event? And then I felt it slowly seep over me, a vague and indefinable feeling of happiness. A feeling of joy and euphoria and lightness of heart. A surge of positivity and bliss that seemed to grow with each mile. The parched aridness of my heart felt irradiated with a Christ like love and compassion. A strong surge of love that reached out to you across the aeons. You were not going to a stranger. It was as if you were going to a place where many, many years ago you had deeply and hopelessly been in love. The intensity of that feeling of love and happiness surprised me. It was like a palpable but joyful wound in the heart. My heart ached with a monotonous languor. Slowly you felt that love radiate towards you and then bathe your being – inundate it in wave after wave of bliss and euphoria. Some months back a Bengali monk had come to Jabalpur. He used to sing simple devotional songs with a rare abandon. He would loose himself in those Sufi lyrics of love addressed to God as the beloved. The simple and devout monk would go into a trance even as he sang. Sometimes he would fall unconscious and had to be carried away. My father had taped his devotional songs and we often used to listen to them at home. Now from nowhere in particular- his beautiful and inspired devotional songs began to course through by being. I felt thrills of intense rapture. Tears of happiness flowed from my eyes. The cadence of that devotional music washed over me in wave after wave of bliss. I left my seat and stood framed in the door of the railway carriage so that the people may not see me.

Tears of love and gratitude bathed my face. It was an extraordinary eruption of love and bliss in the heart. A surge of love that was Trans-human, it seeped up from a deeper level of my own psyche; from the very core of consciousness. It is said in the scriptures that there are seven levels of the human mind as it radiates inwards and encapsulates the human body. The body is contained in the Pranic field, the Pranic Field in the Field of the mind (The Manomaya Kosha). The mind body contains the rational mind, the relational mind, the seat of will and the sixth level of Divine Love and

Ecstasy. The Seventh Level is the level of the Supermind and Serenity. Such feelings of love, euphoria and ecstasy sometimes well up from the sixth level of our minds and surge into our everyday consciousness.

It was a beautiful experience. I was so excited that I could not sleep and must have stood framed in the doorway of the carriage for many hours- the cadence of a divine music coursing through every atom of my being, irrigating the parched field of my consciousness with love and bliss. What a relief it was from the aridness of rationality and the tyranny of reason and doubt. The train sped on into the darkness. It hurtled along the straight lines of the railway tracks that seemed to converge in the distance, at a thousand miles and a thousand years in the past. I was at last on my pilgrimage and I felt joyful and happy. Sometimes a journey is a metaphor whose very straightness and linearity points a way out of the convolutions and confusion of our life. The very straightness of its path seems to lead us out of the cobwebs of our confusion and doubt. It is a release and a catharsis.

Every external pilgrimage is merely allegorical of the final pilgrimage that we have to undertake in the depths of our own consciousness. The final journey from the roots of our spines to the summit of our brains; from the seat of the Mooldhara to the crown of a lotus with a thousand petals. I was tired but happy. The whole compartment had fallen asleep long ago. The wind whipped at my face and rushed through my hair. The wheels beat a soothing mechanical cadence on the rails. At long last I came back and fell asleep on my berth.

11
Initiation

20th of Sep 1974

I pass my hands reverentially over the faded pages of my diary of those years.

How many aeons ago, it all seems now.

At 0430 hours in the morning, the train steamed into the Chalisgaon junction.

The conductor gently shook my arm.

"Chalisgaon", he announced.

I stepped down on the platform and shivered in the cool wetness of dawn. 0430 hours in the morning. Just before daybreak, comes the divine hour of Brahman. The right time for meditation. It was in that hour that I stepped off the train into the sleepy, milk-producing town of Chalisgaon. It was so quiet and still. The entire world seemed to be rolling on the tides of sleep- the deepest and most restful sleep before dawn. The stars still shone brightly but you could see a faint trace of light in the East.

Tea? The vendor pushed a cup towards me.

The steaming hot tea cleared the cobwebs of sleep from my head.

I went to the retiring room, shaved and washed my face. Then I felt it again, like a gentle murmur- the cadence of those devotional songs; I felt again that surge of quiet euphoria and happiness, that wonderful feeling of positivity and joy. The Tonga clip clopped through the deserted streets of the town. The first bus to Patne leaves at 6'0 clock, the tea vendor had said. As I reached the bus stand, the sky was flooded with the diamond light of dawn. I sat down by a window seat in the bus. Within minutes crowds of tribals filled the vehicle, swarthy men with huge Red and Magenta turbans, gypsy women with white bangles that covered their slim arms till their elbows. Surprised faces. Looks of astonishment at the presence of a stranger.

The bus started. It wound through the streets of the sleeping mofussil town. The aroma of spices assailed my nostrils as we passed the bazaar. Then we came into the open fields. In the distance, I saw the vague blue wall of hills rising suddenly and steeply from the plains. The Sayhadri ranges- (to be more precise, the Indryahyadri hills) loomed over the forested expanse. The divine symphony of that music coursed through my being. I felt so happy. It was wonderful to be on this inner adventure. To act upon your pure impulse and inspiration- to transcend the shackles of reason and logic and simply follow the voices in the stillness of your heart. To do with your life as you please. To essay into the unknown with joy in your heart. I felt so euphoric and happy. I did not want to talk to anyone. It would have broken that spell of enchantment. Some inner elixir would have seeped out of my mouth, as it were. The bus came to a halt at the village of Patne. "Where is the Devi Temple?"

"This is as far as the bus goes. You have to walk the rest of the way. The temple is some two kilometers into the forest", said the conductor. Surprised faces. Women drawing water at the well paused to see a total stranger in the village. I walked on. Suddenly, I was out of the village and into the forest. It was so still, so peaceful and serene. The early morning sun shone through the filigree of leaves and creepers. I experienced the full surge of that euphoria. I was all alone now. I almost danced, as I strode along the cart track, going deeper and deeper into the forest.

The magnificent ruins of the Mahadeva temple.

I paused to take in their grandeur. I was so excited. Whom would I meet? What would he be like?

Surges of love and bliss inundated my being. The aridness of my heart suddenly felt irrigated with love.

I walked on

Suddenly, a huge brown snake emerged from the forest, slithering across the dust track and disappeared into the forest beyond.

I stopped in fear momentarily. The snake is the symbol of the secret forces of the soul. It sloughs off its skin and renews itself even as the Atman reincarnates in different forms. It is the ultimate paradox. It symbolizes eternal life and it symbolises death. It is auspicious to see a snake on a spiritual journey.

I resumed my walk. The silence. The utter stillness of the deep forest. The magic of the morning mist and dew.

The devine cadace of those hymns

I was almost running now -impatient to catch a glimpse of my destination. I entered a clearing. I crossed a stream and suddenly, I stopped. The huge basalt cliffs towered over my head in a massive amphitheatre. There, to the left was the ancient Devi temple. The two huge Deepa Stambhas, the pillars of light, towered at the entrance like the sentinels of time. To the right, was a little island in the dry nala bed. It had a dense cluster of trees and two straw-roofed huts. You hesitated. Where should you go, first? You turned to the temple.

A long flight of stone steps. Exquisite sculptures and statues in the courtyard. The inner sanctum. The porous stones were worn smooth. There you came face to face with the huge Alpine faced statue of the Devi. You were surprised.

No, it was not the Mahakali.

It was a statue of the Mahisha sur Mardhini, the Devi in her form as the slayer of the buffalo demon Mahisha Sur. That face! What a strong resemblance it bore to the photograph of the sage.

I was now tense and apprehensive.

I bowed my head to the ground.

What would happen now? Would lights course through my brain? Would I fall in a swoon? I was strangely nervous. I then went out and stood before the sage's hut. The small wicker gate is still there. The straw roofed hut of the classical hermitage is gone now.

"Baba," I called out diffidently.

"Kaun?" Who is it? I heard that clear warbling sound as if of the birds. And a Sufi parable flashed through my brain. One went to the home of the beloved and knocked. "Who is it?" said the voice within. "It is I, I have come", he replied in triumph. "Go away. Your time has not yet come", said the voice. Crestfallen he returned. He fasted and prayed for many years. Then he returned again.

"Who is it?" said the voice.

"It is I", he said hesitatingly "I have come again".

"Go away. Your time has not yet come", said the voice.

He was truly dejected. He came back. He fasted and prayed for 14 long years. His hair grew white and the years mellowed him. He returned finally to the home of the beloved. "Who is it?" said the voice. "It is thyself", he replied gently.

"Enter" said the voice and the gates were thrown open to him.

"Kaun?"

"Who is it", said the warbling voice within the hut. I opened my mouth to speak but no sound came out. The Sufi parable flashed through my brain and I was at a complete loss for words. What should I say in reply?

He came out of his hut.

The broad Alpine face. The vermilion mark on the forehead. The seamless saffron robe. The long, powerful arms that came till his knees. The thousand questions in his eyes.

I touched my forehead to his feet.

The surprise and unspoken questions were writ large all over his visage.

I felt strangled. I just could not speak. Were words necessary? Did we need a formal introduction?

We went inside the audience hut. The painting of the Patne Devi by Rahoul's mother – the fragrance of incense – the deep quiet.

We sat down.

Gently, he took up the unspoken questions.

Who? From where? How?

I had to make a supreme effort to speak. Speaking was like breaking that spell of enchantment. I was tired after my journey. I spoke in brief mono syllables.

A touch. A look. A glance, anything can set that off- the shakti pat that triggers the arousal of our inner energy.

There was a child-like look of uncertainty on his face. How much like that Burmese monk he looked.

"How long will you stay?"

I hesitated "As long as you wish".

"But still...."

I sighed and looked at him in perplexity.

He looked at me for a long time.

Suddenly, he had come to a decision , "You must be tired after your journey. Have you bathed?"

"No".

"Then go and bathe, change into something comfortable".

I drew water from the well and bathed. I had not realised it so far, but I was tired. I changed into a loose kurta and pyjama. The boys had pulled out a cot and put it under the tamarind tree. "You must be tired. Why don't you lie down for a while", said the sage. I did so, and soon was fast asleep. As I slept under the tree, the sage sat silently. He was deep in thought. He kept looking at the sleeping form sprawled out on the cot. For a long time, he sat like that. Then he retired to his hut.

When I got up, the Sun had risen high up in the heavens. I felt refreshed. Some villagers had come to meet him. They were in the audience hut. A small child had come with his mother. "Go touch his feet", she prodded him. Uncertainly, the child got up. The sage put his hand into a box of sweetmeats besides him and offered a fistful to the child. Happily, he scampered up, grabbed the sweets, touched his feet and ran back to his mother and buried his face shyly in her lap. The people broke into smiles and "Ahed" and "Oohed" in delight.

"You seem to be very fond of children", I observed.

"Well, yes. Their minds are so plastic. They can be moulded. With the grownups you can do little. With you and me we can do nothing, really".

I was surprised. As I was to learn later, he never did anything without a purpose. Every act of his was imbued with a deeper meaning.

We got talking.

"I am confused. I sit down to meditate, I close my eyes

but what exactly should you do after that? What is the correct technique?"

"Its our fault, really. We do not speak clearly. Certainly, I will tell you" , he replied.

Aurobindo speaks of a descent of the Force- a descent of the Supermind. The classical texts, however, talk only of the ascent of the Kundalini. What really is the truth?", I asked him.

"Ascent or descent – up or down, aren't these the categories of our measuring intellects?" he replied. "Is there really an 'up or down' in the topology of our consciousness? I do think it is the self-same force. The classical texts describe its ascent. My own Guru's Guru felt that its ultimate action took place in the region of our head. The ascent from the space between the eyebrows to the Crown of our brains was the crucial ascent. Different constitutions experience it differently. It is a highly individual phenomena".

More villagers came in and left.

Then came a group of small boys from the village school. They adored him. A transformation came over him in their presence. His eyes sparkled and shone with mischief. He became a little boy, like them. A little boy who had never known an adolescence or puberty. The more I saw of him, the more he reminded me of Alyosha, the boyish young priest in Dostyvesky's immortal classic "The Brothers Karmazov".

Alyosha. The friend of all the little boys! We moved for lunch to the kitchen. The boys served a simple meal of rice and lentils. As we ate, a baby rat scampered fearlessly around the place. He came to Baba's plate and sniffed curiously. The absolute fearlessness of the tiny animal underlined the total Ahimsa or non-violence of the sage.

"The animals do not seem to fear you," I said.

"Why should they? I am the guest in their realm. Not they in mine".

He retired to his hut for the afternoon.

In the evening, we visited the temple.

Then we came back. I retired to the audience hut for the night. "Baba is calling you", one of the boys said. I hurried over to his hut. It was a small hut with a thatched roof. He was sitting cross legged on the bed. I sat down on the floor with my legs thrown to one side carelessly.

"Sit properly" he commanded. Surprised, I sat down in the lotus posture. "The Atman (soul) enters the body mind complex here at the Brahma randhara (the apperture of Brahman) at the crown of our heads. When we focus our attention here- the sound that we hear is the sound of "Aum" the highest mystic chant. The Atman here is fully cognisant of its identity with Brahman".

"It descends next to the eye-brow centre to the Ajna Chakra – the center between our eyes. When we focus on this, the sound that we hear is "So-ham" "That am I". It is the chant of our breathing – it is the sound of our breath itself. When the Atman descends lower to the Throat centre, here, the sound that we cognise is "koham" "Who am I". The Atman has lost its identity with Brahman. And below the throat centre the Atman loses itself completely in the experience of the lower life and its myriad activities". He continued, "When we begin our meditation, an easy start point is not the crown centre – but here – in the space between the eyebrows. The sound here is not "Aum" but "Soham". This is called the "Ajapa-Japa" the chant of our living beings- it is the sound of our breathing that goes on constantly. Focus on this sound of the breath. It is a natural bio-resonator structured in our body-mind complex". I was astounded. Murthy had casually asked me to begin with Aum and I had found it difficult. The sound of my breath used to intrude upon my consciousness, every time I tried. It was as if he had read my unspoken thoughts- it was as if he was fully aware of all that had happened to me earlier. I almost shivered.

"So, sit down", he continued ,"Gently close your eyes and focus on the sound of your own breath. Watch it as it flows inwards like this- "Sooo" he uttered gently as he drew in his breath and "Haamm" as it exhales. Is there ever a time when we are not breathing? We breathe as long as we live. But are we conscious of the sound of our own breath? It is a pity. For it is a powerful mystic sound. It is a constant chant. It is the refrain of all life".

"Sooo – as you draw in your breath, and Haamm as you exhale. Now all you have to do is sit cross-legged, keep your spine straight and close your eyes. Then, gently focus on your breathing. Mentally chant "Soo" as you breathe in and "Hamm" as you breathe out. Do not shorten or lengthen your breath. Just follow it gently. Just focus on it, softly".

"Now try it", he said.

I closed my eyes. He followed the rhythm of my breathing. Then he began the hypnotic chant "Sooo" as I breathed in and "Hamm" as I exhaled. It had a powerful hypnotic effect. It drew you inwards to the depths of your psyche.

"As you focus on your breath, it will become shallower and shallower. At a point, it will seem to vanish. Your thoughts will tend to drift. Do not struggle to control them. Gently, shift your attention back to the sound of breathing. Remember the slogan "Thoughts may come and thoughts may go, but the breathing goes on for ever". So focus on your breathing now". He let me do it for ten minutes or so. It had a powerful soothing effect. I felt overjoyed.

"The best times for meditation", he said "are the dawn and dusk. When the day and night meet, and it is pleasant and cool. Avoid meditation in the hot part of the day. Do ease your self both before and after meditation. Ensure that you sit in a place where you are not likely to be disturbed by people or the telephone. Do it for fifteen minutes only in the morning and evenings initially. As you increase your practice, you will notice stretches where your breathing has become almost imperceptible, and there are no thoughts and no breathing. That is meditation. No thoughts- no breath. Have you understood?"

I was amazed by the clarity of his exposition. Murthy had asked me to focus on the sound of Aum. Each time I did so, the sound of my own breathing seemed to intrude conspicuously. I noticed it, time and again, but I did not understand.

Until now that is. It was so strange. It was as if Baba had just filled in the blanks in my knowledge. He had explained with the utmost clarity the art of meditation. I, reverentially, touched his feet in gratitude.

"Keep up the practice. Increase the time steadily. You will experience peace. The peace deepens into bliss. The bliss blossoms into Euphoria, and Euphoria turns into Ecstasy. You will have many inner experiences. Record them down, and discuss them with me".

"I have now given you the ticket to your ultimate destination", he said "How far you travel depends entirely on you. You could get down at the first station itself, or go on right till the very end. The travelling has to be done by you. I have only shown you the way".

I bowed reverentially, once again.

"Now, go. Tomorrow you must return home. Your parents must be worried about you. But keep coming and spend more time here".

Outside the stars were blazing forth in an ink black sky. The forest was so silent and still. The trees seemed frozen in the gestures of a mystic dance.

My initiation was complete. I had, at long last, found my great teacher – my guru and spiritual guide. One phase of my life was over. The next had begun. It was exactly the Seventh day after I had met Murthy, and heard his strange prophecy.

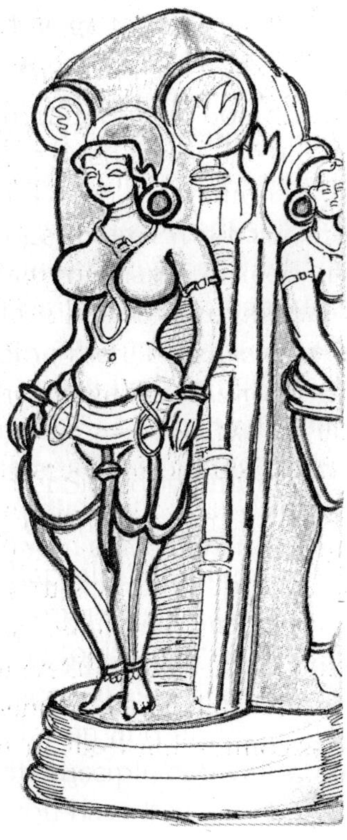

12
Encounters with Ecstasy

(Experiences of the River of Happiness)

Under the benign guidance of the sage of Patne, I began to intensify my meditational practises. I lengthened the meditation sessions till I could sit nonstop for over an hour at a time. He exhorted me to deepen the practice further in my annual leaves. An annual retreat to Patne became a recurring feature of my life. I used to come home on my leave and intensify the meditational practices. When I felt I was ready, I would then go off to Patne to be with him. There was little need for dialogue. What needed to be said, really?

"I have given you the ticket", he had said, "You can travel as far as you like. That depends on the personal effort you put in". So I learned to be silent and still. Sometimes, we did not exchange a word for days. He insisted that his disciples get up well before daybreak. We got up at 0400 hours in the mornings, bathed and greeted our teacher. Then, we went to the Devi temple for Darshan. Thereafter, we would sit down separately for meditation- he in his hut and we in the main audience hall. Some months after I first met him, he had added a third hut for visitors, where guests like me could come and stay and meditate. I somehow preferred to do my meditation in the ancient Devi temple. The shrine had such a positive atmosphere. The stones of the floors were worn smooth and so comfortable to sit on. Just being in Baba's benign presence was a powerful spur to your inner development and unfoldment. His presence was like a catalyst that hastened your inner evolution. By his grace and benign guidance, within a few months, I could sit in meditation continually for hours on end. The very atmosphere was so conducive. The field that emanated from him was so powerful that it aligned your consciousness like a magnet. It induced a deep silence and inner positivity. It induced an inner current of joy.

When you sat down to meditate in his presence, you lost all count of time. You just closed your eyes and sank inwards to a comforting, soothing inner darkness. It was like a cloistered shell of your own, you forgot that you were alone in a deep forest- you felt safe and secure and serene, and so contented. Your eyes felt glued together and you had to make a conscious effort to prise them open after meditation. Your spine remained straight and rigid of its own accord- you lost all sensation of the stone floor on which you were seated. You sat like that for hours on end. When you opened your eyes at last, and looked at your watch, you were often astonished. What had seemed like a session of just 15 or 20 minutes had actually gone on for three or four hours. That was the essential feature of Babas method of meditation. Focussing on the bio-resonator of your own breathing, somehow caused you to lose all sense of time awareness. It had a pronounced effect on your frontal brain lobe. The pitch of sensation in the space between the eyes became so acute that it was almost physical.

The only way to unlearn your reality is to first decondition your mind of its habitual modes of the normal perception of time. All our life experience is threaded upon the linear axis of time. It is this axial progression in time that helps us to organise our life experience. It is a rigidly linear and unidirectional flow. Its conditioning is overwhelming.

It can flow only in one direction- from the past to the present, and into a future that we can not normally foresee.

Baba's method of meditation altered your perception of time. When the ingoing and outgoing breath have been equalised- a resonance is entrained in our brains that powerfully alters our perception of time from an ever onrushing linear flow to an ever-expanding isness of a never ending now. We slip into a different space-time continuum altogether. The Vedic and Upanishadic seers, and later the Buddhist monks, had realised the essential nature of this psychological deconditioning process of outgrowing the rigid and inexorable linearity of time. The tyranny of time is the greatest and most inexorable imposition of our lives. It is the basis of our reality. When we wish to unlearn this reality, we have to consciously adopt a different life style that is designed to free us from the linearity of our time flow, and broaden it to pools and lakes of eternal tranquility.

The pace of our everyday lives is so hectic. We are forever rushing aimlessly to meet deadlines and punishing schedules. We are overwhelmed by the rigid linearity of our time perception. The faster it flows- the more it disorients us and causes us distress. Time is entropic. It destroys and unravels all that we build- it is the basis of our mortality. The Rig Vedic Rishis, the Atharvans and the Buddhist monks had perfected the psychological mechanism of deconditioning our minds of this learnt reality. The secret was a withdrawal from active human civilisation to remote forest retreats. In that ecological environment, they followed a deautomatised routine that was cyclic instead of linear. They got up at fixed times, monotonously chanted the same verses and sutras, meditated, ate their meals and then congregated for ritual chants and meditation. This cyclic routine enforced a new monotony and rhythm that served to de emphasise the linearity of time. It dissolved the essential difference between yesterday, today and tomorrow. It forced the monks instead to focus on the "now" or the present, instead of the past or the future. It emphasised the continuity of a never-ending "isness". Meditative focus on the bio-resonators of the sound of breathing was the ultimate deautomatising experience. One breath is so similar to the next. A focus on the breathing engenders a revolution in our awareness of time by imposing a uniformity on our experience, by doing away with the novelty and difference between one event and the next. It breaks the chain, of the succession of events which normally orders our time awareness.

The frontal lobe of the brain is the seat of our time awareness. It is also the seat of creativity and attention.

The meditative life style of the Buddhist monks was designed to break the succession of the novelty of events and sensation. Such a focus on the Shangrilian "now: upon the tranquility of a never-ending "isness", generated a feeling of peace and bliss. It lengthened the pause between one breath and the next. Long spells of such a meditative, tranquil and placid experience pushed the system to an extremity of hypo-arousal. In a strange paradoxical way, the body-mind system pushed to such extremes of inactivity, underwent a physiological REBOUND. It was pushed to experience states of hyper-arousal and extremes of ecstasy. Ecstasy was the end result of such serene and meditative life styles.

TheExperience of Shunyata

One of the most remarkable experiences that I had,occurred during one of my annual retreats at the Ashram. It was a very quiet evening in Autumn. By dusk, all the people from the village had left. Suddenly, I felt a deep and palpable curtain of silence fall over the horizon. The giant cliffs seemed to have become powerful magnets, that sucked out every decibel of sound from the atmosphere. It was as if a gigantic vaccum-cleaner had opened wide its mouth and sucked in every thing into an obvilion. Dawn and dusk have traditionally been times of great silence at Patne. But there was something radically and qualitatively different about the silence of that evening. The epicentre of that great circle of silence seemed to be the hut of the sage. Great waves of an utter stillness seemed to proceed from there and delete the outlines of the entire universe of sound and form. I was amazed by the sudden onset of this stupendous curtain of silence. Something unusual was happening. It was as if a gravitational black hole had been opened, which was simply drawing everything into itself and oblivion. Yet there was great peace and positivity in that silence. The gates of eternal tranquility seemed to have opened of their own accord. The epicentre of that volcano of silence seemed to centre on his hut. We kept staring at its door. He used to come out every evening, just before sunset and lead us all to the temple for the ritual darshan at dusk. Today, he seemed to have gotten engrossed in his meditation, and the door remained shut. The silence grew deeper and deeper, till we were left amazed at its depth and profundity. The sun sank behind the western cliffs. The shadows lengthened across the forest. Darkness began to steal across the land. He emerged from his hut, after what seemed an eternity. One look at his face left us transfixed. His eyes were glazed and lost in the distance. He hardly seemed to walk. We were awed by the stillness and silence that seemed to emanate from his being. Silently, he came and sat along with us on the parapet walls of the ashram. We sat like that and gazed into the stillness of the forest for what seemed to be an age. Then he whispered as if to himself, "you know it is true," he said softly.

"What?", I asked gently .

"The Shunyata, the great void of the Buddhists. I just experienced it today."

So that explained that great and utter silence that had emanated from him and touched us all that day.

I stared a him in awe . I was transfixed and could not utter a syllable. We sat like that for a long time. Then quietly we retired to our huts and slept, while the stars blazed forth in the utter stillness of that strange night.

This was exactly the lifestyle that Baba set for us in his Ashram. His hermitage was an exact replica of the seats of the Upanishadic seers. The life style he prescribed for us was that followed by the Buddhist monks of yore in their Chaityas and Viharas in the sixth century before the birth of Christ.

The experience of the onrushing and fleeting mode of time, with its constant deadlines, is distressing in the extreme. It causes psychological and physiological ill health. Civilisationally, there comes a time when we have to slow our collective pace and make it more languid and less stressful.

LIVING WITH THE SAGE: THE WISDOM OF HONEY

The discovery of the sage of Patne was a single event that brought about a revolutionary change in my life style. So far, I had dreamed of perfection. I had dreamed of an archetypal sage and an Ashrama in a hut- something like the Rigvedic, Atharvanic, or Buddhist forest retreats of yore. I had despaired of ever finding it. Then, I stumbled upon it suddenly. It became a defining moment of my life. The sage taught me the art of meditation. Today, in hindsight, I realise that he taught me something else that was equally, if not more, precious. He taught me to be silent and still. He taught me to enter in to the deep and eloquent silence of the forest; to soak in the tranquility of the trees; to draw sustenance and living energy from the golden sunlight itself and from the chlorophyll process that turned the rich sunshine to the sap of aliveness. *Vanaspatayah Shantih* " The vegetation and plants bring us peace" By being still and silent in the forest, you got an unforgettable experience of the depth Ecology.

That deep ecological experience was the core of his teachings and life style. There is a symbiotic union between man and nature. The Atharvan(also called the Angirasas)were the forest sages who had first enunciated the Indian tenets of ecology. "All things on this earth are beneficial to one other and to this earth". The central metaphor here is not one of the Darwinian struggle for survival and a fierce and relentless competition for scarce resources. The relationships in nature are symbiotic and supportive. We are all parts of that web of connectivity that ties all life forms together in chains of harmony. The central Eastern metaphor of life is harmony. The Western metaphor is based on discord and struggle and a relentless competition where the strong devour the weak. That is the basic difference in the world views of the Eastern and Western civilisations (or a. least it used to be till the concepts of Ecology gained currency in the West).

Today, Norwegian philosophers like Naess are talking of the concept of "depth Ecology"- an ecological standpoint that stems from an understanding of the universality of consciousness per se. In 1975, I had a deep and profound experience of this depth Ecology. Baba had been asked to write a paper on the Kundalini by a Hindi magazine. He showed it to me. What I read- transformed me forever and remoulded my world view in a radical fashion. He said "Everything in this Universe is conscious. Only the degree of its expression varies. Every quark, every atom, every proton and electron is conscious. There is no such thing as 'Jada' or 'Chetan' as 'sentient' or 'insentient'. Consciousness is universal. It has varying grades of expression, as stratified and mineral matter, as metals, as the water of the rivers, seas and oceans, as microbial life forms; as plants and vegetable life forms that are rooted and static; as reptiles and fish and amphebians, as mammals and primates that are mobile. There is a whole range of the expressions of consciousness. Consciousness or "Chit" is the basic stuff of the cosmos. That is the core concept that underlies the Indian view point on "depth ecology". All things are beneficial to one another because they are forms of the self same consciousness. It was a simple but a profound revelation that changed the moorings of my intellectual landscape in one go. It transformed my world view, and I could only bow in gratitude for the gift of the realisation.

I came to him again in the year 1976, this time with certain basic questions regarding the overall direction of my life. My parents were now pressing me get married and settle down. I was keen to pursue my meditation and was not sure if that would be compatible with a house-holder's existence.

Questions that had seemed so pressing outside seemed to lose their relevance and significance in his presence. " My parents are pressing me for marriage. What should I do?"

"What do you want to do? What is your inclination?"

" I don't know, I am confused. That is why I need your guidance".

"When you are in such a confusion or quandary-do not do anything Just wait for life to resolve the question" he said.

"But that does not answer my direct question to you", I protested.

"Why, ask me? Ask the Devi there in the temple. She will give you the answer", he said.

I opened my mouth to protest, then left it at that. His panacea was simple. Keep meditating. The questions and doubts will resolve themselves of their own accord.

He was happy at my progress in meditation. I could meditate for three to four hours at a stretch now. He exhorted me to now break the sleep cycle - to meditate by night and sleep by day, if required. Night time is most peaceful and tranquil, and ideal for meditation.

I tried earnestly.

The first night I sat meditating till mid-night, but then dozed off. He came to check and found me sleeping.

The next day, he was highly amused. He could spend nights in ceaseless meditation and could not understand my sleepiness. "I thought, soldiers spent whole nights on sleepless vigil. Do you sleep on sentry duty then?" he laughed boyishly. I was deeply mortified and hurt.

Some how, I found the mornings so much more conducive for meditation. I tried again the next night and the next and managed to do a little better. To occupy myself between the sessions of meditation, I used to read some books on Yoga and philosophy. This time I had brought along a copy of the Bhagvad Gita. I was reading through it when I chanced upon a verse that spoke of "*Adhidaiva, Adhibhoota* and *Adhiyagna*." The terms intrigued me. Just then Baba walked into my hut after his morning meditation.

"Baba. What is Adhidaiva? What is Adhibhoot and Adhiyagna?".

He looked at me significantly. Then he smiled and shrugged in his characteristic fashion which seemed to imply "Is this important? " "Just meditate and go on meditating". But still ..." I insisted after some hesitation. He laughed "I don't know" he said simply and that was that. He did not encourage conversation.

I went for meditation to the temple the next day. It was a beautiful day. The sunlight was so limpid-the air so cool and bracing. My meditation proceeded flawlessly like the flow of oil (like "Teldhara" as the classical expression goes). I felt exhilerated. A profound feeling of peace came over me.

Baba used to insist that after sessions of meditation we walk a little into the forest, and ease ourselves. There was a dry nala bed of a stream that ran to the West of the Ashrama. We used to go there for our ablutions. So, after my morning meditation session I walked languidly up that dry nala bed. It was so quiet and peaceful. A dense growth of trees lined both banks of the dry stream. It gave the impression as if you were entering a deep tunnel of vegetation. I was ambling along when I noticed a tree that was heavily laden with scented flowers. Its lavender scent perfumed the air. Humming on the flowers were thousands upon thousands of bees. For some strange reason I stopped below the tree and gazed up at the bees humming on the flowers. They seemed drunk with its perfume. Their sonorous humming sound- the sound of so many bees humming together in unison, was like a chant.

The humming sound of the bees is the best intonation of that mystical chant of "Aum".

"Auummmmmmmm"

My attention was riveted on to that humming sound. I felt transfixed and rooted to the spot.

Something strange and lyrical happened next.

I felt an upsurge of happiness that welled up within like a stream of joy. A laughing, tinkling stream, sparkling in the sunshine, splashing over the rocks and sand-a river of eternal happiness. The Tibetan ky-ling-chhu. I felt as if bubbles of happiness were rising inside my being as they arise in an aquarium- a profusion of bubbles that float upward in the invisible fluid in a never-ending stream. What followed next, was utterly indescribable. The river of happiness flowed into my being. I heard its tinkling music. I heard the sun shine and then, for the first time in my life, I experienced ecstasy. It was beyond any description-I felt deliriously happy and ecstatic. The very air I was breathing had seemed to turn into a divine elixir-the Soma of the Gods. I took deep and joyous breaths to fill my lungs with that rapturous joy.

I had felt euphoria and rapture earlier, but this ecstasy was a peak-experience of a far higher magnitude. It was like a revolution of rapture.-a supernova of ecstasy and happiness.

I stood transfixed, taking in deep, joyous breaths of rapture- my eyes transfigured in an incredible ecstasy that washed over me in a tide of bliss and Ananda. It was a core mystical experience of rapture. Never before in my life, or any time after that, have I ever experienced anything quite like that, It was overwhelming. I was so delighted and exhilarated. I felt besides myself with joy and rapture as if the very air had turned to Soma - the very elixir of life and immortality. I had a fleeting glimpse of the Madhu Brahman, the honey experience of madhu- of honey-of the flowing river of honey-of the flowing river of Soma and ecstasy.This was a very vivid experience of what the classical texts describe as the Ritasya Dhara or the Madhu Dhara (he streams of truth and the ecstasy of honey.) A part of me felt apprehensive. I prayed that I could stay on for ever in that rapturous state and not lose it. I shut my mouth tightly so that the Soma would not flow out of me. It was beautiful beyond compare. What should I do. I felt the peak experience receding slowly.

I should record it.

I rushed to the hut, and whipped out my diary and pen to note down what I was experiencing. As I did so I felt it subside within me-Slowly sink back to its original state-ebb slowly like an inner tide, subside even as a flame subsides. I felt frantic. My God ,I had lost it. I felt bereft and bare-like a sucked out orange-like a fruit drained of all its elixir and juice. I felt drained out, dry and insipid. I came back to normal every day consciousness with a jarring thud, as it were.

What a striking contrast this normal state was to that beatitude and bliss. I felt a state of panic at its withdrawal. I felt a desperate longing to regain that original peak state of beatitude that I had experienced so briefly, and lost. It was gone. I felt panic as never before. I yearned for that state again. In desperation, I ran out of my hut to Baba's place. The door was locked. He was deep in meditation. Possibly the intensity of his meditation had triggered off the experience in me by a process of induction, as it were. I so desperately wanted to tell him about it. I was breathless with excitement. I had touched it momentarily and then lost that divine state. I was feeling panic at the loss. How could one live without that supreme thrill of a self-sustaining rapture that wells up from the deepest depths of our being. I almost wrung my hands in despair. There was no option. I retired to my hut and waited impatiently for him to emerge.

Baba continued to meditate for hours after that When he came out, it was almost noon time. The boys had served lunch in the kitchen. I looked at him- he had still not fully come back to the normal state. He looked remote and far, far away. You opened your mouth to talk, but one look at his face, made you fall silent.

We sat down for our meal. After some time had elapsed I gently interjected. "I had a strange experience today".

He looked up briefly. " What kind of an experience.?"

" I don't know, I was passing beneath that tree with thousands of bees. I felt an incredible ecstasy. I ...... I don't know how to describe it.

"Good! That happens. Now do you understand how the sages spend years after years in the forest. It is because of the experience of this ecstasy. It is this that keeps you here. All talk is a painful interruption. Sometimes you wish the people would go away so that you could go on enjoying that inner state of rapture."

"But..... But it went away", I spluttered in alarm. " I feel drained out, juiceless and insipid. I feel bereft and bare now that the experience is gone. Why?"

"That happens", he said calmly" In the beginning this state comes and it goes". I looked at him anxiously.

"How does one make this state permanent?"

"Keep meditating. That will make it permanent". He said and resumed his meal.

I stopped eating mine. So that was the way. My God, How desperate one felt for regaining that primal state of ecstasy.That longing itself is an agony.

I made an inward resolve there and then. If continued meditation was the only way to do it, then tonight I would sit down in meditation, and not get up till I had made that state permanent. Indeed the world was well lost even for an iota, a tiny fragment of that utter happiness, It was indescribable. Nothing, but nothing could compare with it or touch it even remotely.

I did not tell him. I did not tell anyone. I simply made a solemn resolve. One touch of that divine Soma was enough to cause a revolution in my psyche. It blazed in my being so briefly, and was gone like a meteor . It just left me longing and thirsting for more. Tonight I would sit down and not open my eyes till I had made that blissful state my permanent abode. What do we live for? What do we strive for in our lives?

For happiness.

I had experienced a happiness beyond compare. The flames of Soma had engulfed me momentarily in their ecstasy and rapture. I had touched an inner river of eternal happiness. I had heard its lyrical song and tasted the sweetness that binds the cosmos together like glue. The touch of Soma-the experience of the Madhu Brahman, of the cosmic sweetness which creates the universe out of chaos and entropy; which glues our beings into a functioning whole; which streams out to tie all life forms in the cosmos in shining strands of connectivity. I had that experience. Then, it had subsided as suddenly as it had flared up in my being.

I was left grieving for the wealth that I had lost within.

But not for long. Tonight, I would sit down in meditation. Quietly and without telling anyone, I made a solemn resolve. Tonight I would sit down in the temple and go on meditating till I had made that state permanent and static. That was my firm resolve.

13

The Night of the Snake : Facing the Hara

"Where are you going?" Baba asked me.

I had made silent but careful preparations. I had a light meal, and drank a lot of water. I took a small rug to sit on. Dusk was descending. I had started off for the Devi temple.

"To the temple. I intend meditating the whole night", I said briefly. "I.... I feel sleepy here. I feel better in the temple"

"Oh", he said simply.

I touched his feet and hurried on to the temple. He kept staring at my retreating back. The darkness was gathering swiftly. The stars peeped out in the ink black sky and gazed impassively at the giant cliffs and the huge, silent sentinels of the temple, the Deepa Stambhas - the Pillars of Light.

It was the night of Amavasya- the dark and moonless night of the lunar month. I paid obeisance to the Goddess. Then, I sat down and closed my eyes, I sank within easily and swiftly. I focussed on the breathing. It subsided slowly and faded out imperceptibly. I felt a warm, comforting, familiar darkness within-almost as if I had entered a house - my own personalised cacoon of safety. I felt safe and secure, and without a trace of fear. I rapidly lost all sense of space and time. The cool stones of the temple floor felt soft and malleable.

The Temple Courtyard

The Interior

I meditated on. One hour passed, then another and then another. My eyes felt glued together. I could not open them, even if I tried. My spine was straight and rigid of its own accord. My asan had become firm and fixed. I continued my meditation with a fierce underlying resolve. This was to be it. I had encountered the end state of this path. It had created a revolution in my psyche. That was what one wanted in life. The world was well and truly lost for even an iota of that tremendous happiness. I went on meditating. It is difficult to guess how many hours passed like that. I opened my eyes with a violent start. Something had struck me in the face. It was the soft wing of a bat. There were hundreds of them in that ancient shrine. I was dazed by the sudden, ness of the event. The blood was rushing to my head and face. My legs were locked and jammed stiff. All sensation seemed to have gone out of them. I was somewhat confused and disoriented, and it took me some time to regain my composure.

What had happened?

I looked at the watch. It was well past mid-night. I looked out. It was pitch dark. The trees of the forest seemed frozen into a stony immobility. The entire universe seemed asleep.

I now felt the discomfort in my legs. Locked in the Lotus posture for so many hours, they had lost all sensation. I rubbed them slowly and unlocked them with an effort. I rubbed them till the blood surged back and they tingled. I had been seated like that for almost six or seven hours now.

Let me walk around the temple to get the circulation going. Then I would sit down and resume my meditation, I thought to myself. I got up with an effort and stumbled around in the darkness. My eyes had adjusted to it by now. Outside in the faint glow of the star light, the cliffs looked so massive and gaunt and still. In the forest, you could hear the circadas intone a toneless song. Suddenly, somewhere far away, you heard the startled hoop of an ape- a rustle of feathers and bushes and then silence. What an utter and all-engulfing silence. How utterly alone, you felt. The whole universe was asleep. Only you were awake. You walked to the courtyard behind the temple. Then around to the northern side. Here on a raised parapet, scores of statues dug in the vicinity of the temple, were laid in row after row, by the archeological people. What exquisite statues they were. What expert sculptors must have wrought their artistic forms so many centuries ago. Statues of Gods and Goddesses. Statues of turbaned Dwarpalas with massive earrings, statues of nymphs and dancing women and one particularly arresting statue of a tall, naked yakshi with an elaborate harido and ornaments. The starlight gleamed softly on her full and voluptuous form and sensuous curves. For some strange reason you stopped suddenly. Your gaze riveted itself on that statue and you shivered. You thought of the artistic and sensitive hands of the sculptor who must have crafted it so lovingly with such acute concentration. His breathing must have been totally suspended as he etched the details of her body in stone. That cold stone contained the imprint of warm, living passions that must have animated the artist's breast. And now he was dead and gone. Reduced to ash and as cold as the stone figurine itself. And yet how warm and living the form was still. How many centuries ago must he have died? Yet his creation stayed on. It survived the centuries, and the impress of his passionate nature remained enshrined in the coldness of the stone before your eyes. The longing never dies. We pass away-the longings remain unfulfilled. The seeds of another birth.

I shuddered violently, and hurried on till I reached the temple entrance with its huge towering pillars. Between them one could see the vast expanse of the sleeping forest. Once, this must have been the central market place of the bustling town of Patne. Huge flames from the Deepa Stambhas must have flared up here. This place must have hummed and bustled with activity then. And now?

Where were the ware houses and dwellings and crowded lanes? All you could see was a canopy of trees and a dense profusion of bushes and undergrowth.

I gazed at the stillness for a long time. Then a thought came to me. Let me ease myself in the dry nala bed and then sit down to resume meditation.

Without thinking much about it, I began descending the steps. It was pitch dark. I reached the dry sandy bed, and began groping for my slippers. I could not see a thing . I felt something cool under my foot. Suddenly I felt a hot stab of pain. I lept up in sheer fright. I had distinctly felt two fangs pierce the skin at the arch of my right foot. I found my slippers, and put them on. A scalding pain began to rise from the arch of my foot, and travel slowly upward to my knee.

In panic, I made my way across the sandy nala bed. I eased my self . The pain was increasing steadily but alarmingly. I rushed back up the steps and scampered inside the temple. Under the light of the bulb I examined my foot. I was petrified. There were two distinct fang marks. The blood was oozing out of those needle like pin pricks. The area around them had turned a pinkish blue.

"Snake!"

The terrible thought flashed through my head like a flicker of lightning. I had been bitten by a snake.

There were dangerous and venomous Cobras around. I had seen them. I felt an upsurge of hysteria. Was I going to die then? Was it all over? Was this the end?.

You felt a wave of panic arising.

If it was a Cobra, I was truly finished . There was hardly any point shouting or crying. It was too late any way. Nothing could be done now. I felt an overwhelming sense of despair. How does one die? The thought crossed my mind. As per the texts one is supposed to leave the mortal coil in the lotus posture.

I tried to cross my legs! I could not. My foot was swollen to twice its size. The swelling was rising up to my knee and thigh. I closed my eyes.

That utter darkness within. That stark emptiness. I felt myself sinking into a dark, bottomless well of extinction-of absolute nothingness. In sheer fright, I opened my eyes wide open. That terrible engulfing darkness. Was that death? I riveted my gaze at the bulb. I clung on to the light like a drowning man clutches a reed. I did not dare to close my eyes again after that. Hours of meditation had caused the blood to surge to my head. Events had happened in such a quick succession thereafter. I was dizzy and totally disoriented. I was just 26 and I was dying. "I wish I had seen a bit more of life-possibly lived out a normal life, experienced marriage and then gone". For the second time a shock transfixed my being. I was astounded at myself. Were these my thoughts on the verge of death? Was that what I really wanted? Was that me? A number of my comrades had been wounded in the 1971 war. Curiously I had asked them. "What did you feel when you felt you were dying"? Without exception, they all had echoed the same thought. "I am too young to die. I wish I had seen a little more of life". At 21 year of age that is a normal reaction, I suppose.

For me it was a revelation.

Do we really know our deep hidden intentions? Do we really know, what we want? Do we truly know ourselves? We suddenly encounter ourselves in the mirror of the unexpected. Death is such a mirror. It gives us the sharpest and clearest reflection of ourselves. Sometimes the reflection that we see astonishes us. When we face death-we encounter the level of our true intentions-our Hara, the core that underlies the body-mind energy complex. The basic level is the level of our intention, our purpose, It is here that we encounter our life task and our deeper spiritual purpose. The level of the Hara is the foundation on which our Auric field rests. It is at this level that we set and hold our intentions - our purpose at any given moment and our greater incarnational purpose and life's task. Sometimes, before you encounter the Hara, you have to face death. *You have to squarely face yourself in all truth as you are, and not as you wish to be seen.*

At that point in time, in that ancient shrine, I felt the true despair of death. How much time more would it take me to die? How much time had elapsed since I was bitten by the snake? What snake was it? A Cobra? A Krait or some less harmful creature? I did not dare to close my eyes again. I started staring at the dial of my watch. The red second hand was going round and round. One minute passed, then another and then, another. Was I alive? Or was I dead already? I pinched myself to make sure. I felt it as if from a long way off. Something was wrong. Some 10 or 15 minutes had passed and I was apparently still alive. Could it be a less poisonous snake? Could it be that the Cobra had not been able to inject the full venom? Perhaps, in leaping up I had shaken it off? In that case it would be better to get it treated. I tried to suck the poison out but could not get my mouth to my foot. The whole foot and leg were badly swollen and paining. I tried to press out the poison. A spasm of the most excruciating pain rent the length of my spine. I cried out in pain. May be it was not a very poisonous snake, it would be better to seek some medicine or treatment. At long last, I got up and walked out of the temple and down the steps. Fearfully, I groped for my slippers in the darkness. Was that snake still there? I hurried across the sandy nala bed, my heart beating in my mouth.

At last, I reached the Ashrama and heaved a sigh of relief. In the community of human beings, I felt a tremendous surge of relief. I hobbled up to Baba's hut, and was about to knock, when I stopped. The other night I had decided to stay awake and had fallen asleep by mid-night. Baba had really made fun of me the next day. It had been mortifying. I still could not get over the sense of shame.

I hobbled away. No, I would wake up Sudam the gypsy boy with his wild mop of hair and that rougish look. He was a creature of the forest. I was certain, he would know some herb or some local remedy for snake bite. I went to the main hut and shook him up.

"Sudam! Sudam"

He got up sleepily, and looked at me in surprise. "Something has bitten me. Do see what is it". I showed him my foot. It was badly swollen now and the whole area around the fang marks had turned a bluish purple. "This is a snake" he spluttered confirming my worst fears. "Do you know some herb? Anything to cure it? He shook his head slowly. "I'll call Baba" he said and jumped up. "No, wait" I cried but he was gone in a trice. " Baba! Baba! A snake has bitten Captain Sahib".

"What ?" I heard Baba exclaim within.

Suddenly, I felt extremely foolish and mortified. This was ridiculous. That night I had dozed off and today this. "What is it" Come here" I heard his voice. "Oh, nothing Baba", I hobbled up. I had come out of the temple to ease myself, and this fellow tapped my foot" I tried to make light of it.

"So, he kissed your feet, is it?" His eyes twinkled with merriment but he did not smile.

"Show"

I showed him.

A shadow flitted across his face and he became grim. " "When did this happen?".

"Oh some half an hour ago". He looked at the watch it was 0230 hours in the morning.

"It couldn't have been a Cobra", I said bravely.

"Yes, otherwise you would have been cold and stiff by now", he said matter of factly

" Just give me a pin or a needle," I said.

Sudam gave me a needle. I tired to prick the poison out so that the blood would flow from the fang marks. The pain was unbearable and I had to give up.

Baba asked for a green chilly.

"Here, eat this", he said: I looked at him uncertainly "I cant eat chillies" I protested "I cannot stand them".

"Eat", he insisted.

I bit it. Strangely I felt nothing. No taste at all. Baba tried it himself and recoiled. It was strong.

"Does it taste sweet?" he asked me with visible concern. I tried again "No, tasteless", I reported. "Then it is good. If it tasted sweet then it was a cause for worry". He thought for a while. "Look, some years back, a Sadhu had come here. He saw the snakes around and told me a Sanskrit Mantra that he said can cure snake bite. I have never tried it myself. Do you want to?

" I don't mind" I said.

He sang an exquisitely beautiful invocation in Sanskrit. It was adressed to the Soul of the river Narmada-which, so the legend goes, can heal the poison of snakes. I repeated it after him a number of times. "How do you feel now?" he asked.

"Better", I said. "Good. He looked at the watch again. "Look, if I send Sudam now it will take him some half hour to reach the village. From there it will take five to six hours by bullock cart to reach the town. By that time the first bus should come as it is". "Do you want me to send him now for a doctor"? he asked.

"Do you think one is needed?" I said.

"I think it is going to be all right now". Baba said.

"In that case, I am going" I said and got up with firm resolve.

"Where?" he asked in great surprise.

"To the temple to resume my meditation". I said firmly and hobbled out of his hut.

"Don't". He called out after me "Its of no use now. It is pointless". "I must go, Baba" I said. I was astonished by the steel in my own voice.

He looked at me in intense surprise.

"If you must go, then take a torch" he said after a pause. Common sense is a rare sense. Baba had it in plenty. I could not help smiling grimly. I took a torch and hobbled out painfully.

As I put more distance between myself and other human beings, I felt my burst of courage and bravado desert me. To act brave we need an audience. In loneliness we face despair. And we face ourselves. I reached the foot of the temple steps and nervously flashed the torch light around. There was no sign of the snake mercifully. I went up to the temple. I tried to sit but could not fold my legs. So I sat with my legs extended. I closed my eyes. That sinking feeling, that engulfing darkness. That utter nothingness. I opened my eyes in fright. I tried again. In fact, I tried several times that night, but I gave up in fright. Baba was right. It was pointless now. Around 3 or 3.30 in the morning I decided it was hopeless. I was dizzy and tired and worried. Frankly now I was not at all certain that I would survive. I painfully hobbled back to the Ashrama. I quietly hobbled past Baba's hut. I did not want to wake anyone or make any further nuisance of myself. I lay down in my hut. I was afraid to close my eyes and fall asleep. I was worried I would never get up again. Nevertheless I was so tired and exhausted that I soon fell asleep. In fact I fell into a deep stupor of darkness.

* * *

It was well after sunrise. I felt the sunshine streaming in from the window and alighting on my face and eyes. I heard a gaggle of voices. I saw Baba standing over me with a look of profound concern in his eyes.

My first waking thought was a surge of relief.

'Thank God, I am alive.'

I tried to get up but almost cried out in pain. My foot had swollen to double its size, my calf and thighs were also visibly swollen now. The area of the fang marks was distinctly blue.

"Keep lying down. Don't worry, the Doctor has been informed and is coming". Word had spread like wild fire "Swami ji has been bitten by a snake." Vast multitudes started moving towards the Patne Devi Temple.

I was thirsty. I drank water and then a hot cup of tea. I could hobble around now. Baba called me to his hut.

"What happened last night?", he asked me with concern. I recounted the whole episode in detail. He fell silent for a long time. Then he spoke. "*Yesterday was the night of the Amavasya. The darkest moonless night of the month. People take Sanyasa on such a night. It signifies a ritual death of their one part of life and persona, and their spiritual rebirth into another existence.* Yesterday, you went to meditate to seek a permanence of the state of inner happiness. I did not say anything. You had come here this year asking some basic questions about the further direction of your life. Now the Devi has spoken to you clearly."

"What has she said?" I asked apprehensively. He looked at me significantly.

"The path of Nivritti - the path of renunciation is closed for you. You have to live the iife of a householder".

"Is the Goddess angry?" I asked with concern.

"No, had she been angry, we would have found you cold and stiff and dead the next morning. She has merely answered your question as clearly as she could. A stone will not get up and speak but the circumstances have given us the answer to your question loud and clear". For some strange reason I felt a tremendous sense of rejection, I felt myself sobbing and weeping in great anguish. I felt the sobs heaving my frame and dissolving my face. Baba was alarmed.

"Array, What is this? Last night we saw a soldier laughing in the face of pain and death. What is this? From where has this woman appeared?" I hardly heard him. What he had said, sounded like a sentence. I had been found unfit for the higher life, for the path of release from bondage. We heard some voices outside the hut. "People from the village are coming. Go, wash your face. It does not look nice". I calmed down. "The other day you had asked me what is Adhibhoota?" Baba said. I stopped in the doorway and turned.

"What is it?"

"Adhibhoota is obstacles from the elements. When we are proceeding too fast in our Sadhana and our release is premature, then the very elements rise up to bar our path. It is a law of nature - evolution must proceed at its laid down pace. It is dangerous to speed it up beyond a point. When the obstruction comes from the shining ones, the Gods, the Devas themselves, it is called Adhidaiva and when obstacles come in the performance of our yajnas - it is termed Adhiyajna". "Do you understand now?" he said gently. I looked at him in utter astonishment and shivered from head to foot.

People were coming into the Ashrama now. I hurried up to the hand pump washed my face and rubbed it clean of the traces of the many tears one had shed. Then I sat down in the visitors hut and forced my features into a nonchalant smile.

All life is drama. War is the highest form of drama. All soldiers are scared of death in combat. The drama of war lies in not showing one's fear. Thousands upon thousands of people poured in to the Asharama. Baba their beloved sage had been bitten by a snake! It was a calamity and the whole district turned out to see. "No!No! The snake did not bite me. It bit him - the soldier sitting there". People looked at me in surprise. I smiled weakly and the people sighed in relief. We jested over the events of the night and made light of them. The Doctor arrived with his bag and stethoscope. He was baffled. How was I alive? Should I be given any antivenom injection? Which snake was it? He shook his head. It was late for an antivenom anyway- so he gave me a lot of antibiotics and left. The crowds continued to come till late in the evening.

It was only after night fall that I could sit with Baba again.

"How do miracles happen", he said? "A stone will not get up and speak? The laws of the universe are inviolable. You asked a clear cut question. The events have conspired to give you an unequivocal answer. Sometimes, it becomes difficult for us to know our own intentions. *Our deeper intentions lie beyond the Auric field. They are held at the level of the Hara - the very core of our life purpose. It is at this level of life that we hold our very basic intentions and spiritual purpose. It is at this level of life lies the reason why we chose to be born-the original intention to incarnate that forms the basis of our life, will and purpose. It is this basal intention that holds together the core of our being and aliveness. It is the basis of our desire to live and also to die* _ when we feel we have fulfilled our purpose. Sometimes we have to face death before we truly understand our own intentions at the level of reality. Right and wrong are relative. What matters is that we must be true to ourselves. That is of supreme importance. There is the way of release and there is the path of the world. The way of release is blocked for you for the time being. You have to fulfill your Karma and your destiny in the world outside. Everything in nature happens on its own as it should. Nothing can occur before the time is ripe. "He saw my crestfallen expression and added "There is no cause for despair. You faced your test bravely. Much more bravely than most other people could have done. It is lucky that you are a soldier and your training stood you in good stead. Do not lose heart. The four fold Ashramas prescribe a path for the house holder. The four Ashramas lead us from bachelorhood to the life of a householder, to Vanya prastha or withdrawl from worldly duties. Finally it leads to Sanyasa again, to the ultimate renunciation. There is profit in each path. Each path is uniquely our own. I for one would not change it, for in the ultimate analysis, all paths lead us to the final experience of the cosmic connectivity of all things".

14

The Years of the Golden Oriole : The Sage of the Mystic Plants

Baba was a stern and spartan teacher. He was unsparing with himself and set the most exacting standards in his own personal conduct. He was somewhat impatient with weaklings. He had spent long years in the wilderness of a remote forest - all alone and absolutely without a trace of fear.

It was for this reason that he was fortunately very pleased with me for the way in which I had been able to withstand my ordeal. He felt sorry for my sense of hurt and rejection, at my disqualification as it were for the higher life of the path of Nivritti. The path of "Nivritti" is not open to all. It implies a fulfillment of ones karmic debts. And no one, not even God incarnate,can evade his "*Prarabhadha Karma*". We all have to fulfill our personal destiny. In concrete Biblical terms, what Baba had said to me was very simple. It is better to marry than to burn. It is essential that we are true to ourselves and do not avert our faces from our psychological reality. That is of supreme importance.

In the aftermath of my highly intensified sessions of meditation, I experienced violent arousals and activation of the hypothalmic region. There was a volcanic release of emotions as it were. I experienced what in classical literature are termed as "Bhavas"-states of hyperaffective arousal. I would finish long sessions of meditation-then dissolve in fits of spiritual anguish and sobbing that were surprising in their intensity. At times I encountered fits of rage and bouts of ravenous hunger. All this pointed out to a violent stirring of the hypothalmic region that lies in the core of our brain. I noticed a seasonal cycle of mood swings and energy upswings - peaks in spring, and with a low in the summer and rains. In spring one encountered episodic outbursts of great energy, grandiosity, of creativity and euphoria. This was followed by cyclothymic low of depression and despair and aridness, an inner drying up of the well springs of joy and of creativity.

The Dark Night of the Soul? Having experienced that intensity of ecstasy in the peak experience of Soma, the ordinary, everyday consciousness was such a marked contrast of aridness. The memories of that peak experience haunted you like a distant lodestar. You had touched it, you had felt that eternal flame and then lost it. You had heard the music of that River of Soma. You had heard the tinkling of the Ritasyadharas. (the streams of the Rita consciousness). Vedic literature makes no mention of the Kundalini. It speaks however of the Kala Agni (the fire- the energy of time. That is the bonding energy that creates and holds together our form as a vortex or whirlpool in the flow of space-time). When the Kala Agni rises- it reverses the arrow of time. Our organism is no longer pushed by the past ,(by our genetic record of past mutations). It is now pulled by the potentialities of the future. We become prophetic beings that are pulled by the forces of the future to actualise our evolutionary potential. Vedic verses record the initial experience of Soma. We can not hold that ecstasy for long and suffer relapses to the ordinary consciousness. That leaves us with a haunting feeling of loss and desolation, with a yearning for the return of those streams of Soma and ecstasy- of those *Ritasyadharas* and *Madhudharas*. The neurons of the brain, it appears can not stand up to a sustained dose of these enkephalin and endorphin peptides of ecstasy. They go into a refractory period in which they can not conduct. We feel burnt out and lost. We lose that exalted state, sometimes for years. Those are the years of intense inner anguish and suffering. The loss of that inner beautitude is so poignant. One is left just with those haunting memories of the peak experience and its stark contrast with our everyday consciousness. Most mystic literature, in almost all religions, records this dark night of the soul, this extended "Bardo" as it were, this feeling of being adrift between two worlds and of being able to belong to neither. A Vedic verse clearly states that the body has to be tempered and prepared to hold on to these exalted states of ecstasy. We can not experience them for long with our inherited neural structures. These relapse into long periods of refraction in which they just can not conduct these higher experiences anymore. We experience them briefly and then lose them. The Vedic verse says explicitly:-

"He tastes not the delight
who is not ripe
whose body
has not been tempered
by the flames of the fire.
They alone
can bear that joy,
they alone can enjoy
the rapture
who have been tempered
by the flame".

It is a long and difficult period of inner suffering. New neuron circuits have to come up to become a channel of expression of that inner state of ecstasy in a more permanent manner. It is as if the Dark side of the Force bars our path. These hostile and adversarial elements retard our progress until we are fully ripe and ready to overcome their resistance. Many Vedic verses describe this inner struggle as a heroic battle against the Dark side of the Force, against the Vritras and Panis. There is an element of heroism in this inner war. At the experiential and subjective level, what we undergo are long years of anguish and inner suffering- a feeling of "burn-out" and exhaustion, a sense of great loss and suffering, a haunting feeling of rejection and tantalising memories of the peak experiences of ecstasy which we felt, and then lost. The grace and guidance of a living guide or a Guru is most essential to see one through this phase. I was most lucky to have his grace during this period that went on for many years.

The external circumstances of my life however took a distinct change for the better. A surprising and deeply satisfying surge of positivity changed every aspect of my life. I felt the power of the sages benediction and blessings in all spheres of my life-worldly, spiritual and material. These were really the best years of my life. I got a prestigious posting to the Indian Military Academy at Dehradun, as an instructor. I got a golden opportunity to read books on philosophy and psychology at the Academy's vast library This helped me understand the various experiences I had had with the sage.

In the year 1978, with my teachers blessings, I got married and entered the life of a householder. I was extremely lucky and fortunate in that my wife was sweetness incarnate, and helped me in every way in my spiritual and academic pursuits. We set up house and were very happy together. Baba exhorted us to divinise all aspects of our lives. That divinity should be all-inclusive. We should offer all our acts to the divine as a homage, as a yajna, as an offering of ourselves. Patne used to get very hot in summer. Baba desired to spend the summer months at a cool place. We prevailed upon him to come to Dehradun. The President of the Forest Research Institute at Dehradun, a saintly gentleman called Mr Vyas, offered him his bungalow at the Rajpur Road. It was a quiet and peaceful location. It gave me and my wife a golden opportunity to drive up on our scooter to his Rajpur Road residence, and spend the evenings with him. The deep silence of his meditations soon left its impress on the surrounding vegetation. The place was transformed. Those were beautiful and halcyon days. We had a lovely house with a balcony overlooking the Tons river.

It is a strange coincidence of history. The modern Indian Militancy Academy is located at the same historic spot where Dronacharya - the great preceptor of the Kauravas and Pandavas, had set up a military training camp on the banks of the Tons river some 3000 years ago. The word Dehradun in fact, comes from the word "Dera Drona" - the camp of Drona. From the balcony of our house, one got a beautiful view of the Tons river, and the hills of Mussoorie and Chakrata. On the trees opposite our balcony we would often see a beautiful Golden bird. This was the Golden Oriole. Mellow sunshine filled our existence. These were really the most blessed years of our lives.

Rahoul's mother (Didi Contractor) who later renounced the world and became Ma Dayananda, came to meet Swamiji and stayed with us. She was a lady of great academic and spiritual accomplishment. With an IQ of over 157, she was on first name basis with many Nobel prize laureates. Her study of the Sanskrit texts and Indian and Chinese philosophy, was remarkable for its depth and sweep of learning. She was a gifted artist, and a very sensitive and intelligent human being, and it was always educative to listen to her. She had some remarkable spiritual experiences of déjà vu. She helped me to understand my inner experiences and place them in context.

Major (later Major General) Hardev Lidder and his wife met Swamiji at Dehradoon and became his most devoted and ardent disciples in the years to come. Their lives also underwent a total transformation. Lidder gave up smoking and drinking, and bacame a vegetarian. His health improved greatly, and he felt a distinct upsurge of positivity in his circumstances, both worldly and spiritual. A Sikh by faith, Lidder's outstanding quality was his total devotion to his guru. It was a devotion that came to him easily and naturally due to the cultural imprinting of his faith. Some years later, with the sage's blessings, Lidder was able to make a pilgrimage to the holy Mansarowar lake in Tibet.

Personally, I felt a great upsurge of inner energy. I could work tirelessly for hours on end and felt a great upsurge of positivity and creativity. These were the years when we experienced the grace of the sage in its fullest measure.

The Sage of the Mystic Plants

One of the most remarkable people that I met in Baba's orbit was Mr. Vaid. He was a tall, handsome old man with a shock of flowing silver white hair and a musical sing song voice. Gentle, soft spoken and pleasant by nature, Vaid was a scientist at the Forest Research Institute of Dehradun. He was a creative and gifted human being and a good writer and an accomplished photographer. His pictures of the Orchid plants of Sikkim has been made into postage stamps. He was a photojournalist and was deeply involved in a number of research projects on the sacred and mystical plants of the Indian Folklore. Two of these plants were his life's work, as it were. He was deeply involved in unravelling the identity of the Soma plant- the most sacred psychotropic plant of the Rig Vedic Aryans. His second major project concerned the identity of the mythical Kalpa Vriksha - the sacred wishing Tree - the Ashwatha tree that lives for an age.

The Scientist and the Sage

I chanced upon Vaid in one of his encounters with Baba. He had come to seek the sage's views on the identity of the Soma plant. It was a fascinating series of dialogues between the scientist and the sage. Vaid's enthusiastic search for these mystic plants was his life's mission. He had spent his entire life span in this quest. He was very widely read, and had a remarkably penetrating insight. I was so captivated and enthralled by his quest for the magical Soma plant that I came to all his sessions with Baba and then followed it up with long discussions with him at his quiet bungalow amongst the stately trees of the Forest Research Institute in Dehradun. He opened up for me a whole magical new world of sacred plants and their folklore. It was an ethno-universe of surprising diversity and richness. Soma is one of the most remarkable plants of the Ancient Rig Vedic Aryans. It was supposedly a psychotropic plant whose ingestion conferred experiences of remarkable ecstasy, mood elevation, grandiosity and euphoria and prompted great upsurges of creativity-that supposedly led to the prodigious and inspired poetic output of the Vedic seers. Today, we have no clue to the real identity of this sacred plant. What was it? A psychotropic mushroom, a creeper plant or a sacred Ephedra? Historical accounts seem to suggest that it used to be ground in pestle and mortar, and taken with milk or curds as part of ritual sacrifices, it caused the most remarkable upsurges of euphoria and ecstasy and triggered off heightened mood elevations that led to inspiration and intense creative upsurges.

R Gordon Wasson, a German Botanist, had earlier studied the Rig Vedic verses in praise of the Soma plant to build up a morphological description of the plant from the clues in the Vedic verses. Based upon these poetic clues-Wasson identified the Soma plant as the Fly Agaric Mushroom (Latin: Amanita Muscaria). This is a striking blood red Mushroom with white flecks. These flecks expand till after a few weeks the whole plant turns milky white. The Fly Agaric Mushroom is a psychotropic plant that was used by the Shamanist witch doctors of Central Asia, as part of their magic rituals. This psychotropic mushroom is also found in the Nilgiri hills of South India. Another School of thought identifies Soma as an Ephedra Plant found in Iran, Afghanistan, Baluchistan, North Western Kashmir and Tibet. This Ephedra bush was identified as the "Hoama" of the Zorastrians. It is an Alkoloidal plant that causes mood elevation, euphoria and heightened alertness. People who ingest this plant can do with very little sleep and turn highly creative.

Vaid, Studied the poetic clues of the Rig Vedic verses in praise of Soma. Canto IX or the Soma Sukta contains the bulk of these references. Soma is variously described as "Hari the Sun." At places it is also likened to the Silver Moon. It has the hide of a bull. It is seated on the mountain tops. From these clues, Vaid had built up a remarkably different morphological picture of the mythical plant. In excited session after session, Vaid demolished the thesis of Wasson. With the help of numerous photographs he put across his version. Soma was not a psychotropic, mushroom he concluded. The "Soma Lata" was a creeper found in the lower slopes of the Himalayas. It has psychotropic properties that caused a release of Enkephalins-the opiates of the human brain that triggered off experiences of ecstasy and hightened creativity in the Rig Vedic Aryans.

Baba was deeply impressed by the research work of Mr Vaid. However, from the experiential point of view, he felt that Soma has an internal and an external dimension. Prolonged sessions of meditation, the sage said, unleashed the experience of ineffable ecstasy in our psyches. At the physical level, these ecstatic experiences could be triggered off by the massive release of endorphins and enkephalins- the opiates of the human brain. Since these were naturally occurring poly peptides- these were not habituating or addictive and served to enhance creativity and insight. Baba agreed with the scientist that surely these neuro-chemicals of the human brain must have had their equivalents in the plant kingdom. Surely, the ancients must have known some botanical plants that replicated the bio chemistry of these remarkable inner experiences. To that extent, these could be externally induced/reinforced/magnified or strengthened. However, the internal generation of these bio chemicals he felt, was the more natural process, and he was not in favour of external intervention by psychotropic plants. The experiences of Soma, Baba felt were mediated by the process of meditation. Just two years ago I had personally encountered this remarkable experience of ecstasy under Baba's personal guidance. The discussions on the mythical Soma plant therefore held a profound experiential relevance for me personally, and I listened to the two of them in absolute fascination.

The Ashwahta Tree : The Kalpa Vriksha

Vaid's second, remarkable thesis pertained to the mythical wishing tree-or the Kalpa Vriksha. Lord Krishna says in the Gita, "Amongst the mountains, I am the Meru; amongst the trees, I am the Ashwatha". The tree of the Indo-Aryans, the Ashwatha tree finds repeated mentions in the Atharva Veda. Its branches are used in magical rituals said to drive away foes. The identity of this tree was the ruling passion of Vaid's life. He had spent years in search of this tree. His methodology was simple. Construct a morphology of this tree by studying the references in the classical texts and then try and unravel the identity of this king of all plants. Vaid read some historical records of the Ellora caves where he found mention of sculptures depicting the Ashwata tree.

THE KALPA VRIKSHA
with roots above and branches below

THE ASHWATA TREE

Vaid visited the Ellora caves. In the Jain group of caves he saw the wonderous statue of the Indrani-(The consort of Lord Indra) seated under the mythical Kalpa Vriksha -the wish fulfilling tree. It is a beautiful statue carved, in very great detail. Vaid was fascinated. An avid photographer he photographed this sculpted depiction of the tree to build a data bank of morphological clues. He spent hours studying that sculpture, and interacted in great detail with the guide Archeologist of the Ellora Caves. The historians variously identified the mythical wishing tree with the Banyan, the Peepul or the Mango tree. The Banyan is called Nygrodha in Sanskrit. It is recorded as a separate tree in the Atharva Veda. The Aswatha tree is altogether different. Vaid was not convinced. The tree sculpture depicted leaves in bunches of five with fruit of various shapes and sizes growing concurrently on the tree. Some fruits were shaped like Mangoes. Some like large Brinjals, some like the Gourd. Vaid was fascinated. The tree was not the Banyan, for the leaf structure was different, and it had no hanging roots. The Mango tree does not have fruits of such diverse shapes and sizes. The ancient sculptors of Ellora showed remarkable acuity and powers of observation. If each hair and trinket on the Indrani statue had been etched in such realistic detail, the same powers of observation should extend to the background sculpture of the tree also. The ancient artists must have applied their acute powers of observation to record the details of the morphological structure of the tree itself. Vaid was certain that the Ellora sculptors had used actual models to help them sculpt their remarkable statues. Vaid spent months studying these sculptures, in particular the depiction of the Kalpa Vriksha Tree. He went year after year to the Ellora caves, convinced that the clue lay in the Jain carving somewhere. One day he was coming out of the Ellora Caves after a days tiring work. Suddenly he stopped at the entrance. He felt rooted to the spot. There were two giant trees which had those same bunches of leaves and the myriad sized fruits. In all probablity these trees had served as the inspiration for the sculptors of Ellora. Vaid had after so many years, solved the myth of the mythical Kalpatru-the Kalpa tree.

The tree was the "Bao Bab"-basically an African tree which lives for 5000 years (a Kalpa or an age by itself). "With roots above and branches below". This tree sheds its leaves and then gives a bizzare look as if it has been uprooted and kept inverted with its roots up in the sky and branches spreading below the earth. At any one time it has fruits in several stages of growth and development. Some look like little Mangoes, other are round and big as Brinjals; other long and cylendrical like Gourd. The fruit is callled the monkey bread. The monkeys are very fond of it. The Ellora sculpture of this tree shows monkeys eating this fruit. The bark of this tree is like paper. It peels off and can be used as writing paper or even as crude cloth by tribals. The tree grows to enormous size and girth, its diameter almost reaching a hundred meters. Sometimes its main trunk becomes hollow and stores water like a well. In fact so many are the uses of this tree that it could well qualify for the title of the wish-fulfilling tree.

Vaid felt that the traders of the prehistoric Indus Valley Civilisation had extensive contacts with Africa-especially the region of Tanzania where this tree is found in large numbers. They must have introduced this remarkable tree in India. The Bao Bab is indeed a fantastic tree. The very fact that it lives for an age (over 5000 years) qualifies it for the title of the Kalpa Vriksha-or the tree that lives for a Kalpa-an aeon or an age. Its latin name is Adansonia Digetale.

Baba and all of us used to hear Mr Vaids discourses on this subject with avid interest and fascination. Baba felt that the Kalpa Vriksha was a symbol of meditation. The mythical Kalpa Vriksha could be understood at many levels . At the metaphorical level, the tree was allegorical. It represented the tree architecture of the human mind. The human nervous system branches out in roots and axons -thus replicating the tree architecture that we encounter in the plant world. The longivity of the Bao-Bab tree and its many useful functions (water storage, fruit, bark, habitat, shelter etc) made it a classical wish-fulfilling tree for our physical needs. There are thus many hierarchial levels of viewing reality. Once we throw a stone in a lake, it causes a series of concentric ripples. Each one of these ripples is a full circle and represents a different order of meaning. Baba said most of the verses of the Geeta were like that. They were multi-dimensional and had many levels of meaning. As one lived and grew and meditated more upon them, the meaning would grow and enlarge with our personal maturation of understanding and experience. The Kalpa Vriksha is a similar multi, dimensional symbol. It is a dynamic image, and has diverse interpretations. It is a symbol thrown up by the collective racial unconscious. At one level it represents the whole creation, the unfolded cosmos that germinates from a tiny seed of potentiality. . *At the psychological level, it represents the structure of the human mind. The roots above seem to reach up to the energic field to draw Prana and susteinance. The branches below are the nerve path-ways that bifurcate literally in roots, nodes and axons to transmit their flow of mind energy*. At the physical level the Bao Bab tree fulfills our wants and gives us food, water, shade and shelter.

Vaid was a rare, creative genius. He expounded his theories at length to Baba. Baba was deeply impressed. At his Ashram he planted two Bao-Bab trees at Patne. Later he planted two more such trees at his Ashram in Kalimath. These trees have grown over the years. 5000 years later, they will still be around to remind us of the saintly personage who planted them, and also of the Botanical scientist who spent a life time in search of the mythical plants of the ancient

Indian civilisation. The tall and gentle Mr Vaid was one of the many remarkable people that we encountered in Babas orbit. In his house, in a densly forested patch of the Forest Research Institute at Deharadun, in that peace and quiet he would often keep us spell-bound with his expositions on these ancient, mythical plants. He encouraged me to read the verses extolling the properties of the divine Soma plant. When I read these, the most inspired and uplifting sections of the Rig Veda, I was struck by the remarkable descriptions of the peak ecstasy experiences that they described. Thus for example, verse 9.1.7 of the Rig Veda says

"This exhilerating Nectar
this ambrosia of bliss
inspires deep reverence
in our hearts
and fills our body with
pure serene thoughts and emotions."

And again verse 9.1.1 of the Rig Veda exclaims

"O Blissful Lord
fill our hearts
with thine nectar
of bliss
which uplifts the soul
on its streams
of spiritual ecstasy
to the heavenly "heights
of bliss"

Verse 9.2.4 of the Rig Veda says

"The heavenly streams of Soma
breathe life into every grain
of this universe
every drop
of the vast expanse of the Sea.
Every wave that dances with joy

sings only of the glory
of this divine splendour of Soma."

And again verse 9.2.6 compares it to a fountain of the life force

"O this wonderous lustrous
unceasing fountain
of the Life Force.
This benign power
that shines through
the golden rays of the Sun."

The next verse continues

"Soma spreads the joyous bliss
of pure knowledge.
It uplifts the soul
on the streams of spiritual ecstasy
to the highest heaven."

The one verse that struck me as a deep echo of my own brief but intense experience of ecstasy convinced me that it was the same core experience that the Vedic Seers were trying to verbalise. Only in their case, it was not brief, fleeting and transient like mine, it was a permanent state of bliss and beatitude. It flowed like a river of happiness. Thus:-

"Yoked to the melodies
of the music of the spheres
Soma flows silently
like the waves of a river

(Rig Veda 9.3.2)

"As it flows,
the river speeds up
like a chariot
to shower its gifts of
ecstasy to all-
Its voice is heard by the multiutdes

(Rig Veda 9.3.5)

I am more than convinced today that the Rig Vedic seers, like the lengendary Shuna Shepa, were sages who were constant in the state of inner ecstasy and bliss (*'Annanda Stambha'*). This inner state of ecstasy and ceaseless happiness that welled up from within the heart like a river of happiness-a tinkling, singing stream of joy, not only imparted a peak experience of self-generated bliss, but also made the experiencing consciousness highly creative and sensitive to the aesthetic trigger. That is how the forest sages who recorded the Vedas and Upanishads have left behind such beautiful and remarkable poetry. Their descriptions of dawn and rain and the clouds are imbued with an ineffable joy. Thus:-

"The Bright dawn
heralds a new day
Its rosy lances have opened
the Golden Gate of the Sun.
and lit up the path of action

Awaken sleeper, the slumber
and darkness are over,
life beckons
May each dawn
lead us from triumph to triumph".
(Rig Veda 1.113.16)

"Radiant at sacrifices
like the rays of dawn
wishing to be lustrous
they shine
with ornaments.
Hastening on, like
Spears, that glisten.
They measure out
form afar
the vast distances.

(Rig Veda 10.78.7)

In the wake of that peak experience I had felt upsurges of this rhythmic and patterned speech of poetry that seems to well up of its own accord. This peak experience entrains such episodic upsurges of creative expression with primitive and archaic rhythms that emerge like ancient tom toms from the depths of the collective unconscious -heavy with alliterations and metaphors The urge for poetic expression is intimetaly linked to that state of euphoria or ecstasy which is invariably its precursor. It is a kind of a repeatable phenomena. Prolonged sessions of meditation heighten sensitivity to the aesthetic trigger and make the experiencer ecstatic and highly creative and prolific in his output. Echoes of the Vedic pattern of poetry are again encountered in the Middle ages in the lyrical outpourings of Indian saints like Kabir and Meera Bai who expressed the same creative upsurges not in classical Sanskrit but in the simple language of the masses.

The key question is, was the ecstatic experience of Soma triggered off by the meditation alone? My teacher had given me a very brief glimpse of that peak experience of bliss. He lived in it for all his life. In those years of the forest, he lived as if in a perennial state of bliss and ecstasy-of a unitary consciousness where he felt himself constantly in touch with the creative cosmic core of love, sweetness and bliss. The magic Madhu - the Honey-the sweetness that is the glue that binds together the disparate forces of this cosmos and gives rise to an ordered and patterned universe. Like the ancient Rig Vedic seers, he lived in that marvellous state of cosmic connectivity. On the vast internet of cosmic-consciousness you can connect to any field and source of any knowledge and tap any information domain, you desire. It expresses itself in insight and the rhythmic and patterned speech that is enshrined in Vedic poetry. Past, present and future have little, relevance for this consciousness. It lives in a never-ending isness- a morning force of dawn and goes into varying shades of bliss as the shadows of the trees lengthen with the march of the Sun. You can experience each day its many moods and shades of sunlit euphoria. When this force rises in our beings- it expresses itself as a great river of happiness and contentment. It heightens our creativity. To give it a conscious outlet and channel-the Rig Vedic seers tried to express it in superlative poetic output and philosophy. The Buddhist monks sought release in art-in frescoes, paintings and sculptures of extraordinary beauty and power.

The key question that Vaid, the Botanical scientist raised was, is there a plant equivalent that has the Alkeloids that can trigger off the remarkable upsurges of Enkephalins and Endorphins in our brains that lead to such an experience? My own teacher told me that the route to this creative and ecstatic state was via deep meditation. Mr Vaid said that there was an alternate route through the plant kingdom that entrained a similar experience. The ancient Vedic Rishis and seers knew these sacred plants and perhaps used them extensively. The sages who composed the Atharva Veda in particular are called the Atharvans or the Angirases. They wrote innumerable verses recording details of many mystic plants and magical herbs of healing. These included the Prishniparni herb, the Kushta, the Ashwatha tree, the Playksha and Khadura trees, and the king of all medicinal plants which was called Soma. Soma, was a remarkable plant -a divine plant-the king of all the medicines. Whosoever found this remarkable plant had found a treasure of bliss and immortality, and the remarkable gift of ecstasy and creative experience. The ancient Rig Vedic Aryans knew the secrets of this plant. It seems to have been lost for ever. Vaid told us he had at last succeeded in rediscovering this plant. He had documented his research-thousands of pages of neatly typed notes and diagrams. Suddenly, he passed away. With-in a few months, his wife followed him. With her, were lost all those papers. I made so many attempts to trace them out and get them published, but like Vaid, the scientist himself, they had gone into the sunset. All that I remembered was the brief, very brief but tantalising experience of that state of Soma which my teacher had given me. The state he knew so well. The state in which he lived so long. The state that came to him so naturally from the depths of his meditation, and not some external intervention by psychotropic plants which could prove to be habit forming and addictive.

Many years later, after both Vaid and Baba had passed away, I was posted in the Nilgiris. There I saw for myself the bright Red Mushrooms that the German Botanist, Gordon Wasson said were the real Soma plants. I gathered them reverentially in the memory of Vaid, and my great teacher, but I did not ever dare to try their psychotropic properties. My teacher was emphatic on that score. *In the field of consciousness, we must never, never use any external crutches that bring about dependency and can damage our psychic structures.* The way to the Soma experience lies in the experience of the states of deep meditation. We must revive that lost art of deep meditation. That was the cenral theme of my teacher's message to humanity. Soma remains the last unsolved riddle of Indology. Soma is mentioned as Haoma in Zorastrian Religion. The Zend Avesta also mentions Atharuvans (Atharvans). The Zorastrian Haoma or Hum has been identified as the Ephedra – a bush of leafless jointed twigs, a mass of branches and sprigs. It has a pleasant pine like aroma and astringent taste. When covered with male flowers the bush is golden coloured. Ephidrine ($C_{10}H_{15}ON$) is extracted from it. Ephidrine is soluble in water, and can be taken orally. It stimulates the nervous system and leads to heightened alertness and euphoria. This Ephedra is found in Iran, Afghanistan, Baluchistan, Western Tibet and Kashmir. Many years after Baba passed away, I was posted to Kishtwar in Kashmir, where I chanced upon the Maru or the Marud

Vridha River. This river finds mention in the famous Nadi Sukta of the Rig Veda. Tradition has it that a large number of the verses of the Atharva Veda that deal with medicinal and psychotropic plants, were composed here. I have not lost my fascination for this wonderous plant, and to this day. my search for it continues, unabated. The truth however, is that our own brain cells secrete that Soma elixir in meditation. We therefore need to seek within and not without for the real and true Soma. In fact a Rig Vedic verse asserts :—

> *"They think they have tasted*
> *the Soma when they crush*
> *the plants.*
> *Fools! The True Soma,*
> *the Brahmins alone*
> *know that one.*
> *No one, tastes the true Soma,*

15
The Palki Celebrations : The Exoteric Phase

In the year 1978, Baba had shifted his Ashram to the larger island that lay to the West of the first Ashram site. A regular bus service had now started to come right upto the shrine, Scores of pilgrims now came each day, to visit the shrine, but even more, to meet the remarkable sage of Patne. His fame grew and spread far and wide to all the adjoining districts. The people looked upon him as a classical Rishi or sage who had come to revive the parched spiritual consciousness of the Khandesh region of Maharashtra. With each passing day, the crowds grew and grew. The sage had now completed one phase of his life. It was the esoteric phase in which he had retired to the solitude of the deep forest for extensive meditation and Sadhana. He spent 12 long years in deep meditation. His Ojas- the spiritual power, grew by degrees. Those of us who lived close to him could distinctly feel the upsurge. Masses of men were moving in the direction of the Shrine. He had caused a historic revival of the ancient pilgrimage centre. In the first place, he had saved the temple from the floods, and now because of him the crowds and throngs had begun to converge upon this shrine in droves. The State govt and local authorities were deeply impressed by the revival that this sage had wrought single-handedly. *The temple at Patne was to Pranvananda what Arunachala was to the Ramana Maharishi. It was his place of power. It was his Tapobhoomi.*

Being one of his earlier disciples, I was a little saddened in one way. The great solitude and tranquility of the Tapovana was now filled by the clamour of the pilgrims, peasants and even tourists. Patne figured now as a tourist spot in the Illustrated Weekly, as part of the series on "the India that you do not know". Only in the early mornings before the first bus came and the late evenings (after the last bus has departed) could you experience that great peace and calm of the earlier years. The magic transformation would occur afresh. The peace began to get lost in the increasing din of the crowds and the clamour of the voices

The people looked upon him as a divine incarnation. His fame spread like perfume. Any time he came out of his Asharam, the people would swarm in droves to get a glimpse of him, and touch their foreheads to his feet. He was fast becoming a living legend- a kind of a living god. Many regarded him as the reincarnation of Bhasakaracharya. A little harried by the crowds, the sage had shifted deeper inside the forest. The second Ashram-was much larger but still in the classical mould of straw roofed huts. The design was unique. Everyone sat on the floor, so the windows were kept at floor level. This permitted the sunlight and fresh forest breeze to inundate the interiors. There was a large Darshan hall and hut where Baba met the visitors. The guests stayed in one corner of it. The kitchens were adjacent. Behind it was a huge well with electric pumps installed for drawing up the water. Baba's hut was tucked away in a quiet corner. It was an elegant blend of the classical and the modern. A beautiful red statue of Lord Ganesha, the local deity of Maharashtra (the Lord of the mind) adorned its entrance. He had his own altar and meditation room underground-so that he could withdraw into total solitude. In the Ashram were planted a lot of ornamental trees and shrubs. Blood red Bougenvillas adorned the fences. There was a dense glade of Chandan(Sandalwood) trees. The vegetation and shrubs here were so thick that they totally screened you off from sight. Baba used to have a mattress spread here and reclined in total solitude, savouring the green peace and tranquility of the forest-letting the chlorophyll transform the sunlight into ecstasy.

The Ashram had carefully been designed for the second phase of his lifes mission. He had thought long and deeply on the subject. In his own quiet and firm way, he now began a conscious transformation from the esoteric to the exoteric phase. He did not want to be an elitist sage. He wanted the impact of his actions to reach out to the masses, the simple peasants and tribals of the area. He realised that if he *confined his field of action to yoga and deep meditation, he would only touch the lives of a small and esoterically inclined minority. Elitist Ashrams catered not for the local populace but the more affluent outsiders. Baba was averse to such a situation. An Ashram divinises and uplifts the life of the community.* In the Second phase, his aim was mass action to reach out to the common multitudes of Maharashtra, to involve them in religious activity and experience in a way that touched their lives completely.

The Palki Celebrations

Towards this end, he showed a deep insight into the Hindu ethos and its love for festivals and celebrations. It is these festivals that involve the whole community per se in a collective action that serves to uplift the mass consciousness of the multitudes. Sermons on Yoga and the Gita would reach out to just a small segment of the middle classes. He wanted to reach out to the peasants and tribal folk, the farmers, the milkmen and herdsmen of the area-to uplift the general consciousness. The way in which he succeeded in reaching out to the masses in Maharashtra was remarkable and awe inspiring.

The bane of Hindu society he felt were the barriers and

divisions of caste and class. These had fragmented the society and unleashed caste conflict and oppression. The caste system, he was convinced had outlived its utility and corroded the Hindu polity. There was an urgent need to make it more egalitarian; to evolve a set of religious practices which involved a free mixing of the high and the low and the rich and the poor. The highly stratified structures of Indian society were its bane. *Hinduism, he felt, had need to learn much from the Sikh egalitarian ethos*. Towards this end he initiated an annual festival of the Palki. It was a beautiful and elegant conception. He had spent his earlier phase of Sadhna at the Sapta Shringad Shrine of the Raja Rajeshwari Devi high up in the Maharashtra plateau. He spoke to the temple authorities there. Each year they agreed to bring a Palki procession of a silver replica of the Spatshring Devi's statue in a Palki"(palenquin) to visit her sister-the Devi of Patne. The Palki was brought in a massive procession. The entire people of Patne and Chalisgaon and the neighbouring districts received this Palki procession at the outskirts of the town. It was then taken in procession throughout the town with Baba accompanying the Palki itself. People would come out in thousands to see their living god, their own Buddha-like being who emerged once a year from his forest Ashram. There was a stampede to touch his feet, to bow to him. The crush of humanity used to be stupendous and frightening. The Palki procession would weave its way through the town of Chalisgaon and then come to the Patne Shrine. A huge camp was established to receive the Palki.

The next day the Sapta Shring Devis Palki was taken to the Patne Devi Shrine. The Priests of the hill shrine would pray at the Patne Devi Salter and the priest of the local diety would perform the puja of the visiting Raja Rajeshwari. Parallel to this, a massive yagya of the Mahakali used to be performed to spread Sattwa into the atmosphere. The chant of Vedic hymns and Devi stotras would fill the air along with the rich aroma of incense and the aroma of oblations fed to the sacrificial fires. In the afternoon, a "langar" used to be held for all people. A mass community kitchen was established. All people who came there, peasants and tribals, officers and peons, the high and low, young and old, were fed on leaf plates in the Sikh tradition of the Langar. Baba's disciples pooled their efforts to feed the guests and local people who came to the festival. Each year the number of people thronging to the festival grew. From a few thousands in the end of the decade of the 1970s it had grown to almost a lakh and more by the end of the decade of the 1980s. The local farmers used to load rice and chapatties in tractor trollies. The fires would burn through out the night and day to feed the multitudes. The food was treated as sacrament by the people and they swarmed to be fed from the Guru's "Langar" or community kitchen.

The high point of the whole programme was the evening function in the Ashram lawns itself. A stage used to be set up. One of the most famous Bhajan singers of Maharshtra, was called each year as the guest of honour. He would sing devotional songs for the whole night as the multitudes joined in a chant that reverberated through the forest. Baba sat up the whole night on an elevated stage. The next morning the Palki procession would depart back for Sapta Shringad.

12 years of Sanyas:

On 28 Aug 1980 Baba had completed 12 years of Sanayasa. The 12th year of renunciation has great mystical significance. This event was celebrated in a very big way. The local people of Chalisgaon and neighboring districts organised a very grand celebration to commemorate this occasion. The local media in Maharashtra was full of this rivivalist event and its epochal significance. Baba started attracting a lot of attention now. Baba invited me for the Palki

Festival in the winter of 1982. It was an awesome spectacle of mass action. He had reached out to the multitudes and set in motion the masses of almost three or four districts of Chalisgaon, Jalgoan, Nasik and Dhulia. When I first saw the throngs and crowds, I was a bit frightened. It was like a mini Kumbha Mela. The crush of humanity was so stupendous. The people were enraptured and enthralled by this traditional revival of an old festive form of social action. The rich and poor, the high and low all joined in to execute the festivities and programmes with military precision and traditional grace.

I, who had seen a totally different facet of the Ashram in the earlier phase ,was baffled. When the crowds had gone I could not help asking him about this massive transformation from the esoteric to the exoteric. He was so mystic and scientific in his outlook. Yet now I found him turning to traditional ceremonial forms and mass rituals. His explanation was lucid. His aim,he said, was to reach out to the masses and multitudes. At their spiritual levels of development, festivities were the best way to involve people in all walks of life. Gokhle and Tilak had used the same form to harness the social and spiritual energies of the people of Maharashtra. They loved celebrations. This gave them all a common purpose to direct their energies to. It popularised the shrine. Chalisgaon was a backward district inhabited by tribal people. Baba wanted to uplift their collective consciousness. He wanted to erode the barriers of caste and class. Hence he insisted upon the langar -the high and low, the rich and poor, the healthy and infirm sitting down together to break bread cooked in community kitchens, served by the devout as a "Prasada", a sacramental offering without any distinction of caste, creed or even race and religion. It was a beautiful conception. His diagnostic skills and traditional solutions were elegant and aesthetic.

What had to be seen to be believed was the mass

upsurge of euphoria that his very presence unleashed. It was like the milk maids of Brinda Ban. The Boys and girls danced in abandon, and surged forth to touch his feet or just touch his person. Thousand upon thousands of them. Each and every one participated and contributed in his own way. It was something curious, he unleashed his spiritual energies so that he could reach out to as many people as possible. He did not make a bee line to the West, to bring in foreign disciples and the dollars and close circuit televisions. He aimed at unleashing a mass action programme at the very grass roots to reach out to the multitudes of that tribal district. His Ashram was a vortex of spiritual bliss. From there the Satwik consciousness seemed to radiate and spread over the entire region. In the mass crush of humanity, you encountered a highly charged spiritual atmosphere. The crowds grew euphoric in his presence. The more you saw of these festive celebrations, the more you thought of Krishna, the divine cowhead of Vrindaban. His charisma simply radiated in love. No one who came near him could fail to be touched by the Christ-like love and compassion that radiated from his being. It was a mass celebration of love and the joy of life. It was a beautiful and elegant conception. As the years passed-the word began to spread. Baba in truth was the incarnation of Vishnu-the Avatara phenomenon of our age.

What is Vishnu Consciousness? It is the consciousness of civilisational revival and renewal. When-ever the civilisational consciousness of India grows tired, dissipated and spent, charismatic beings arise to revive the collective consciousness and renew the drained energies of the people. The Vishnu consciousness therefore is the consciousness of a civilisational renewal and revival. To that extent Baba represented just such a consciousness of revival. He was very classical and traditional. Yet he had correctly diagnosed the ills of the caste-ridden Hindu polity. His method of mass action was to reach out to the masses by involving them in festive celebrations and collective social activity where they shed inhibitions of caste and creed. He insisted on self-discipline and perfection in all that was done. His Ashrama was a classical fusion of the ancient and the modern-the best in technology synthesised with the ancient Indian civilisational form. His skills as an engineer and technocrat, were blended with his deep knowledge of the classical scriptures and tradition to make a perfect blend of the ancient and the modern. A synthesis that represented a classical revival. He insisted on remaining a local and regional phenomena for he felt his duty was to the common people who had given him shelter. *As a saint, he had a symbiotic linkage with the local and regional community. His task, as a sage, was to divinise society. He devised a perfect method to reach out to the masses in a way that would involve them whole-heartedly in the relgious life and process.* The traditional and local art forms were on full display on such occasions, the dancers, bards and singers, the acrobats and eunuchs all came out in their traditional finery to participate joyously in the festival-the week long annual celebrations that involved a whole community. And the throngs poured out to express their affection and love for their sage. In all my years, I have not seen anything like that mass euphoria and upsurge of religiosity. And behind the celebrations was a *deeper underlying purpose, a clear message for Hindu society to cast away its barriers of caste and creed and join spontaneously in an upsurge of religiosity that bordered on collective euphoria*. To do this he had revived the traditional festive forms and celebrations to harness the energy of the local society and focus its emotions collectively on a holy enterprise. This has been the classical Hindu method to set into motion mass movements that reach out to the multitudes. The Kumbha and Ardha Kumbha melas are such conceptions of generating religious mass action and establishing traditions that will renew the faith of the multitudes. To those of us who had seen the mystic sage in his earlier phase of solitude, it was a staggering transformation, but one that followed the classical pattern. The mystic withdraws from society for his deep meditations. He gains his insights from the distance. He then returns to society to spread his charisma and spiritual energy amongst the masses, and divinise life at the grass roots level. *From a recluse mystic and stern ascetic, Pranvananda, the sage of Patne, became a saint of the masses.* The peasants and tribals of the region now worshipped the very ground that he walked upon. Till the end he remained classical and traditional, the very embodiment of the ancient Indian way of life.

Some two decades ago, he had set out to prove that the ancient Indian ideal of renunciation was still relevant in this day and age. By the end of the 1980s he had reached out to lakhs and lakhs of people, and with each who came to him he developed a special relationship of love and deep affection. In his presence, you felt an upsurge of Christ-like love and purity. The honey of his deep meditations attracted the multitudes like bees to his innate spiritual sweetness.

His entire life was a quest for ultimate perfection. He wanted to live as a flawless exemplar of the ancient traditions. The sage draws his sustainence from the local community. His first duty therefore is not to distant audiences in the cities and foreign lands but to the local people. The very presence of a sage in the community divinises the social intercourse and uplifts the consciousness of the region. As a sage who had settled down in a forest in Maharashtra, he owed a deep sense of loyalty and gratitude to the local populace. His foremost interaction therefore was with them. He was a Bengali but to serve his adopted community, the community that gave him shelter, sustenance and reverence, he learnt the Marathi language. He could speak it flawlessly, and subsequently he composed devotional hymns in Marathi. He geared the Ashram activities to involve the local people, the poorest of the poor as it were, was involved in these mass celebrations that were designed to elicit a mass response.

"You do not seek the origin of a
river
and you do not seek the
origins of a sage".

BOOK THREE
THE SAGA OF SUSHANTA

"The Guru is Brahman
The Guru is Vishnu.
The Guru is Mahesh.
The Guru indeed is
the manifest Para Brahman
To such a Guru
I offer my salutations".

Bholagiri Ashram, Haridwar

16

The Sage Recollects : Chanelling the Descent

The transformation from the mystic to the level of mass action was a little too staggering. I requested him to permit me to visit his Ashram in the quieter phases after the Palki festivities and celebrations, when the crowds thinned out. He agreed graciously. So, I now visited him along with the family once each year to spend a few days at the Ashram. We had been blessed with a boy and a girl-lovely children who grew up in his care. He was their God father. They adored him. He totally charmed the children. He had named them and was their inspiration. I was keen that the children be exposed to his spiritual ambience as much as possible. A beautiful forest Rest House called Leelawati(named after the daughter of the Mathematical sage Bhaskaracharya) had been constructed near the temple by the Forest Deptt. So had guest rooms for pilgrims and distant guests. We came and stayed there each year. It was a joy to be able to live in his forest retreat. He knew the individual needs of each disciple. For me his instructions were simple-solitude. A sheet would be spread amongst the dense grove of sandalwood trees so that I could sit alone and meditate and write. He encouraged me to spend the whole day alone and by myself. He encouraged me to write. In fact, this came as a command from him. Meditation, especially deep meditation, unleashes large tracts of creative energies in our beings. These must be given a useful outlet. A channel has to be created for the passage of this energy which must be usefully expended in a way that ennobles and uplifts.

In fact, in year 1977 itself (even before my marriage) I had received a sudden summons from him to come to his Ashram for the Kojagiri or Guru Purnima celebrations. It is a unique Indian tradition. On this full moon day, disciples from far and near, gather at their guru's Ashram to honour him. In the night, when the full moon emerges from behind the hills, the disciples gather in the open and boil milk collectively. It is boiled in an open vessel on which the moon beams must fall. This milk is then drunk as sacrament by all the disciples. That year, some of the closet disciples had gathered there at his Forest Retreat at Patne. It was a beautiful moonlit night. The blue sheen of the full moon on the forest was so soothing. The cliffs glinted as if they had been coated in silver and encased in the moonlight for eternity. The peacocks cried out in the forest as we honoured our classical teacher.

He called me to his hut for a personal audience. He came straight to the point. "I have called you to tell you that the time has come when you must begin to write. You must record your experiences. In the beginning, it will come and go. You will fill up pages and then throw them aside. The output will wax and wane, and vary in quality till you develop the channel. Then the books and writings will come in a steady stream-a glissade. They will flow down of their own accord. "I was quite astonished by his prophecy. But that was exactly how it came to pass. I took his command seriously, and began to write. I filled up registers and then threw them away in disgust. I made a conscious effort to open myself to the info-sphere as it were- to open my mind and call for that descent of the Divine Richas or inspirations.

I tried what is called "automatic writing". The initial attempts were disappointing. There were flashes in between and some tracts of good writings and flow, interspersed with the very average. Then, it began to flow in a steady stream over the years.

I had been doing very deep meditation under his guidance, and it had stirred up deep forces in the psyche. I had a very strange experience. It seemed to me that a whole mass of fully formed books were beginning to descend on my mind all at once. They came fused and jumbled together in parts that were random, the end often preceding the beginning. They began to descend on my mind all at once in a glissade as it were. At the onset I was hard put to just keep pace- so many themes descended as it were, fused and jumbled together on my mind. I had to receive them and then filter and organise them into separate works. It was a strange experience. The writings seemed to descend from a sphere where they pre-existed in a fully formed fashion, in a kind of an infosphere. When you sought them, the concepts and thoughts descended in a mass, you had only to differentiate and edit the flow-and give it a linear and sequential order. Over the years that followed,from the initial mass of jumbled ideas that descended concurrently as it were, one was able to differentiate and extract ten different books which were later published.

In the year 1979 my son was born. Just before his birth I felt inspired to express my meditational experiences through the medium of poetry in my native tongue. I was pleasantly surprised to encounter those classical patterns and rythms, the Sanskritic alloterations and metaphor-rich language bearing the Vedic inspirational imprint. This patterned and rythmic speech does appear to be a derivative of the meditationally-aroused consciousness. It is curious how these innate rythms have a universality of stylistic form which is a constant in all ages and times. It is constant because the inspirational source - the dimension of the mind from which these descend, is constant. *The Vedas speak of the concept of the Richas. These are the divine inspirations, the fully formed creative ideas, concepts and archetypes which preexsist in the infosphere. Our minds serve as the channells to bring down these concepts and archetypes, to give them mentalised expressions, to verbalise them and bring them, down to the human plane. The writer acts merely as a lightning conductor or a medium and channel of descent.*

What is important is a conscious development of a channel of expression which serves as an outlet for the creative energies aroused in the psyche by the process of deep meditation. Such a channel of expression is an imperative need for anyone who wishes to proceed on the path of higher yoga. This was true of the Rig Vedic Seers, the Buddhist monks and the popular sages of the Middle ages like Kabir and Meera. The creative upsurges in most cases were preceded by the onset of euphoric states of mood elevation and even ecstasy. This Soma experience seems to well up from deep within the psyche. As the consciousness is pushed to one extreme of ergotropic hypo-arousal, it rebounds to the opposite level of hyper-arousal. Thus bouts of great tranquility engendered by meditative practices unleash experiences of intense ecstasy. Conversely, physical ecstasy or peaks of atheletic effort produce euphoric states of bliss. quieude and tranquility.

Thus, an Olympic athelete strains himself to the utmost for his leap. He strains every muscle and sinew, he focusses all his energies and emotions for a supreme effort. He pole vaults over the record mark. As he falls down and lands on the mattress- he suddenly slips into a paradoxical experience of quiet euphoria- in the midst of the shouting, exultant crowds- he slips into a peak experience of quietude, inner happiness and deep satisfaction. A peak of physical experience and deep activity causes the consciousness to rebound to its very opposite state of intense tranquility. *This "Rebound" experience of consciousness is well known to the mystics*. Perhaps it has something to do with the paradoxical nature of consciousness itself (even like the paradoxical nature of light - it is a wave and it is a particle. When we focus on the particle aspect - the wave aspect phases out and vice versa).

Even so, the human consciousness pushed to one extreme of quietude and stillness and deep tranquility, suddenly rebounds to its very opposite extreme of intense emotional or creative activity. Possibly, it has something to do with the paradoxical, quantum nature of consciousness. However, his emphatic instructions to me to develop a channel of expression was a great boon in dealing with the arousal of the creative energies in the psyche. This facet is highly visible in Buddhism. The energies unleashed by collective and individual meditations were given a flow and full form in the Creative Arts- in sculpture and painting, in architecture. Buddhism had unleashed a cultural explosion of art in India-the festive frescoes of Ajanta, the exquisite sculptures of Ellora, the cave paintings and stupas. Meditative cultures have expressed themselves in great upsurges of art. Creativity is unleashed by meditation. It can either be wasted in procreative excesses or be channelled into mental creativity- into art, architecture and writing. All art needs focussed attention and concentration. Concentration is an essential step in Yoga. It leads to meditation. Meditation spurs creativity- that leads to artistic expressions. Baba's technique was simple. He directed that I spend entire days in solitude and tranquility. I used to simply lie down in the limpid sunlight that streams in the forest, and open my mind to offer a channel for the Richas, the archetypal concepts and knowledge free floating in the infosphere of the collective unconscious. "We do not choose writing", he said "writing chooses us". We prepare our minds to act as channels so that the autonomous tracts of knowledge waiting to seek expression at this plane can descend. It is a minor variation of the Aurobindo's theme of the descent of the Supermind . In mythology, the descent of the sacred River Ganga upon the head of Shiva- provides a beautiful metaphor for this process of channelling. The ancient Vedic seers used to open their minds in the deep *silence to receive the downflow of these Richas-these streams of knowledge, these autonomous, pre programmed tracts of knowledge from the cosmic info sphere of the universal consciousness. "We donot invent the knowledge and order in the Universe. We merely become instruments for its expression and unfoldment*. Our task is merely to perfect the instruments (or to use the terminology of the Gita) to become "Nimittas" the channels for the expression of the divine will.

Einstien's earth-shaking equation, $E=MC^2$, established the relationship between Mass and Energy. What we see around ourselves however is a trinity. It is a cosmic trinity of Mass, Energy and Information. There is a vast infosphere which lies behind the observed universe of mass and energy. The order in this universe comes from that infosphere. That information is infinite and limitless. More and more of the information keeps descending into our universe of mass and energy to counter the ravages of entropy. All minds (human, animal or vegetable) are conduits for the descent of information. What we need today is a new Einstien's equation, that will establish the true relationship between the trinity of Mass, Energy and Information.

He asked me to carefully record my inner experiences. It was essential to form a data bank of such experiences-so that it would be available to the future generations-so that we could apply the tools of modern scientific knowledge to understand the true nature of these experiences. As an Engineer, he well understood the concepts of modern Physics which implied that the observing consciousness can not be left out of the scientific observations. There is no such thing as a truly objective observation. The consciousness of the observer can not be excluded from the observation. As Heisenberg tells us, each act of observation distorts and changes the system being so observed.

Modern Physics has so far confined itself to the external phenomena. Meditation deals with consciousness itself. The discipline of Yoga can be treated like a series of repeatable psycho-somatic experiments. The scientific method can well be applied to this field. *The first requirement for such an enterprise would be to record our experiences clinically*. Our initial struggles and failures would all then be important learning steps in dealing with the consciousness itself. It was towards this end that he exhorted me to record in clinical detail my own experiences. I started keeping detailed notes in accordance with his instructions.

I then summoned up the courage to ask him to let me record his personal experiences. He was very hesitant. The higher order of experiences as it is, do not lend themselves to expression in verbal constructs. Very rarely could these be transmitted, they must be experienced, he said. Nevertheless I persisted. What then of his earlier experiences? What of his own formative experiences in the early stages of his Sadhna? Of his struggles and the years before he took Sanyasa.

"When I took Sanyasa" he said "I ritually died to the life that I had lived before".

"But the real learning experience, the experience to which we lesser mortals could relate, lay precisely in that early phase", I persisted. May be I should not have. An ancient proverb says "one does not trace the source of a river. One does not similarly seek out the origins of a sage." But I persisted. He seemed pained-but for some reason, I kept returning to this theme.

One day he relented at long last.

He called me to his hut. I was indeed blessed to receive beautiful glimpses of his early years. These were as remarkable as I had expected them to be. In fact, much more so. The complete story of Pranvananda, the sage of Patne, now filled out at long last.

17
The Legend of Sushanta

It was a beautiful and extraordinary life right from its origins. The story began in a small hamlet in Bengal-near Kumar Pu kur, where the last of our really great ones-Ramakrishna had been born in the nineteenth century. Baba was born on 12 Oct 1941 in the ancestral house of his mother in the native village Harinavi. This incidentally was the village where eminent Indians like Netaji Subash Chandra Bose and Pandit Shivnath Shah had been born. When Sushanta was only three years old, his mother died. Baba remembered his father's ancestral house in Behala, Calcutta. It was a huge ancient mansion with countless rooms. The Mukherjees were a very rich family of Bengali Brahmins-very rich and very pious. They could trace their family history back to some 32 generations for atleast a 650 years span. In the clan were some very illustrious ancestors of the eminence of the Late C.V.Bannerjee (First President of the Indian National Congress) and Ashutosh Mukherjee, former Vice chancellor of the Calcutta University. For the last 225 years they had been living in the ancestral mansion at Behala in Calcutta. The house was a picture of antiquity. There were huge old portraits in the galleries and halls of the ancestors. The house had countless pots and pans and brass and copper utensils which people borrowed for marriages and social functions. There was the old Victorian furniture of polished mahogany and the air of deep quiet that settled over everything.

Baba was born 'Sushanta Mukerjee'. His father was the fourth of seven brothers. It was a well-knit, joint family. However, Baba's father had married against the wishes of his family. They felt the bride's family was no match for that ancient clan. His father had been ostracised. He had left the ancestral home in Calcutta, and started his own business in the mica mines. Three years after Baba was born, his mother passed away. The elder Mukerjee was very distraught. About this time, the "family" began to seek reconciliation. The reason was simple. The family did not as yet have a male heir. The eldest brother of Baba's father was the only other brother who had married. He had only a daughter. The rest of his uncles had refused to marry. Out of his four uncles, three had tried to take Sanyasa. The mystic calling ran in the genes of this clan of Brahmins. The joint family was presided over by the wife of Baba's eldest uncle. Her name was Bimla Devi. She was a "grand dame" in the classical mould. She was called "Baro Ma" by the whole family. Of all the persons in his life, she had the greatest influence on Baba. She was a regal personality, tall stately and beautiful. She had long black tresses that fell below her waist. In the Bengalee tradition she usually wore white silk sarees with a red blouse. She was a saintly person of lofty character. It was she who insisted that Baba's father must be brought back to the fold. The clan needed a male heir to continue the family line. So the emissaries began to come to Baba's father. They pleaded with him to return to the fold. The distraught elder Mukrejee needed someone to help him bring up his infant son. So the reconciliation took place at long last.

Baro Ma adopted the young "Sushanta". He was then just five years old. She took the infant Baba in her own care and brought him up as her own son. She showered love on the orphaned child and doted on him. She was the one person he was most deeply attached and devoted to. For not only was she his surrogate mother-she was also the first teacher who insisted on absolute moral purity in thought, deed and action.

Sushanta was a precocious and lively child but given to moods of deep introspection. His class mates called him a "Bhavavadi". He would seemingly go into trances and witness the future. He would blurt out what was going to happen, and it invariably came true. He was an extraordinarily, gifted child. He recalled the first experience he had with the great sages. They first came to him in a dream. It was an extraordinary vision. He saw two tall sages with flowing white hair and beards. Their gaze was penetrating and serene. He felt waves of love emanate from these tall sages and a great silence. Gently, they reached out to him. They whispered the sacred mantras in his ears and told him to meditate upon these. They told him that he would take Sanayasa and renounce the world. Then, as quietly as they had come, they vanished. He still remembered the bright and vivid colours of that vision. How much more real than reality itself it had felt. How deep and vibrant. It left a lasting and indelible imprint upon his life. Visions of these tall sages came to him on many critical occassions in his life. It was they who had told him of his destined path. He would renounce the world. He was to became a Sanyasi. That was his life's mission.

Young Sushanta went to school. Baro Ma used to talk to him at great length every day when he returned. She insisted on his speaking the truth and upholding a very high standard of moral purity. She was very conscious of her duty to supervise his upbringing in the most perfect manner. He was a lively child full of energy and a keen sense of humour. He enjoyed teasing the pompous. One of his teachers was once taking a class on literature. He spoke of the "Bengani colour" (The violet colour of Brinjals). What is the colour of the Brinjal, sir? Young Sushanta asked with an air of assumed innocence. "What? You don't know the colour of the Brinjal?"

"No, Sir" said Sushanta in all earnestness. The old teacher frowned. He thought of an alternate way to describe the violet colour of the Brinjal , but Sushanta shook his head. "Oh, very well then", he took out a rupee coin "Here just run over to the market, buy a Brinjal for me, and come and show it to the whole class".

Young Sushanta scampered out to the market place. He hurriedly inspected the pile of shining violet, coloured-Brinjals. Suddenly, he saw one of those freak ones that are white in colour. Naughtily, he picked it up and rushed back to the class. "Have you brought the Brinjal, Sushanta?" said the teacher "Now, show it to the class". Sushanta held up the white Brinjal aloft, and the whole class burst into peals of laughter. "What?" the old teacher was astonished. Despite his annoyance, he could not supress a smile. In later years, the sage used to recount sometimes such happy incidents of his childhood.

One of the most vivid episode he recalled however, was that of his youngest uncle called Surendra. Mysticlly inclined by disposition, his uncle was forever engaged in deep meditation. He often spoke of renouncing and becoming a Sanyasin. Young Sushanta loved him deeply. His uncle Surendra refused to be enmeshed in the bonds of wedlock and worldly life. The entire family was worried that he would seek to escape from their protective mantle, and run away to become a sanyasin-an exemplar-who would uphold the validity of this ancient tradition in this modern day and age. One day, there was a great commotion in the house. His uncle Surenedra had escaped. He had given every body the slip and gone away to become a sanyasin-free as a bird clothed only in its own feathers ! The women began to lament. A curse seemed to have come over the house of the Mukerjees. Two of the elder boys had already vanished without a trace. Now, the third was gone. Search parties were sent out in all directions. The police was informed. Relatives, in distant palces, were rung up. But there was no news of him for many months after that.

Then, one day they brought Surendra back-almost like a prisoner. His face was emaciated, his hair was distraught, his clothes torn and soiled. He had sought the refuge of the eternal life-hoping that the cosmos itself would attend to his every need- as he had surrendered to it his will. But it did not. He had to starve. Sanyasa was no longer a vibrant and living tradition in this land. There was poverty and misery. The pious people did not have enough to eat themselves. How could they look after saints and sages and wandering sadhus? Beggars there were a plenty-but they were the dregs of this earth. The lost and the damned. In India, in the land of the Budha himself, there was no further place for the ideal of renunciation, there were no great sanghas and orders of monks, no learned monasteries catering to mystic and spiritual pursuits. Such a calling was an historical anachronism-in India. Industrialisation had destroyed the self-sufficient rural economies which generated a sufficient surplus that could enable the local societies to sustain their monks and sages in the forest. That symbiotic linkage had gone. In the grinding poverties of the cities and slums, men struggled to keep body and soul together. They had little time, inclination or the economic means to cater for sages. His uncle Surendera was heart-broken. He would not speak to anyone. He had trusted the infinite -he had cast off his fetters. In return, he did not get liberation and joy and freedom. All he got was hunger and privation and want. A month later, he died-a broken man. Young Sushanta was deeply moved by this tragic event. He was shaken to the core of his being. Deep within his being was the conviction that one day he was destined to be a Sanyasi. He was destined to renounce the world. This was indeed his destiny. There was no escape from his destiny. But, was this the end he would meet?

When he had grown old enough to ask about his own mother, Baro Ma led him to the alter of the Maha Kali - the Cosmic Mother. This, is your true mother, she said. It was a defining moment for Sushanta. For the young child - she became his mother. He would speak to her, converse with her and share his hurt. Baro Ma was stern in discipline. If Sushanta was naughty, she would tell everyone -"No one is to speak to him".

Sushanta would feel terrible. But he was very self-willed. He would equally refuse to speak to others. Inside him, the little child would feel crushed. "Make them speak to me mother" he would entreat the Mahakali. "Make them speak to me. "I will not speak to them". He was very stubborn. Invariably, the others would relent in this test of wills.

When this tragic event occurred, and his uncle Surendera passed away, he came to the alter of the Devi. Silently and accusingly he gazed at her "He trusted you. Why did you let him down like this? Why did you not take care of him?" "Will you do the same to me when my time comes?" He felt hot tears roll down his cheeks. He must have dozed off in between. Somewhere in the mist he heard her speak. *"He suffered for he did not really trust me. He was afraid. You can not approach me with fear, only with love and total trust."* Slowly, he gazed up at the four, armed image. One of its hands is always raised in the "Abhay dan Mudra" the mudra that frees us from fear. Fear is the greatest fetter. Fear brings failure. Fear brings death. Fear makes us mortal. Freedom from fear is our true liberation.

Sushanta Mukerjee excelled in school. His forte was mathematics. Invariably, he used to top the class and score the highest marks. He had an innate feel for numbers. Many years later, he had shown me a book on Vedic Mathematics. Maths is an innate language. The symbolism of Mathematics was his second nature. An amusing incident happened once. He was in high school. He had given his maths exam. For once he had thoroughly spoilt his paper. He was mortified and crestfallen. He enjoyed winning- coming first in the class everytime. They used to announce the results in class and this was a critical exam. For some strange reason he was overcome with grief. He came home and sat quietly before the family altar. He gazed imploringly at the four-armed statue, his real mother, as Baro Ma had told him. Tearfully, the young Sushanta made a boyish request. "Please mother, I do not want to fail in this exam. I want to maintain my record of coming first and topping always. Please save me from this humiliation." The papers were evaluated. He went with a thudding heart to the class. It was mortifying. Sushanta, the acknowledged maths wizard was going to fail. What an utter humiliation! What a disaster it was". The maths teacher (who incidentally was very fond of him) began to read out the marks. He sat with down-cast, his heart beating in his mouth. "Sushanta Mukerjee - 90 percent marks the highest once again". As usual he had topped the class". Sushanta was shocked. He knew he had done badly. How could this happen. His class mates clapped and cheered. The class over, Sushanta hurried after his teacher. "Sir ! Sir there must be some mistake. I..." "I know Sushanta, Frankly I am very sorry. I know you must have done cent per cent correct and were expecting 100 out of 100. But my boy, I am deeply embarrassed. Well, its like this you see. Yesterday, I had kept the papers on my table to correct. Yours was lying in the middle of the table. My youngest daughter- she is only three, you see. - She.. well, She spilt the whole bottle of ink on your paper. Frankly, I could not decipher a thing. The paper was soaked through. So well, I ..ah.. I gave you marks based upon your earlier performance. I am most apologetic my boy. I am really sorry."

Sushanta gazed at him, his mouth open with

astonishment. Yesterday evening he had prayed to the Devi with such fervour to save him from the humiliation of failure". By slow degrees, through a series of such coincidences, he realised that he had established an on-going dialogue with the nameless void. The nameless void he had personified in the form of his own mother. The void is your mother. This four-armed statue is her form. Speak to her when you are in distress. She will always hear your call. "That is what Baro Ma had said".

Sushanta's father was a great scholar of Vedanta. He was highly learned in the classical scriptures and enjoyed spiritual conversations with his son. His hobby was Astrology. He was excellent at casting horoscopes and his predictions were uncannily true. His maths was excellent and this, so people said, was what lent such accuracy to his astrological predictions. His business interests however kept him extremely busy. His fortunes fluctuated wildly. Most of the time, he did exceedingly well. Wealth and goods flowed into the house - so would friends and hangers on. Suddenly, the business would collapse. The hangers on would vanish - the flow of friends would reduce to a trickle. The lavish parties at the Calcutta clubs would cease. These ups and downs, taught a great amount of inner balance to the young Sushanta. He saw the precariousness of relationships built on selfishness and wealth.

Ramakrishna Parmahansa, the last of our really great ones had left a profound impression upon Sushanta. Every other day, he would take the bus to Dakshineshwar. He would bathe in the brown, warm waters of the Ganga and then have the Darshana of the Maha Kali - the powerful diety of Dakshineshwar. He would spend hours in meditation there. "The milk of the cow - in essence pervades its whole body - but it is at the udders alone that we receive it easily and naturally". Like wise the cosmic mother permeates every atom and quark in the cosmos, but at these selected shrines

- it is so easy to touch that infinity. It is easy to establish a personalised equation with the void. Scores and scores of people come to a shrine. They come with pious thoughts and noble aspirations. These cling to the walls and floors of the shrine and add to its power and positivity. It only grows with the years. It increases ever more "with the increasing throngs of pilgrims, it acquires a life of its own".

18

The Last of the "Mohicans"

Sushanta finished Matriculation in 1959 and went on to join an Engineering Institute. His brilliant academic career continued. He notched up achievement after achievement. His whole family doted upon him. He was the sole male heir- the last of the Mukerjees - the only heir to a family fortune worth lakhs.

Baro Ma doted upon Sushanta. She was most anxious about his welfare. His every whim was attended to with alacrity. He was the only male progney who would carry forward the line of the Mukerjees, the pious and learned Brahmins from Behala Calcutta. However deep, deep down in his heart Sushanta knew that this was not to be. For many, many years earlier, the tall and august sages had appeared to him in that vivid vision and informed him of his destined path. As he grew, so grew the conviction in his heart. He had to renounce this life and seek the life of the 'Sanyasin'. He continued to work deligently at his studies but the life of the spirit held a deep thrall for him. He frequented the temples and the monastries. He met the wandering sages and sadhus that he still chanced upon in Calcutta. He spoke to them with an urgency born of a clear realisation of his lifes mission. Somewhere around his penultimate years in the Engineering College he began his annual pilgrimage to Rishikesh and Badrinath.

At Rishikesh he met a young Sanyasi. One look at him

kindled a long friendship - no introductions were needed. Sushanta was sometimes troubled by the movements of the lower vital. The Sadhu addressed his unspoken questions on his own accord. There after he demonstrated to him some Yogic Asnas which enhance self control and temperance. He gave him a number of useful practical tips on Brahmacharya and meditation. Such aids often come of their own accord in our spiritual lives;sometimes prayed for, sometimes unsought. In Haridwar, in Rishikesh, in Rudra Prayag and Badrinath he sought to contact the eternal stream of the Hindu consciousness. He sought to put himself in touch with the vibrant tradition that had come down unbroken for the past 5000 years. It had suffered the vecettitudes of invasions and persecutions but the essential structure had withstood the concerted onslaught of Islam. India is the rare case of Muslim rule where a large segment of the subjugated population retained its original religious way of life. A far greater cultural impact came with the advent of British rule and modernity. The ancient traditional structures of an agricultural society had come under attack as never before. Their continued validity in the modern day and age were now openly questioned. The mind set of the enslaved sought to view its own cultural context as inferior. The culture of the Western conqueror was regarded as vastly superior. It was this deep rooted civilisational inferiority complex that revivalists like Ramakrishna, Vivekananda and Dayananda and reinterpretors and synthesisors like Aurobindo had tried to reverse and transform. They were only partially successful. The colonisation and subsequent industrialisation of Indian society had led to a destruction of its historic cultural and civilisational context and traditional structures. The entire stable structure of Hindu society has been shaken to the core, first by the impact of Islam and then by the impact of modernity. Modernisation is often equated with Westernisation. The original Indian culture, he felt, was getting subsumed and inundated with the cultural invasion of Western mores and forms.

In his travels Sushanta pondered deeply over these issues. Yet Hinduism had an eternal core of aliveness that would enable it to withstand the onslaught of modernity and renew itself as it had done time and again. The process of the civilisational renewal and renaissance, is indeed at the core of the Indian concept of Avatarahood. The so called incarnation of the Godhead in human form implies a social revolution; a reform movement of revival and regeneration. A deeper analysis shows that Indian and Eastern Philosophical thought is far closer to the modern view point of Quantum Mechanics and the New Physics. Fritzof Capra, Gary Zukov, Romain Roland and a score of other Western thinkers have pointed out the tremendous similarities between ancient Eastern, mystic philosophies and the New Physics. The modern Systems view of Life is far closer to Hindu philosophical thought than the outmoded Newtonian- Cartesian Mechanistic Paradigm ever was.

What was needed, was a revalidation of the ancient Indian ideals and traditions in the modern setting. The institution of Sanyasa or renunciation, had to be shown to be as valid in the modern times as it was in the Rig Vedic, Upanishadic or Buddhist periods of Indian history. Sushanta sat for hours on the banks of the Blue-Green Ganga in Haridwar and the musically named Prayags (the confluences) of Rudra Prayag, Dev Prayag, Karna Prayag, Nand Prayag and Vishnu Prayag. The sacred rivers have such poetic names - the Alak nanda, the Bhagirathi- the Mandakini, the Bhilganga and the Pindarganga. Truly, this section of the Himalayas is called the "Deva Bhoomi" the land of the Gods. It is a cradle of the Hindu civilisation and ethos. These rivers are the metaphors of its eternal flow and life.

Sushanta came back home. A deep silence seemed to have engulfed him. He felt himself in touch with the collective unconscious of the Hindu race. He wanted to live and breathe its traditions and myths. Then tragedy befell. In 1963 Baro Ma fell sick and was soon on her death bed. Sushanta was distraught. This was the deepest emotional attachment of his lonely life. She was the well spring and embodiment of all love and affection. She was deeply concerned about him.

Tradition decrees that before renouncing the world, a Sanyasin is required to take the permission of only two people- his mother (if he is unmarried) and his wife, if he is a house holder. If they withhold permission, the way of renunciation is barred. It is only with their willing consent that success can be achieved in Sanyasa. When he realised that Baro Ma was about to pass away from this earth, he went to her alone as she lay on her deathbed. Even in her last days there was a kind of a spiritual glow and radiance that emanated from her being. She looked up at him with deep concern and love as he sat besides her and held her hand. He hesitated.

"Baro Ma, Ever since I grew old enough to understand things - I have felt this deep seated inner conviction and urge. I have to take Sanyasa - I have to renounce life. That is my destiny. Your permission and blessings are essential for this". He breathed deeply. "Will you please give me the permission to renounce life after you are gone?" He held his breath for what seemed an eternity.

The stately old lady said nothing. Only tears rolled down her cheeks. Sushanta felt terribly distressed.

But she smiled through her tears.

" I had always known it son. I knew it was your destiny. That is why I took so much care to ensure that you would never stray from the path of moral purtiy", She looked at him with deep affection. "You have my permission son. May the Devi bless you with success in this noble endeavour". She closed her eyes. On her face was an expression of indescribeable peace and tranquility. Sushanta squeezed her hand gently. A few days later she passed away. With her went the last bonds that tied him to the worldly life. Before going however, she had said to him "Sanyasa, my son is not an escape from life. It is not the refuge of the weak. It is for the conqueror. It is for the hero. Before you renounce, you must prove that you have mastered this life. It is not that one has been driven by defeat and despair to flee into an escape. It is that one has achieved and having achieved, renounced it all as a token of his mastery. You must prove that to the world before you renounce this life."

He had heard her with rapt attention. Then solomenly he had nodded and touched her feet.

"It will be as you wish mother".

He completed his engineering studies in 1963 with flying colours. At the campus interviews itself he was picked up by a multinational company. Jessops and Company were good employers. They liked this sincere and diligent young man and he rapidly moved up in the hierarchy. He had a good academic career and now he had an excellent and well paying job. He travelled a lot. Once each year he would go to this favourite pilgrimage spot at Badrinath- the ancient Dham- one of the most sacred shrines of Hinduism. He kept a track of the major Hindu festivals. He visited the Aradha Kumbhas and then he was even able to attend a Purna Kumbha Mela in 1966. The Kumbha Mela is one of the unique Institutions of Hinduism. Every 12 years it seeks to bring together a mighty conclave of the pious and the faithful to the banks of the sacred rivers of India. Millions upon millions bear down to the banks of the Ganga, to renew themselves spiritually in the stream of the eternal Hindu consciousness.

Sadhus and Sanyasis of all shades and orders, congregate at these vast concourses, to preach their doctrines and share their spiritual experiences. The disciples seek out their gurus. The gurus search in turn, for worthy disciples to teach . The vast multitudes that congregate upon these bathing ghats in their millions come with pious thoughts. This civilisational outpouring constitutes another psychological Ganga of the spirit that renews our tiered consciousness and uplifts us. It is a cyclic ritual of renewal and regeneration. Sushanta participated in this ritual of renaissance. The Purna Kumbha Mela of 1966 was a land mark spiritual event in his life. He joyously immersed himself in the surging sea of pious humanity. The cries of Har ! Har ! Gange ! rent the air. He sat on the sandy embankments of this great Indian river and meditated. The Ganga represents the perenial, the eternal stream of the Hindu Consciousness. The Ganga is the soul of the Hindu civilisation and embodies in its flow its immortal spirit of enquiry and spiritual striving. He met a number of Sadhus and Sanyasis. They looked upon him and smiled – as if he was one of their own already. They encouraged him to live the eternal life, to escape from the fetters and bondage of a worldly existence and seek the liberation of a total renunciation. It would come on its own – in its own good time. This Purna Kumbha Mela of 1966 left an indelible stamp upon his consciousness. He realised the ancient method of the Indian sages who had striven to preserve our civilisational heritage and our innate sense of unity as a people through these cyclic rituals of renewal and the celebration of life per se. most of our Hindu festivals are plugged in to the rythms of the seasonal cycle. These are rooted in the relics of our past as a great agricultural civilisation. Each year, the festivals of spring mean the renewal of hope. There are festivals for sowing and harvesting. There is the festival that marks the end of the rains, and the onset of clear skies that are studded with stars.

Festivals and celebrations of life constitute the primal techniques of mass mobilisation in this ancient civilisation. The Kumbha and the Ardha Kumbha were such deliberate cultural events that had been set in motion to keep the faith alive and vibrant. These celebrations, set millions upon millions upon the move- from the North and South and the East and West of this subcontinent. These wove the fabric of our civilisational and cultural unity even in the midst of a striking and bewildering diversity. The Kumbha concourse, thus forms a seminal land mark event in his life. He had made it a point to attend all the Ardha kumbha and Purna kumbha melas that occurred in his life time. The Kumbha symbolism is deeply mystical. It signifies the pot of nectar that emerged from the churning of the ocean of Samsara by the Gods and the Titans. The nectar in the Kumbha signifies our immortality. Both the Gods and the Titans battled for it. One legend has that one of the Gods (Jayanta) assumed the form of a rook and stole it. He flew for 12 days from place to place. Drops of Nectar fell at Prayag, Hardwar, Nasik and Ujaini and sanctified these places with immortality. Millions of Hindus converge at these sites for the vast concourses of the melas of the Ardha Kumbha and the Purna Kumbha (at Prayag). In fact the movement of these pious millions is a reaffirmation of the living vibrancy of the Hindu faith and its power to move masses of men (if not mountains). It is a very ancient tradition. The Chinese traveller Hiuen Tsang, recorded his impressions of the Kumbha Mela in the time of Harshavardhan, as far back as the Seventh Century AD. He wrote of the congregation of almost half a million people on the Banks of the Prayag. It was in the Ninth Century that the Great Adi Shankracharya, gave the present form to this massive concourse of the Hindu civilisation. He had established the four well known monastries in the four cardinal directions of the Indian subcontinent (Jyotir math in the North, Sringeri math in the South, Goverdhan math in the East and Sharda math in the West.). The great Shankracharya thought in civilisational terms. Hence the establishment of these four cardinal monastries and their manning by saints from the other parts of the country. He divided the Sadhus and Sanyasis into 10 orders (Dashnamis- Saraswati, Puri, Bano, Tirtha, Giri, Parvata, Bharti, Aranya, Ashram and Sagara). These orders were exhorted to assemble regularly at the Kumbha Melas with the two fold purpose of maintaning contact with the sadhus of the other dominations, and fortifying the faith of the lay aspirants. The Kumbha is therefore, a great living tradition of the Hindu civilisation and Sushanta was greatly moved by its power and piety. The Kumbha Mela over he returned home. But the images of the pious and surging masses of humanity and the bearded faces of the Seers and Sanyasis continued to haunt his dreams for months afterwards.

And even while he lived in this world and progressed materially he was all the time deeply conscious of his resolve and firm commitment to the ideal of Sanyasa. He never, for an instant forgot his destiny. He never had any doubt - it was a calm certainty.

He had kept his intention a close secret. Only Baro Ma had known about it, and now she was gone. In his ancestral home, in his well furnished room with a huge mehagony bed and soft mattresses, he used to lock the door and then quietly sleep on the floor. He was toughening himself. Preparing himself for the austere life of renunciation. He was strengthening himself to face upto hardship. At the dinner table he would deliberately eat very little, so that he would accustom himself to the pangs of hunger. So that he would not be overcome- like his uncle Surendra had been, and return home, a picture of abject defeat and betrayal.

He clearly remembered the last words of Baro Ma "Seek perfection in all that you do; Perfection in all your actions.

Never settle for anything that is less than perfect". He had nodded silently. He was a last of the "Mohicans", the last of the Mukerjee clan. Perfection would not just be his perennial quest but his spiritual emblem in later life. His entire life and works, represented this perennial and never ending quest for excellence.

19

Dialogues with the Sea

Testing the Connectivity

The year 1966 was drawing to a close. One day, his father sent for Sushanta. He entered his study to find him bent over his table. It was covered with sheets of paper. He had been casting a horoscope. His mathematical calculations and charts were scrawled all over the pages. He was poring over the charts - his brows knit in deep thought.

"Yes, father?" Sushanta said gently to announce his presence.

The elder Brahmin whirled around "Ah there you are" he looked at his son fondly. How he had grown. How the years had passed. How much of his mother he had in his visage. His eyes misted over.

But there was work at hand. He cleared his throat and took one final look at the charts in front of him.

"Sushanta, are you dissatisfied with your job? Are you contemplating a change?"

"No Baba, but why do you ask?"

"I don't know. I have been going over your natal chart. It speaks of a change- a major change in the direction of your life. And the time is almost upon us. That is why I asked."

Sushanta was awed by the accuracy of the man's mathematical predictions. He was also afraid that his face may betray his deeply hidden intention of seeking renunciation.

"Do you want a change of job?"

"Not really - not for just now at least".

His father gazed at his face quizzicaly. "Curious that the stars should say so. "Are you happy? Are you well?"

"Yes, Baba"

"Oh", he seemed to be at a loss for words. Somehow there were deep barriers of silence between him and his son. Like his mother, he was so quiet and uncommunicative. But, his eyes said it all.

For some reason the elder Mukerjee was troubled by the way Sushanta averted his gaze, "Very well then. I thought, I must ask".

The audience was at an end.

Sushanta was sleeping regularly on the floor now. This audience with his father reminded him how close at hand was the time of ultimate reckoning. Did he really believe in his destiny? Did he really have the will, the nerve to just walk out one day and never, never give a backward glance? And what lay ahead? What was the future, to be? He thought of his youngest uncle, Surendra. "Madness? Death? "He shivered. Surendra's fault had been that he did not trust the void. Did Sushanta? He used to be deeply troubled. He would take long walks sometimes on the shores of the sea. Sometimes along the banks of the Green-brown Ganga Sometimes he would take long walks, late in the nights, when the streets were empty and bare, when the crowds had gone and the street lamps cast lonely pools of light in the sadness of the dark. He often thought of Baro Ma. He thought of the serenity on her face, and then the tears in her eyes. He looked at the decaying ancestral Mansion. Decay! That was the first thought that came to him - the first gestalt- the chief impression that he had whenever he looked at his ancestral house.

Had he died already to this life? Was he just clinging to the empty shell like a spirit - like a ghost haunting a derelict and decaying mansion? His path lay elsewhere. His destiny was different. It was beckoning now with an urgency that was intense and overwhelming. And yet when we come to the actual point of decision we are overcome with so many doubts and nagging thoughts of confusion. Are you sure that is what you want? Was that right? Was that really his destiny? Or was that just a childish impulse? That vision - was it just a figment of his imagination?

The sheer overwhelming reality of it all. It lingered with him to this day. Could it be really untrue?

"Sushanta, your food is getting cold".

At the dinner table he was remote and far, far away. That was the way he used to be those days. Pensive, indrawn, lost in deep thought. Struggling with a resolution. Wrestling with a decision. Teetering on the threshold. Peering into the brink, suddenly afraid of himself and his intention.

He remembered those dismal scenes. His youngest uncle being brought back home, a wreck, emaciated, hungry and with that desperate, hunted look in his eyes. Betrayed by the void. Led to madness by voices he chose to trust.

And yet, when he had gone to the Kumbha mela, he had met those sadhus and bearded sages. They had accosted him lovingly as one of their own. He felt happy in their company. His destiny lay there with them. He felt so sure in Haridwar, in Badrinath, in any of the confluences of the streams with such musical and feminine names - the Alaknanda, the Mandakini, the Bhagirathi. Their waters flowed with such certainity. With such focus and longing towards a predetermined goal - the Sea. Did they ever, for a moment entertain even the shadow of a doubt? The destiny of the rivers lies in the Sea. They make their own way. They cut their own gorges, they fashion their own flood plains, and in their deltas they seek their final deliverance.

One day, he went to the sea shore. It was near sunset. The vast expanse of the sea stretched away till the horizon. The waves rose and fell. He sat on the shore. The wind flew through his silken mop of hair. He looked up at the Blue void of the sky. "Are you there?" he whispered to himself. "Will you protect me?" Sometimes, he felt like a Parachutist who is framed in the doorway of an aeroplane, a few thousand feet up in the sky-waiting tensely to jump. He jumps on one simple faith - that his parachute will open. That it will blossom like a white orchid and gently sway him down with the breeze, like cotton seed. But, what if it does not open? Would he become a "Roman candle"? Would he crash to the ground like a rock, and be smashed to smithreens on the hard and unrelenting surface of reality? He got up in great agitation. "Are you there?", he looked up at the sky once again. "Will you take care of me - O Cosmic mother?" Or will you forsake me? He started walking towards the sea into the raging waters.

Suddenly, deep within him, everything felt very silent. He did not hear the tumult of the sea any more. He did not hear the breakers crashing upon the shore. He did not see the boiling, frothing foam as it swept past his feet and back, sucking away the grains of sand. He heard himself asking from a great distance. "Give me a sign. Tell me you are there". For some strange reason, he articulated silently a prayer. "Give me a sign. If you will take care of me - Give me- give me a coconut just now". He looked up at the emptiness of the blue sky. He was standing knee deep in the sea waters. He felt something coarse and wet and round. He looked down with a start. It was a coconut that had been washed ashore.

Reverently, he had picked up the coconut and brought it home. He felt a great feeling of peace and calm confidence. A quiet happiness deep within himself. He ate the milk white flesh of the fruit. It tasted like nothing he had ever eaten before. That was all he had that day. Some days passed. He was lost in the rush of work. He was working to discharge all his worldly responsibilities now. To pay off his debts. To write all the unwritten letters. To meet the people he had said he would meet, and in the process the certitude seemed to desert him once more. In the busy bustle of life in Calcutta, how remote and far away a life of renunciation seemed. How distant and unreal. Was he sure the coconut could be nothing but a mere coincidence? A pure accident. Was he reading too much meaning into unrelated cues? Was he looking for meaning where none, in fact, existed? This was too simple a test. He had to make very sure. The sheer enormity of the step itself frightened him. It often gave him cold feet. He had a comfortable home, a secure job. Renunciation in this day and age? Would they not call him a drop out? Failure? One who had fled from his responsibilities? Responsibilities!

It was the year 1967. In the Calcutta office he was now the number four in the hierarchy, just promoted from the junior-most rungs of managerial trainees. The two men above him were middle-aged and miles his senior. The boss of the office was an irascible old man, and a hard task master. One day Sushanta was sitting in the Dakshineshwar temple. The doubts had resurfaced. Was he reading too much into a simple coincidence? To make very sure, he must set the void an impossible task. One that could not be fulfilled by a mere accident or happpenstance. A test that would give him a positive and certain indication. He thought long and hard. "Before I go, I want to be the head of this office" - he said to himself. 'So make me.' This was infact impossible. No mere accident could cause it. Only a military coup. He smiled as he thought of his hard driving boss – a typical and a traditional authoritarian. The Jessops, however, were a construction company, not a military organisation. There was simply no scope for such a coup. "This was a difficult test" he smiled grimly to the diety."Give me a sign, O Cosmic mother, If that indeed is my destiny - give me a clear and unmistakable sign through this test. Make me - if you can - the head of this office before I leave".

Sushanta Mukerjee was just 26.

A few days later, a strange series of happenings took place at the Jessops firms branch office in Calcutta. Sushants irate and irascible boss, was denied his next promotion. In a fit of pique, the old man put in his resignation. Not for a day, not a single day, would he serve under his juniors. The company accepted his resignation. The decision had been anticipated. What had not been foreseen was the violent personality clash that look place between the number two and three. There was some confusion about their inter se seniority. They belonged to different branches and simply could not see eye to eye with one another. The number two was appointed the officiating boss. Promptly the number three put in his resignation. This was more than the management had bargained for. They were at their wit's end. The new boss was being posted in from another city and he could not come for a few months still. A representative of the Management came over to resolve the tussle and smoothen the ruffled feathers. He hit upon an original idea. Young Sushanta Mukerjee, the number four would officiate in a purely symbolic manner. He would sign the papers and be the nominal head till the inter se seniority between his superiors could be sorted out.

Sushanta was so junior and such an amiable person, that number two and three readily agreed to this arrangement as a temporary, face-saving formula. Sushanta was truly astonished to find himself officiating as the head of the Jessops branch office at 26 years. He shivered slightly when he got the news. With this episode, his mind was well and truly made up. He felt elated and happy. It was not a void that he had been talking to. It was a warm and comforting presence- it lived within you and it lived without. It knew your innermost thoughts and needs and wants. It was everywhere - most near and most far. It was connected at once, with all points of the Cosmos. It was a web of connectivity. It plugged in your desires to the sources of their fulfillment, but only and only if you placed implicit trust in its innate goodness. *Only if you relinquished your own obtrusive little ego- your island of separateness from the sea of infinity. The infinity of consciousness in which we all live for ever, only then did it come forth to nurture, to protect, to feed and clothe and guide, as the eternal companion* – the one, at once most near and most far.

He undertook his last pilgrimage as a lay person in Oct 1966. It was late in the season. A winter chill had set in the air. People advised him against venturing to the mountain shrine so late in the season. But he want all the same. It was a beautiful experience – so serene, sublime and divine. Blissful hymns coursed through his being. With each step that he took upon the way, he became more certain that he had taken the right decision. It had begun to snow at Joshimath. The shops were closed and shuttered. Yet, he felt no apprehension. It was as if he was part of a beautiful dream of perfection. A pious lady saw him and asked him home. The old couple covered him with blankets as he lay shivering in the night. The next day he had a beautiful darshan at the Badrinath Shrine. The tall, gaunt peaks of Nar and Narayan loomed into the glorious blue sky. The clouds had cleared up – the Sun shone through in a euphoric stream of light and bliss and benediction. He met the Sadhus. They took one look at his rapture suffused face and embraced him as one of their own. They seemed to sense intuitively what was going on within him. They did not say a word, but the happiness in their eyes, endorsed his decision.

20
Dialogues on the Ganga

A verse from the Rig Veda says "Soma flows towards all virtuous thoughts and blesses them with bliss. It becomes the soul force of all righteous thoughts and actions". (Rig Veda 9.6.8)

All righteous resolves and actions attract the flow of that Soma of bliss, along the numberless channels of cosmic connectivity; the channells that tie us to the web of cosmic life. *Every yearning finds an echo in eternity. Every anguished cry for redemption, comes back to us, charged from the sources of eternal ecstasy and happiness.*

Whenever we make a pious resolve and then act upon it with conviction, we seem to plug into those streams of cosmic consciousness that underlie, the visible universe. In this entropic, decaying universe there is a core of aliveness, order and creativity that is eternal. That for ever renews our spirits and refashions the order and harmony, we have lost in struggles for survival against the forces of entropy. These indeed are the two mega trends of the cosmos. The trend towards entropy, disorder and dissolution. And the equally evident trend towards wholeness, order and integration. This order manifests from the underlying substratum of cosmic creativity, that expresses itself as ecstasy, as opposed to the entropic forces of death and dissolution. Ecstasy celebrates the eternal life and is its chief leitmotif. The Madhu Brahman, is the expression of the underlying sweetness and ecstasy of the earth, the Sun, and the infinities of space. Vedic Metaphysics recognises only two primal forces- the forces of Soma- that attract, cohere, bring together and gravitate. They are the *Sneha tattwa* of the cosmos. And the forces of Agni. These are the forces of entropy, that burn, tear apart, rend asunder and spread out all that there is.

At long last Sushantas doubts were laid to rest. The "vikshepa" the tossing of the mind ceased to torment him. He had come to a noble and pious resolve: to live up to his destiny. He would be a Sanyasi – a recluse and a hermit. In the post-modern age, he would proclaim, by his living example, the validity of the ancient Indian tradition and the classical way of life. He would be an exemplar. He would strive for utmost perfection. He would strive to live the divine life. His actions would speak far louder than his words. He was all set now to prepare himself for the life of the recluse.

And as the Rig Veda proclaims so clearly- every pious resolve is met by an outflow of that euphoric stream of encouragement from within. It wells up in our being. It overcomes our fears and doubts. It fills our life with positivity, hope and optimism. It dispels the dark clouds of fear, foreboding and gloom. We learn to trust. We set aside our reason and open ourselves to the promptings of new, trans-human faculties that usually lie dormant in most men. Faculties that take us beyond the time warp- of the past, the present and the future. Faculties that take us beyond the eternal experience of entropy, to the underlying universal sources of creative order, organisation and bliss. We sink inwards to the levels of the implicate order, we encounter the wholeness of the cosmos-its underlying order, harmony and joy. It is not a mere conjecture. It is an experience of life itself. Beyond the realm of entropy, we encounter a higher ecology, far higher than the confines of this earth - it stretches into eternity, and ineffable ecstasy - it comes from the experience of the Madhu Brahman- the Honey of the ultimate integral experience of cosmic connectivity.

The remarkable experiences of the strange synchronity of events, come in the wake of such core experiences of inner ecstasy. These in turn stem from an enlargement and deepening of the floor levels of our consciousness. That is the secret of meditation. Sushanta felt euphoric and happy. He had now placed complete trust in the void. Meticulously, thought-fully, he now went about his life - methodically closing this chapter, recounting all left over obligations and promises; freeing himself of all lingering karmic debts; the promised visit, the promised call, the last letter, were all carefully carried out. He was leaving and like all things in his life he wanted his going to be as perfect.

19th of August 1967. He completed all his work in his office and then asked for long leave to visit his "friend". He handed over charge, took one last look around his office and then left for ever—there wasn't a single paper pending on his desk. This thoroughness and ceaseless quest for perfection was the hallmark of all that he did in life.

He came back home, carrying that atmosphere of peace and euphoria with him, like a personalised cloud of joy - an aura of bliss. He moved about as if in a dream. He walked through every room of the ancient ancestral house, with its overpowering sense of entropy and decay. In the evening he went to his room. All he took was a painting of the Mahakali, in her blue, four armed form. This had been his surrogate mother. From Baro Ma he had taken the permission. There was no need to ask anyone else. The scriptures sanctioned that path. He left behind a small note.

"I am going to meet a friend".

"I did not tell a lie", he told me. "Isn't God our greatest friend- our dearest companion? I had left home to meet - the eternal Sakha- the eternal friend, witness and companion", he said innocently.

He caught a train to Delhi. The next morning he got down at Haridwar. It was a beautiful and glorious morning. It was the Rakhi Purnima. He took a rickshaw and went to the blue green Ganga. How crystal clear and pure she is here in the upper reaches. Along the banks of the Ganga are numerous temples and Ashramas. He went past each, stopping every now and then, to go inside. Was this the place he had to go to? He went from one monastry to another-searching, anxiously looking, somewhere he felt the euphoria subside. No, no fear, no foreboding he would trust her implicitly. Silently, he prayed.

The rickshaw was going past the Bholagiri Asharma. There is a massive temple of Red sand stone - shaped like a classical chariot with four cupolas with intricate motifs and designs. Behind the temple is the monastry. Sushanta stopped the rickshaw. He did not get down. Appraisingly he looked up at the complex. There was a tall gaunt, old man in a saffron robe standing at the gate. He looked at him from behind his high powered spectacles. There was a strange and amused expression in his eyes. The two looked at one another for what seemed an eternity. This was Vrijananda, the tall Pahari Baba- the recluse from the hills. The old man had been a govt. servant for long years. After retirement he had renounced the world and stayed at the Bholagiri Ashrama- a stern old ascetic whose eyes, for some strange reason, always twinkled with an inexplicable merriment. The old man was leaning on the gate, his arms carelessly flung across its top. "You want to stay here", he asked simply. "Yes, I do", said Sushanta. It was all as simple as that. He had entered the new life.

Back in the ancestral mansion at Behala Calcutta, there was a commotion. The last of the Mukerjee clan had fled. Knowing his reclusive disposition, they all guessed instinctively at what had happened. The family had been through this before. But this time it was catastrophic.

Sushanta was the last male heir- the only one who could carry the family line and name forward. He had no right to do this. Search parties were dispatched in all directions. Some went to Joshimath and Badrinath, some to the other shrines in Bengal and his other favourite haunts. There was no sign of him. He had vanished without a trace. The search continued, however.

Some months later they traced him down. One of his Father's friend, a most learned scholar of the Vedas came to fetch him. Sushanta firmly refused to go back. His decision was final and irrevocable, he said. He had to fulfill his destiny in the world. His uncle, a silver-haired Brahmin was a great scholar and renowned mystic.

"Convince me that the path you have taken is right and I will go away without saying another word", he said. "The path to salvation can equally be taken through the way of the house holder. That, in fact, is the way of action. You can not escape from the performance of action. You must do your duty" said the old man.

They went to the banks of the Ganga. A great "shastrartha" (debate) started. The monks of the Bholagiri Ashrama gathered around to listen, with deep interest and fascination, to the elemental dialogue between two scholars par excellence. "Let the Gita be the scriptural authority for our decisions", said the old man. If you can convince me of the correctness of your stand, you can take Sanyasa. If not, I have booked two seats for Calcutta and you are going back with me. Sushanta agreed, and they started. The old man quoted shloka after shloka from the Gita to expound the correctness of his view."One does not have to flee from life to seek salvation. One can be as attached to his renunciation as the other is to his possessions. "The way to salvation, said the Lord, is through the path of action. No one can live without performing action. Why was he seeking an escape from life and its duties?" he demanded.

The verses of the Geeta are very pithy, cryptic and multidimensional. The compressed Sanskrit texts are open to several interpretations, depending upon the overall context in which they are read. Each verse therefore is open to diverse interpretations. It is, Baba had told me, like the concentric ripples that arise when a stone is thrown in a lake. Each concentric circle is like a different level of meaning. As we live and grow, the meaning of the verses changes constantly in the context of our life experiences. Each verse from the Geeta, the old man quoted, was given an alternate interpretation by Sushanta. He went ahead and quoted other verses from the Geeta which implied the validity of renunciation.

The monks of the Bholagiri Ashrama were amazed by this debate. They had not seen such a classical "shasthratha" in all their lives. What was at stake was the future path in the life for Sushanta. If he lost, he would have to return to the life he had left behind. The debate started in the morning. It stretched on, into the afternoon. Towards evening, when the shadows were lengthening, the old man got up with an intense sigh "Enough! I see the depth of your conviction Sushanta," he said quietly. "This indeed seems to be your destiny". Sushanta got up too. Suddenly he saw the sorrow in the gaunt and wrinkled face of his uncle. He fell silent and hung his head down. "By your act of renunciation", the old man said in his sing song voice "you have put an end to your family line. Go then, follow the promptings of your heart. Become a sanyasi - if that indeed is your destiny". "But remember"? he said sternly "We would want you to be a perfect sage - an exemplar."

Sushanta fell at his feet.

The old man raised him up and embraced him tightly. Sushanta felt the hot, silent tears upon his shoulder. He felt, as never before, a deep, deep wound in his breast.

Then the old man turned around and left silently. He never looked back even once. That was the last time in his life that Baba saw him, and for some reason, he stood rooted to the spot. Even as he vanished from view he continued to stare at his retreating back.

Long after the old man was gone, he stood alone on the banks of the Blue Green Ganga - staring into the vacancy of space.

A week later, he got the last letter from his father.

It said, "Sushanta, by your actions you have put an end to our family line. There is no one left to carry the torch further. So be it. Be a monk, if that indeed, is your destiny. But remember, we would not want you to be an ordinary mendicant. There are many beggers upon the streets. If you become one of them – you will get our "Abhishap" – our curse. But if you become an exemplar then indeed you shall have our blessings. Ashirwad- I bless you."

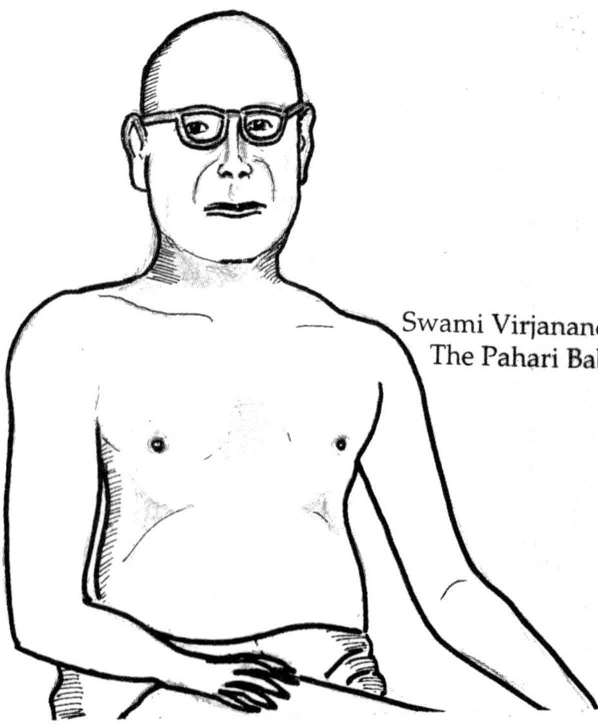

Swami Virjananda Saraswati.
The Pahari Baba

"May my motherland
grant me the lusture of Gold
May her autumnal sighs
inspire our dreams
and memories"

(Atharva Veda 12.1. 18)

BOOK FOUR
THE PEACE THAT PASSETH UNDERSTANDING

The Nearest one,
He is far, he is within
He is without all things
This multi farious universe
this creation itself
is his eternal poetry.

(Atharva Veda 10.8.32)

Patne Devi Temple – The Deepa Stambhas

21

Analysing the Supermind : Descent or Ascent

The milk-producing town of Chalisgaon was transformed by the sage into a modern "Vrindavan". Peace, positivity and sattwa spread through the region like a palpable influence. You could feel it as you stepped down onto the Railway station itself. You would feel it growing stronger as you sat in the bus and moved towards Patne. As you saw the amphitheatre of hills rising above the carpet of green forests- you felt its full surge. The deep and profound meditations of the sage had divinised the atmosphere . it had surcharged the air with the positive influence of "Sattwa"- the "Guna"(the quality) of harmony and orderliness. This influence was at its peak, in his initial years when he was in seclusion and involved in deep meditation. Sometimes, he would meditate for the whole night, night after night. He saw people only once a fortnight on the occasion of the full moon. The number of people who visited the temple were few and far in between. Slowly, however, he had transformed the place. He had wrought a miracle of sorts, by turning those desolate ruins into a thriving, bustling spot of pilgrimage.By slow degrees the crowds had started pouring in. What had started as a trickle, soon turned into a torrent and then a flood. After finishing 12 years of solitude and intense sadhana - he publically announced the on set of a new phase. The sage came out of his seclusion. The esoteric and mystic phase was over. The exoteric phase began from the decade of the 1980s onwards. He made a concerted effort to reach out to the masses, to involve them in religious activity and endeavour - in a mass, collective movement aesthetically designed to elecit maximum participation of the commonfolk. He tapped the Indian fondness for festivals and celebrations to further this purpose. The Palki festival that he started gradually acquired the proportions of a mini Kumbha Mela. His keen, diagnostic abilities had penetratingly analysed the ills of the social situation. The caste system was an anchronism, he felt. It was a divisive and corrosive influence which had outlived its utility.

He wanted Hindu society to adopt a more egalitarian outlook. He wanted it to emulate the Sikh tradition of mass worship and service at community kitchens and festivals in which the whole society took part. Subtly, he designed the framework of the Palki celebrations, in such a manner as would encourage a free mixing of the rich and poor, the high and low. In this subtle manner, he tried to erode the barriers of caste and creed and reach out not just to all the Hindus, but all human beings, regardless of religion, caste or creed.

These mass celebrations, required a major mobilisation of the population and resources of the region and the collective effort of all the people, of not just the district of Chalisgaon but also the neighbouring districts of Dhulia, Nasik and Jalgaon. It was a monumental upsurge that one witnessed. To set in motion such a mass mobilisation was a feat of social engineering and transformation. He did it so beautifully and single handedly. The whole conception of the Palki festival, was so elegant and aesthetic. It unleashed the creative energies of an entire community.

The dancers danced in gay abandon. The bards and singers sang the traditional songs and chants. The acrobats performed their stunts. Others looked after the community kitchen. Yet others rolled up their sleeves to serve the food to the multitudes, the poor, the destitutes and the tribals. Others cleaned up the place and decorated the Ashrama and temple with buntings and flowers. Others got together to perform the yajna- the classical sacrifice. The Brahmins and priests chanted the Vedic hymns. The grand finale was a night long session of bhajanas and community singing.

Most modern Ashrams in India, cater to elitist clientales. They have little to do with the local population. Guards and walls and fences usually keep out the common folk and the local people from these elitist and exclusive Ashramas. Not so at his Ashrama at Patne. He depended upon the local community and he felt deeply obliged. It was his duty to serve the community that supported him. It was a symbiotic relationship of trust and mutual dependency between the saint and society. It was the classical relationship. He was ever so perfect in his conduct and faithfully discharged his obligations towards the local society and folk. I attended only a few of these Palki festivals. I was a little non-plussed by the crush of humanity, that burst upon the place. In the beginning, I was a little horrified. At this rate, this shrine, this ancient Tapovana - the forest of meditation, would begin to look like any other crowded place of Indian pilgrimage. The crowds and throngs would invade the peace of the place and rend it to shreds. It would never be the same again. Those of us who had witnessed its utter peace and profundity, were a little distressed and disoriented by this staggering transformation.

I frankly asked him. I had expected that phase of silence, sublimity and prestine grandeur to continue unbroken. Patiently he explained his rationale. He did not want to confine spiritual striving to an elitist circle. He owed a duty to these simple peasants and tribals. He was duty bound to reach out to them and touch and transform their lives. The only way to achieve this mass participation was through such festivals. It was the traditional way. All the major Hindu festivals were celebrated with dignity and classical ceremonies at his ashrama. The Guru Purnima was a special occasion each year. The Palki festival however was the major event of the year and a big draw for the people.

I, however, had requested his permission to visit him in the quieter phases. He had agreed readily. "We all have our own path. Indian philosophy recognises the difference between men and temperaments. Some are mystically inclined. The path of Raja Yoga or Kundalini Yoga would suit them. The intellectuals would find satisfaction in Vedanta and Jnana. The emotive people would find the best expression in Bhakti and devotion- in such celebrations of religion. Those given to action, would follow the path of Karma Yoga. At your stage of spiritual development, you need a retreat - at least once or twice a year. Withdraw into the solitude and turn inwards. Explore the inner spaces within. To me, he set a specific task. Build up a bank of experiental knowledge on the aspects of meditation and the arousal of the kundallini. Try and reinterpret it, in the light of modern scientific knowledge. The Dharma is constant. It does not change. It only has to be reinterpreted in the language of the age- so that it becomes intelligble to the people; so that its relevance is re established. The language of this industrial age is science. He asked me to reinterprett religious experience in scientific terms.

I tried to meet him at least twice in a year- once with my family- so that the children would see him, spend time with him and thereby acquire the right imprinting and "sanskaras". He was remarkable with the children. Almost like the Pied piper of Hamlin. They simply adored him. The second time around, I would come alone. I used this period as a retreat. His instructions were simple. Get up well before day-break, bathe and meditate in the temple for one to two hours. Then I would retire to a quiet corner of the Ashrama and spread a mattress either in the Chandan glade (the glade of Sandalwood trees) or under a small shady tree near the rear fence of the Ashrama. I would spend the whole day alone in solitude - either reading or writing or just simply soaking in the filtered sunlight, as it streamed in through the filigeree of the leaves. Often, I would feel inspired to write poetry. I would feel the onset of those ancient upsurges of patterned speech - the Sanskritic eruptions rich in alliterations and metaphors.

The Madhu Vidya (The Wisdom of Honey)

He taught me to experience the peace of the plants. He taught me to soak in the sunshine and cholorophyll. He taught me to be peaceful and euphoric. With this simple method- he gave me a remarkable insight into the ancient Vedic concept of Madhu Vidya- the wisdom of honey. This is enshrined in the dialogue between Rishi Dhadhangya and the Ashwins (the twin gods) that is cited in the Atharva Veda. Its basic tenets are beautiful, elegant and simple. "All living things in this universe are beneficial (Madhu) to one another and to this Earth "That is the essence of the Indian outlook on ecology. Every time I went to him, I felt a unique experience of deep happiness and joy. I used to lose all count of time. My need for sleep would get reduced significantly. I felt states of grandosity and euphoria. I felt highly creative and wrote a lot. The experience would peak around ten in the mornings. Then I would leave the glade of trees and sit in his presence in the audience hut. Sometimes he would call me to his living hut for a personal audience to discuss my experiences. The more I meditated, the more convinced I was, that the classical Kundalini experience was earlier encountered in the Rig Vedic period, as the Soma experience and the descent of the Supermind. Aurobindo, in fact, identifies the Agni in the Vedic hymns as the Supermind. A verse from the Rig Veda says

"The supermind—
that light supreme
descends.
from the regions
above our beings.
It loosens the knot
in our heads.
It unloosens the knot
in our hearts.
It descends
into the knots in our navels
It transfigures our beings
in bliss and joy."
(Rig Veda 1.24.15)

Here is a very graphic description, not of an ascent of the force but of its descent. This verse describes the opening of the chakras not from below but above. The knots are the "granthis" of classical literature. Aurobindo felt that it was the self-same force. The Vedic seers described its descent from above. The later Tantric seekers described its ascent from below. Aurobindo felt that it was dangerous taking it up from the lower centres of consciousness to the higher. Yet most of the classical yogic literature described an ascent of the force-not descent.

Could it perhaps operate both ways? My teacher thought as much. One day when I was wrestling with this conundrum at his Ashrama - he sent for me.

"My own guru", he said "was Muktananda. His guru was the great Avandhuta Nityanda. And his guru in turn was a great sanyasi - the little known Swami Shivananda. He hailed from Andhra Pradesh. He spent a whole life time roaming and meditating in the dense forests along the Godawari. He was a great 'Anubhavi' - one who has experienced these things, rather than read or heard of them.

His experiences were recorded by one of his disciples in this book". He pulled out a slim volume from his collection. "Here read this. Personally I have found my own experiences to be quite similar".

I read that book in detail. Initially it made little sense. But he asked me to read it again. This time around the core of the argument crystallised. The real action of the Kundalini (or Agnim force) takes place not so much in the body but in the energy field. Physically, the real centres of all the transformations, are located in our brain. What we encounter lower down in the body are just their reflections. The lower chakras are unimportant. Their controlling centres lie in the brain - in the region of the head. Swami Shivanada gave a curious analogy. "When you wish to check the land records of a village, you can go to the village itself. However you can do even better than that. You can go directly to the district headquarters, where all the land records are available together. Thus it is with the brain. All the controlling centres are here. What happens in the lower chakras is nothing but an echo or reflection of the changes taking place here. The book went on to elaborate upon the seat of the soul. It lies not in the heart. *The real heart is here. In the core of our brains- in the cavities and ventricles of the brain is seated that cortical rider - the Purusha, the Atman, the supreme person that is shaped like the thumb.* That is the hologramic entity. The energy of consciousness is coiled about him metaphorically, even as a snake coils around the Shivalinga. That is the real self-the Purusha- the immortal Atman. The flame like person, the Vedic Agnim.

The Descent of the Ganga

The book spoke of the metaphor of the descent of the Ganga. The Bhagirathi came down to this earth from the higher regions of the mind. More than the physical stream, it is a cosmic stream- a spiritual descent of the force from the higher regions of immortality, to the lower earth planes. The myths and legends describe the force of its descent. So great was the force, that the Gods asked Shiva to bear the shock of its descent upon his head. The spiritual force of the Ganga descended upon him. It generated the enkephalins of ecstasy as also the strong poisons of entropy - The "Hala-hala visha" which Shiva drank. (Hence his blue colour) -his throat turned a deep blue and to this date he is called the Neel Kantha - the one with the blue neck. Could it possibly be, that the descent of the Ganga, was a metaphor for the descent of the force - for the descent of the Supermind? As Baba had said - Is there really an up or down in the topology of our consciousness? Which way it opens - whether from above or below depends upon the nature of the psycho-somatic organism and its innate evolutionary disposition that directs the flow and guides it unfoldment. Baba explained this to me with the help of another analogy. This one is from quantum mechanics. An electron can exist in various energy shells or orbitals that lie around the nucleus. Generally it stays in the lowest energy state. When it is excited (by an induction or photon of energy) its jumps up to the next orbital. It can not however stay in that state for long. It has to come down. As it comes down, the potential energy difference between the two levels is given off, as a quanta of energy. So it is with the consciousness. It can exist in many different states (waking, dream, deep sleep and Turyiavastha the Transcendental State).

Habitually, it rests at the lowest level. However, when we meditate, our consciousness jumps up to the higher planes. It can not stay there for long. When it comes back to the original state - the difference between the two states is experienced as a descent of the force, as a charge of energy. It happens at the energic levels. It is experienced in the brain, as an eruption of neurotransmitters and peptides, the (enkephalins and endorphins) the integral opiates of the human brain.

I met Baba again after reading the book which recorded the experiences of Swami Sivananda (the guru of Nityanda and Muktananda). "But what exactly is your personal experience in this field? I would beseech you to be more specific", I asked. He hesitated. "Some of these transcendental experiences are so difficult to verbalise or transmit. In truth they can only be experienced or induced - they can rarely be described in any satisfactory fashion. They deal with the consciousness directly - not through its mind map of symbols and words. They are reality themselves. All this is an expression of that reality". "Nevertheless", I persisted. "Please tell me of the nature of the Kundalini experience as you have felt it within your being". He paused to gather his thoughts "The dichotomy of the Vedic and Tantric approach is apparent. The Vedic approach as reinterpreted by Aurobindo - mentions the descent of the Supramental Force - a coming down of the Supermind to the earth plane of consciousness. The classical texts, the Tantras are equally emphatic about a reversal of the normal downward flow and orientation of the human energy field (possibly brought about by gravity). The field is reversed and reoriented. The Polarity is changed. Such a person in whom this transformation has occurred is called an "Urdhvaretas" - one in whom the flow is upwards -one in whom the field has been inverted. This certainly points out to an ascent or a rise phenomena "What of my own experience?" he continued "Prolonged mditation releases great tracts of bliss and happiness. This is the ecstatic Soma experience of the Vedas. You have felt surges of the same process yourself. I have not specifically experienced or felt the kundalini shakti rising up - from the Muldhara through centre after centre, climbing up the spine as it were, from the sacral or the sex centre". "But I have certainly experienced its rise from the centre between the eyes - the classical Ajna chakra - to the 'Brahma Randhara' - (the apperture of Brahma) at the summit of the brain. The crown centre - the Sahsrara or the thousand pettalled lotus lies above the head. I have felt this centre. It has a typical motion as if of an eccentric wheel". He paused to let it sink in. "So I can not say of the detailed organisation of the lower Chakras-their number of petals, their colours etc. Were these just useful images to focus our attention at particular nerve centres or plexsuses along our cerebro-spinal axis? I am not sure. The endo crine glands are co-located at these chakra sites. Focussed or directed attention upon these sites, could lead to their hyper arousal and hyper activity- leading to a massive production of their specific harmones. This could be the level of action at the purely physiological plane.

Theoretically, therefore, one could focus attention upon the site of the endocrine glands, and seek to acquire conscious control of their autonomous functioning. Imagine the result of such a process. If you wanted to increase aggression levels - you could focus on the Manipur a chakra (colocated with the Adrenal gland sites). Or for hyper pro-creative activity- attention could be foccussed on the sacral centre (or the Gonads-the classical Swadishthana chakra). This is my conjecture".

"What I have experienced is the top two chakras personally. I have also experienced the "Neela Bindu" or the Blue Pearl or the Glittering Blue dot of the colour of the sky. This is indeed a fascinating experience. Once your mind has become highly focussed and still in meditation, you suddenly encounter this beautiful experience. In the darkness within, you suddenly see a Brilliant Blue dot - a glittering Blue pearl as it were, that appears in the space between your eyes. It is fascinating and hypnotic - your entire attention gets riveted onto this "pearl". You can keep watching it in fascination for hours and hours. This comes as a great sign of fixity in yoga and meditation. This "Neela Bindu" experience is often described in the esoteric texts. I have experienced it most vividly myself and can vouch for the truth and beauty of this experience. It fills you with absorption, it focusses your entire mental, emotional and psychic energies on to a point. It gives great coherence to your thoughts.

It imparts them dynamism. You are established in the Truth. The converse also happens -what you speak becomes the truth. But as far as the 'ascent' or 'descent' question is concerned. Please go back to what Shivananda Maharaja has said so emphatically in his records. Don't waste your time or energies in the centres below the head. Nothing lies there". He has been emphatic upon that point. I want you to consider this deeply. Where is the true sexual centre? Modern physiology tells us that it is not in the Gonads. They are not the primary sexual cetnre. It is in the Pituary and Hypothalmus. The Gonadotropic hormones are secreted there. It is these which entrain the Gonads to secrete Testosterone or Ostrogen. Yes, there is a feed back loop involved - but please try and understand what I am trying to point out repeatedly. The true sexual energy centre -lies not in the sacral centre at the lower end of the spine but in the CORE of the Brain - in the Hypothalmus, Pineal, Petuitary centres. This is, or should be, the true seat of the Kundalini shakti. What you are seeing at the terminal end of the spine - is NOT the CAUSE, it is the EFFECT".

He paused. I felt electrified. This was indeed a revolutionary insight into the Kundalini process.

"Could it be possible that the ancient Tantric sages mistook the effects for the causes", I asked. The effects take place in the terminal regions of the spine. They lead to hyper arousals. But the real source, the real action of the Kundalini, as per my experience he said lies in the core of our brain". "The critical and crucial ascent", he emphasised strongly " is from this centre behind our eyebrows to the centre above our brains". "And yet we must understand the basic difficulty in all these verbal models. You are dealing with Eucledean Geometrie's three dimensional model of consciousness. You are confining yourself to the three (four) dimensional space and time. The structures of consciousness lie not in the body but in the human Energy Field or the Morphogenetic Field. That is the cause. What you see is the effect in the body. The field transcends our three dimensional reality. If we focus only on the body, we could get our directions entirely wrong. They would be true only at the level of the body. Even at this level there is scope for confusion. The Gondas are not the real centres of reproductive power or the creative psycho- sexual energies. The Gonads are activated by the Gonado-tropic hormones released by the Pituitary complex. So the classical image of the kundalini axis with its base in the psycho-sexual centre at the lower end of the spine and its summit in the brain is not the entire truth. It is only partially true. The real seat of the Kundalini seems to lie in the reptilian core of our brains - in the complex of three key psychic structures, the Pituitary, the Pineal and the Hypothalmus glands .Each of these endocrine structures is paired -(like our eyes, nostrils, ears, brain lobes etc) These are probable stereo-pair analogues, which help us to express the next higher dimension. Thus two dimensional photographs (arranged in a stereo pair with the 60 percent overlap) generate the three dimensional view when viewed through a stereoscope.

Is the real physiological kundalini axis localised in the six inches or so of space between the base or core of our brain and its summit? That indeed is my personal experience. I have felt it this way. The rest is conjecture".

"Even in these few inches of ascent our experiences can be radically different. I am convinced that it is greatly dependent upon the angle of the ascent. Each of these angular paths would traverse different regions of the brain cortex, and so generate radically different experiences. Even here, the direction of travel in the field is even more important. He paused and reflected deeply. "Could it be a concurrent ascent and descent? Aurobindo speaks of the descent of the Force and ascent of consciousness. It is best explained by his classical motif of two intersecting triangles (The basal cosmogram of the Sri Yantra) that symbolise the concurrent movements of ascent and descent. What do you wish to focus on? The ascent or the descent? Could it be, that like light, these phenomena have a dual nature. Zoom on one and the other zooms out of focus. See it as a particle and you can not see it as a wave. See it as a wave and you can not see it as a particle. Yet it is both. Reality is paradoxical. Light is a paradox. So is consciousness. The supreme energy - the real organising and synthesising force in the universe - is a far greater paradox. Do you still wish to argue about it?" He quoted a Rig Vedic verse.

"The mind soars to those summits

and dizzy heights

then it falls like a wounded bird.

What really shall I speak

and what shall I think?" He paused significantly.

"Hence my first piece of advise to you was - do not talk about reality. Experience reality. The very experience will change you for ever. It will fill you with wonder and awe. You will find it impossible to construct verbal models to describe that overwhelming experience of reality. That evolution creates a revolution in our psyches. That is the essential difference between Eastern and Western philosophy. "Wise is not learned. Learned is not wise" said Lao Tzu. "What can be spoken of is not the truth. The truth lies beyond", he continued. "I can verbalise only so much of my experience. For the rest you have to experience it yourself. You desire to reexpress the classical truths in the language of modern scientific thought. The masters of Quantum Mechanics are still struggling to express their mathematical insights. They are struggling to reinterpret these matehmatical insight in common sense verbal models. Common sense seems to be the first casualty. We must guard against over simplification". He smiled gently like the Buddha. He again emphasised the experiential aspect of their phenomena and dissuaded me from the theorising aspects. Experientially, when, we enter into forest retreats, we first encounter peace and tranquility. This leads to Bliss and Euphoria. Most creative inspirations came in the euphoric phase. This' deepens into ecstasy. Prolonged spells of ecstasy lead to an exteriorisation of the conciousness—you suddenly find yourself outside your body.

My final understanding of this theoretical conundrum came some 12 years after his passing away. Those were years of intense inner suffering and anguish. However, I was again posted in the Himalayas, this time in the Kishtwar region of J&K. The famous Marud Vridha (Maru) river of the Nadi Sukta of the Rig Veda, flows here. Tradition has it, that a large number of the verses of the Atharva Veda, were composed here. Coincidentally, one was then carrying out a deep personal study of the Atharva Veda. I prayed to my teacher's memory often to seek his inspiration. The revelations came finally from the Atharva Veda. The Vedas do not speak of the Kundalini. They speak instead of the rise of the Kala Agni- (the Fire, the energy of time). The rise of the Kala Agni leads to the descent of Soma upon our consciousness. The Agni rises and the Soma comes down. That mystifying conundrum had been resolved after decades of struggle. Our biological forms remain constant even as the matter in them changes continually. They are like whirlpools in the continual flow of Space-Time. The energy of Time binds and holds our forms into a degree of constancy. The residual energy of Time is locked up in our beings. Meditation unleashes it. This dormant "Fire of Time" is kinetized by the meditative process. The Kala Agni rises. It reverses the arrow of time. From biological life-forms that are driven by the past- (by the inherited digital knowledge of our genes), we become prophetic organisms that are pulled forward by the future evolutionary potentials inherent in our Morphogenetic fields. Normaly information from the past steps forth quantum mechanically to guide and shape the unfoldment of our biological forms in the present. When the Kala Agni rises- a revolution in our time perception occurs. The arrow of time is reversed dramatically. It normally flows from the past, to the present and into the Future. Now the Future shape steps back quantum mechanically to guide and propel the unfoldment of our biological forms in the present. We become prophetic beings or future impelled (not past driven) biological organisms. As the Kala Agni- the energy of time is kinetized (our Kundalini rises) the Soma descends from the Field- the super mind comes down with its quantas of ecstasy, super coherence and intelligence. A deluge, a super nova of Enkephalins and Endorphins erupt in our brains. We experience the ecstasies of Soma- we experience the lyrical transports of rapture and we encounter the next steps in our evolutionary Odessy.The Vedas celebrated it as the descent of the streams of joy and ecstasy, the coming down of the Ritasya Dharas and the Madhu Dharas; the descent of the sacred steams of heaven.The ancient paradox was resolved at long last: the Kala-Agni rises, the streams of Soma come down. We encounter ecstasy.

However Baba's enunciations remained the most crystal clear exposition of this phenomena because it was experiential. Briefly summarised, he said :—

Prolonged periods of seclusion, meditation and freedom

from time stress, lead to an intense internalisation of the consciousness.

Overtime, this results in :—

* Experiences of deep peace and serenity.
* These deepen into Euphoria and highly creative states.
* The Euphoria deepens into ecstasy.
* Prolonged spell of ecstasy can lead to an exteriorisation of the consciousness in the form of out of the Body Experiences.

The Kali Temple

22

In the Footsteps of the Master

In those years with Baba, I was fortunate enough to benefit from his deep insight into the nature of the Kundalini experience and the nature of consciousness itself. These philosophical insights have been compiled separately in another book to present a sequential unfoldment of his mystical thought and experience.

The years with the sage transformed my life. I requested his permission to go to the places he had been to and soak in the atmosphere. I expressed a desire to write about his life and times. He was hesitant but agreed on the condition that the book be published only after his demise. The first person I went to was Madhuakar Joshi - the Guide Archeologist of Ellora. He gave me fascinating glimpses of the history of the Patne Devi temple, the Pitangalya Vihara and the adjoining regions. This was the field of Babas meditation and Sadhana - his "Karma Bhoomi." Joshi took me around the Ellora Caves, and his deep study and learning and his marvellous narrations made those Chaitya caves and Hindu and Jain Temples come alive. I lived and breathed the historical lore of the place. There was no one more competent than him to narrate the history of the Patne Devi Temple and Bhaskara-charya, and the sage's early days at the shrine.

Next I went to Bombay to meet Koregaonkar Kaka. One of the original disciples of Nityanda, he had been an ardent follower of Swami Muktananda Paramahansa in his earlier phase, before he acquired international fame and renown in the West. Koregaonkar Kaka was a crusty old bachelor - deeply devoted to the spiritual life. He was a great admirer of Baba (Swami Pranvanadna Saraswati) and till his death he used to make it a point to be with him, for a week or two each year. He knew all the details of his stay at Ganeshpuri.

Next, I took the train to Ganeshpuri. Swami Muktanandas Ashram was a palatial complex. It had gold plated roofs on which the sun glinted the whole daylong. It was a mammoth spiritual organisation run with ruthless efficiency and military discipline. A signpost at the Gate advised you to leave your shoes and your ego, outside the Ashrama gate. Guards stopped me at the gate and took my message to Ma Dayananda Saraswati (Rahoul's mother). She was one of the most ardent admirers of the sage of Patne and one of the senior, original disciples of Baba Muktananda. I was accomodated for two days at the Ashrama. It had a strictly enforced routine. Almost 90 percent of its inmates were foreigners. Indians were few and far in between - a marked contrast from my guru's simple but classical Ashrama and his emphasis on the need for close symbiotic bonds between the sage and the local society. The guards here kept the locals, the peasants, the tribals and the poor out. To that extent I quietly preferred my own guru's simpler but more classical and egalitarian Ashram which was so much more in tune with the classical Indian concepts of the traditional Rig Vedic Gurukul. It was open to all, regardless of wealth and material well-being. Ganeshpuri, in contrast, was magnificient and opulent and very elect. It had close circuit televisions, workshops, seminars and spiritual siddhi courses-(for a steep price in dollars of course). Yet the atmosphere was positive and uplifting. It was grand and sublime-a Westernised transcreation of the Indian concept of "Swarga" (Heaven). The western ladies tied their hair in top knots like Rishi Kanyas and all wore saris. The best feature was the Arti-the collective singing of devotional songs in the evening. On the stage, talented ladies played the sitar and the Veena while the entire Ashram inmates sang from 'Roman English', renditions of Hindi Bhajans and Sanskrit chants. In the morning, people did collective meditation in the hall. The collective chanting of Shlokas was the most beautiful experience of the Ganeshpuri Ashrama. It was the best synthesis of the East and the West. It had a powerful spiritually uplifting atmosphere. renowned Master Muktananda was a great mystical adept with a powerful aura that could act as a catylist for engendering spiritual experiences. No one really returned from his presence without an experience. The ambience of his Ashram was indeed very positive, powerful and uplifting. With his dynamised power of the mind, he had concretised his dreams of vast Ashrams. One was deeply impressed by the organisation, the discipline and the grandeur of the marble floored Ashram. After 40 years of intense sadhna, Baba Muktananda had turned to "Digvijay"-the phase of prossletysation, as he travelled widely to spread the knowledge of the Kundalini to America, Australia and Europe. He set up one of the richest spiritual conglomerate empires. It was beautiful and grand. What I missed dearly however, was the personal touch. Here you felt insignificant and part of a crowd of seekers "literally goose stepping" to God. I saw what my own Guru had left behind. Had he stayed on, he would have possibly inherited the mantle of Muktananda and the marble floored and gold roofed Ashrams. When Ashrams grow so big- the normal social dynamics come into full play. Envy, jealousy and in the end palace intrigues and succession wars are some of the normal sequence of steps that do follow (unless the Guru is very strict in the criterion for selection of his closest aides and successors). The level of personal devotion and psychophancy, sometimes becomes a far greater criterion than spiritual merit or progress in sadhna. It is virtually impossible for the head of such a large chain of Ashrams to personally attend to each of his disciples. In the end, succession disputes brought a sad controversy to the Ashram affairs. Nevertheless, Muktananada must go down as a part of the Indian renaissance. His forays in the west, set in motion serious research into the Kundalini phenomena. Inspired by his persona, scientist of renown like Lee Sanella and Yitzhak Bentov applied their minds and scientific techniques to a deep study of this Kundalini phenomena. A tremendous amount of spiritual literature was generated. The social dynamics of this spiritual organisation, however went awry, possibly due to the controversial selection and perhaps the incomplete grooming of successors. This led to unseemly controversies after the passing away of the Guru, which caused great emotional hurt to a number of the followers of Muktananda Paramahansa.

Many years ago Baba, (Swami Pranvananda), had possibilly seen all this coming in the future. The sage of Patne had left well in time. The sage had made a conscious choice to leave a gold roofed and Palatial Ashram for a dense forest and a grass roofed hut. In itself it was a worthy act of renunciation-the second in his short life.

Ma Dayananda spent long hours with me. She told me about the early days of the Ganeshpuri Ashram and the early spiritual career of my guru under the stern tutelage of the sage of Ganeshpuri. She described in detail the Diksha ceremony of his Sanyasa-how the Mahamandaleshwar of Nasik, Swami Akhandananda Saraswati had ordained him as a sanyasi of the Dashnami order of monks, formed by the great Adi Shankracharya himself. She described his transformation from Sushanta to Swami Pranvananda Saraswati. She described how they had shaved his flowing, silken hair, and how he had emerged as the very picture of a

Buddhist monk, something right out of the frescoes of Ajanta. Her son Rahoul used to stay at the Ganeshpuri Ashram in those days. As it began to grow, he too found the crowds oppressive. The early days of peace and quiet and the perennial company of any master, are beyond compare. It is usually difficult for the earlier phase disciples, to forget their closeness to the master and settle for sharing and rationing their time with the thousands of people who flock to these spiritual centres later. When material wealth and worldly status begin to make a difference in the levels of proxmity to the master, then it deeply hurts the true aspirants. In this regard, the great master Nityananda, was a model. Once a very rich but worldly man came to meet him. He almost forced his way into his chambers, offering to throw his wealth at his feet. The sages response was characteristic of the "Avadhoota". He was lying on his couch. He simply rolled over and turned his back to the merchant in disgust.

Unfortunately, as the Ganeshpuri Ashram began to grow and expand, some of its inmates keenly felt that spiritual merit was taking a backseat in the selection of people who had proximity to the master. In the last phases, it came to the fore very strongly. Manipulative practises led some people to feel emotionally hurt and exploited. Others felt that it was acquiring a cult overtones.

Nityananda had seen it coming many years earlier and warned the great master to be of his coming test in his spiritual progress. Swami Pranvandanda Saraswati saw it coming next. He was the first to leave-just as the Ashram had really begun to grow and expand in an astounding fashion. His guru Muktananda Paramahansa was equally astounded by his favourite disciple's decision to leave.

What is generally not known is, how deeply attached Muktananda was to this young and idealistic Sanyasi of Patne. He really doted upon him as his own son. Ma

Dayananda said she had seen Pranvananda at one time as Muktananda's successor. He would indeed have been a worthy successor. How many paths in our lives do we break off without knowing that in the stillness of our hearts they will be continued forever. Large organisations, where the picking order is decided by the proximity and the grace of the sole spiritual master, are bound to lead to situations of emotional hurt. The social dynamics of such organisations, have a familiar pattern and rhythm. Too strongly dependent upon the charisma of a single person, the cult organisations generally tend to break up in the absence of the original master. The cohering focus is the personality of the master, and after his passing, this focus is entirely lost, and the organisation tends to unravel. A lot depends on the master's judicious selection of his disciples and successors and the transitional/succession mechanisms that he creates. This was sadly lacking at the Ganeshpuri Ashram. In that authoritarian spiritual set up, there was no one qualified or really groomed to entirely take the place of the original master. Unfortunately, after his passing(for a period) the Ashram politics became quite ugly and distressing. The power play was spiritually most unedifying and deeply hurtful to the thousands of devotees of the Ashram. The end had become apparent even in Muktananda's life-time itself. Ma Dayananda, was like wise forced to leave the Ashrama in the early eighties, confused, bewildered and hurt.

She was a lady of remarkable intelligence and learning. India had been her home for over five decades. Her knowledge and mastery of the classical scriptures was as great as her knowledge of science, arts and psychology. A lady of exceptional brilliance and intelligence, it was education to sit with her. From her own extensive experience in spiritual practices, she was able to offer me many useful insights, to reinterpret the psychological experiences of the meditational practices in the light of modern scientific thought. A tremendous amount of work was being done on these lines at the Ganeshpuri Ashram. With her help, I was able to go through the works of Dr Lee Sanella, Itzhak Bentov and some Japanese scientists on the aspect of the reinterpretation of the kundalini in modern scientific terms. This was perhaps the most useful and lasting contribution of the Ganeshpuri Ashram.

I came back to Patne from Ganeshpuri. Two days later, I climbed up to Saptashringad Devi shrine. It is a gruelling climb of some four to five hours. It is a dominating conical peak. It is said that Markanday Rishi, wrote the Markandya Puran here. The temple itself is situated on the peak of the lofty Deccan Plateau which soars up above the flat Maharashtrian plains like the sheer rockface of the Grand Canyon. The sheer heights and space are breath-taking in their stark splendour. The wind and rain have carved these plateaus into fairy land scapes. A little crowded street-an alley and then the second Ashram. Koregaonkar Kaka had told me of the events at this second halting place after Baba's flight from the Bholagiri Ashram and Ganeshpuri. It was a deeply spiritual journey for me-tracing the foot steps of my master in his wanderings after he took sanyasa.

In those days I was still posted at the Indian Military Academy in Dehradoon. In Dec 1980 I had received my posting order back to my unit. The last journey that my wife and my little son Aditya undertook from Dehradun, was to the Bholagiri Ashram in Haridwar, the Bluegreen Ganga; the brick red structures of the Bholagiri temple and the Ashram—I stood staring at the temple cupolas for a long time. I gazed at the banks of the sacred Ganga, where the long debate had taken place between Sushanta and his learned uncle on the relevance of renunciation in this day and age. I could see it all happening in front of my eyes, as elemental a dialogue as any that one could encounter in an epic or myth. What is duty? What is action? And what then is renunciation? What indeed is the purpose of renunciation? What is the relevance of renunciation in this day and age? In all his life, the person Baba Pranvananda revered most deeply, was the tall, old Pahari Baba-Swami Virjananda Saraswati. I was most keen to meet this saintly personage. I walked up to the Ashrama. I met the inmates. An old Bengali Swami with white hair and flowing white beard met me. His Hindi was halting and broken. "Where is Swami Virjanand?" I enquired. "The Pahari Baba? The Hill man?" "Yes", I nodded excitedly. "Ah" He said sadly "The body is gone (Deha Gayee). The Atman has shed its vesture and taken to wing".

"When?" I was deeply shocked.

"Just two days ago", he said. When he saw the look of shock on my face he was concerned.

"You must be from his family", he said.

My eyes misted over. Beyond physical relationships, there is a deeper spiritual kinship and a larger spiritual family that we belong to. "Yes, I am", I said with down-cast eyes. Silently he led me to his room. "Here", he said. "This is the only worldly possession that he had. This is a photograph of the Pahari Baba". I took it and touched it to my forehead. Reverentially, I brought it back and gave it to my guru in Patne, a few months later. He was deeply pained to hear of the passing of the Pahari Baba. After Baro Ma, it was this saintly old man that he remembered with the deepest affection. A great sadness came over him as he heard of the passing of his teachers and loved ones. Somehow, he was never quite the same after that.

23

The Social Dynamics and Economics of Ashram Life

My teacher was deeply saddened to hear of the succession struggles at the Muktananda Ashram at Ganeshpuri. The social dynamics of such Ashram societies have to be carefully managed. In those days somehow, he was very averse to the idea of creating organisations and structures which could decay and deteriorate after the passing away of the founder, and thereby bring disrepute upon his name. A number of the followers of Swami Muktananda were deeply bereaved and bewildered at his passing. Many of them came to attend the Palki celebrations at Patne. Many of them wanted to stay at his Ashram, but he was most unwilling to create a mini Ganeshpuri at Patne. There was too much of the "group mind" at work in Ganeshprui. There was too concerted an effort to efface the individual ego, in the quest for belonging to a group centered upon a highly charismatic master. Such cult dynamics tend to get a little negative, unless spiritual standards and yard sticks are strictly enforced. It would also be essential for the founding guru to exercise discrimination in selecting and grooming his followers with great care. Many advanced masters eschew mass action, and prefer to groom a very small circle of carefully selected acolytes. That was the strict practice in the Rig Vedic and Upanishadic period. With the Buddha, the trend towards mass organisations and large monasteries had first started in India. But that was indeed a different age of peace, plenty and prosperity. The Indian civilisation was vibrant and at a pinnacle of sophistication in culture, art and philosophical thought. The synthesis of the spiritual and material aspects of life was so deep rooted that it was difficult to separate the two into the material and ecclesiastical divisions of western society. Between the Sangha, the order of monks in their Viharas and Chaityas, (those flourishing monasteries and centres of learning) and the society at large, there were strong symbiotic linkages. The Indian society of the Buddha's period was deeply mystical. It willingly supported a creative minority of monks in leisure, so that they could devote themselves whole heartedly to their spiritual pursuits. It was the trading community that was the bedrock of support to Buddhism in India. Later, the Great Adi Shankracharya, realised the spiritual hunger of the Indian people. He uprooted Buddhism but in the process made Hinduism so much closer to Buddhism. He established the order of Hindu Monks. He established Ashrams in the four corners of India, in diverse regions to promote the cultural unity of India. Baba came from the same Dashnami order founded by the great Adi Shankrachary himself. Was it not his duty to leave behind a viable order and an Ashram? We asked him. He would listen attentively. Then he would shrug. It was all the Devi's wish. Things would happen when She willed. He did not wish to burden himself by exercising his intentionality and therefore his separateness from the cosmos. He felt, it was the duty of the disciples to consecrate the memory of their guru and spread his teachings. We felt depressed at times. Only he could mobilise the resources and energies of the people for a mammoth undertaking like this. Not one of us felt equal to the task. He was supremely unconcerned. He felt his prime task was to involve the masses at large, and uplift their consciousness. His field of action, he felt, lay amongst these poor peasants and tribals who had given him shelter and supported his mystical endeavours in every way possible. How could an Ashram ever close its doors to the poor and the destitutes? How could it leave out the impoverished tribals and cater only to the rich and affluent or focus only upon the foreigners?

As the Patne Forest Ashram increased its scale of activities, there was a need for a number of permanent working hands for its maintenance and up keep. Baba was a stern disciplinarian. He wanted everything to be neat and clean, and kept in perfect order. Some families of the local villages and town had accordingly sent their children to stay at his Ashram and serve the sage. It was in the Gurukul tradition. He was deeply attached to these children. He took great care to see that they upheld their moral purity. These boys in turn, served the Ashram with great zeal and devotion. They worshipped the sage like a living god. They swept the place clean of dead leaves, at least four times a day: they watered the plants and cooked the food. They looked after the visitors and pilgrims, and they took part in the celebrations with great zeal and enthusiasm. Some of them were orphans, some had no homes. Their sole focus of emotional attachment was Baba. He was the centre of their universe. Shivaji was the earliest of these boys. Sudam was another. However, he was of a more fiery and tempestuous temperament. Baba therefore asked me to enroll him in the Army. Shivaji stayed on and became his most devoted attendant. His parents had given him to the sage. So had the other parents given their children. Baba hoped that in time they would grow up to be the neucleus of the Ashram and continue his work.

He was deeply attached to these village boys. Over time, they became his blind spot. They could do no wrong. The boys were simple. Some local merchants began to spoil these innocent children. They started showering gifts upon them, in the hope that the sage would be pleased and give them his blessings which would transform their lives and business. As the fame of the sage spread, the type of people who thronged to his Ashram naturally included a lot of these miracle seekers and those who sought his blessings for purely material gain and advancement. The harassed sage told them plainly that he performed no miracles. The greatest miracle that he knew was the rising of the Sun each day. Was that glorious sight not a miracle enough for all mankind? He was exasperated by these quests for miracles, and quite blunt in his refusal. Yet in his quest for mass mobilisation and reaching out for the common masses, he needed the practical support of the local traders, artisans, workers and influential men to help him organise these massive celebrations that were acquiring the proportions of a mini Kumbha mela with each passing year. He came to rely upon some of them more and more.

One of his greatest pillars of strength was the legendary Anil Dada Deshmukh, the scion of one of the landlord families of Chalisgaon. He owned a number of sugar factories, and vast farms and agricultural lands. A spiritually inclined man of deeply practical mein, he and his family were an excellent blend of modernity and traditions. Till the very end, he was one of the main pillars of support to Swamiji. The other was the Jain merchant Shard Shah. Right from Baba's earliest days at Patne, he and his wife had religiously come almost every other day to the sage. They had contributed greatly to the construction and expansion of his modest Ashram and the construction of Guest rooms for visitors and pilgrims who had begun to flock to Patne Devi in thousands. The sage was deeply impressed by their devotion. His blessings caused Sharad Shah's modest business to flourish in an amazing fashion. Shah himself was astonished. He was a Jain by faith but his knowledge of the Hindu and Buddhist lore was deep. He deemed himself a mere channel for the realisation of Baba's projects. The wealth, he felt had come by his grace and for his purpose. He spared no expenses to support the Ashrama activities.

The number of local worker and devotees was enormous. There was Shebu Choudhary, the old wrestler turned union leader of the Auto-Taxi drivers. He and his family, worshipped the sage and participated most actively in organising the Ashram celebrations. There was Mohan Seth the ardent Sindhi merchant and devotee whose simplicity and deep sincerity had made him so close to the sage. These celebrations were the means Baba had devised to elecit mass participation and mobilisation in the classical Hindu way. One of the most enthusiastic workers proved to be Colonel (later Major General) Hardev Lidder. A Sikh by faith, he was deeply steeped in the Sikh, ethos of service to the Guru and to the community. In the years that followed he participated very actively in the Palki celebrations and grew very close to Swamiji. He loved the Guru's concept of Sewa to the community and the Langar or Community kitchen. As a Sikh, he participated enthusiasticaly. He endorsed the sage's attempts to strike at the barriers and divisions of caste and creed and even religion and give rise to a more egalitarian society. Spiritual striving can not become a monopoly of the privileged few. In this respect Swamiji took Hinduism even closer to Buddhism. In fact he was quite clear that the Buddha, indeed was the Ninth incarnation of Vishnu. His own deep meditational experiences had given him the glimpses of the Great Shunyata, the utter Voidness of Buddhist philosophical thought. Baba's diagnosis of the spiritual malaise in India, was penetrating and deep. His solution was elegant and simple, indeed so simple that at first sight, it hardly seemed a solution at all. It was simply a collective celebration of life that elicited the mass participation of the entire community. This was the traditional Hindu way of energising masses of men. The seasonal festivals in India are celebrated in tune with the changing moods of nature as expressed through the seasonal cycles of the year. Life has its innate circadian rhythms. These rhythms are diurnal, monthly and even annual. In Astrological terms, sometimes they pass through seven year cycles of experience. The Indian tradition has identified these phase transitions in the circadian rhythms of nature. Most Indian festivals coincide with the Agricultural process cycle. Spring and harvesting are traditional occasions of celebrations in pastoral societies the world over. Spring, Rain, Autumn and the calmness of winter all get fixed in the minds of men through these seasonal celebrations.

Personally, I must confess, I was initially put off by the massive onrush, the stampede of crowds that milled on to Patne. They rudely disturbed the tenor of my annual retreats and it was impossible to meditate in such crowds and festivals. Yet the congregation of almost a million people for a common spiritual purpose has its own effect of spiritual synergy that uplifts the mass consciousness. Individual acts of liberation were now beyond his pale. His aim was the regeneration and uplift of the consciousness of the regional society at large. He was aiming at mass mobilisation. The mass upsurge has little place for the individual. I had therefore opted out of these celebrations regretfully. It is only in hindsight, that I was able to see the extraordinary design and purpose in his remarkably simple solution. He had started an Indian cultural renaissance in the Hindu heartland of Maharashtra. It has a message and relevance for the whole of India-a relevance that we understood only when we saw the later intensification of the caste conflict in the years that followed. In the early 1980's however, Mandal had not as yet burst upon the Indian civilisational landscape. The sharp polarisation of castes and caste conflict had not reared their ugly head. Indian society was still relatively stable. With modernity, people were beginning to forget and outgrow their birth ordained divisions of caste and creed. Pranvananda's vision of a casteless and egalitarian Indian society then, was prophetic. Incidentally, so was the choice of his Karmabhoomi. The district of Chalisgaon has a very large percentage of scheduled tribes and scheduled castes in its population mix. The sage of Patne had chosen to make this his home and centre of spiritual action. No top down reformation for him, he wanted to proceed upwards, right from the very grass roots of Indian society, in the remote villages and forests.

He was nevertheless gracious enough to accept my non-participation in the social regeneration efforts. He let me continue undisturbed in the mystical pursuits of his earlier years.

He busied himself in now spreading and radiating the satwa, the positivity and peace he had accumulated in the twelve long years of his Sadhna. He mobilised the masses to irrigate that human flood with the peace and positivity of his meditations. With peace and positivity came prosperity. The milk cooperative and sugarcane factories brought a minor economic miracle of sorts and transformed life in the region of Chalisgaon. From a small mofussil town, it became a fairly prosperous and bustling city. It was now a major milk-producing centre that met the milk needs of the metropolis of Mumbai.

24

Entropy : The Shadow of the Magus

And so, the Palki festivals continued. They grew bigger every year. The crowds increased by leaps and bounds. Patne became the vortex of a whirlpool of humanity as it were. They all thronged to the shrine, to the forest retreat of the sage. They all carried away with them, a part of its peace, positivity and harmony. The sage had rescued the shrine. He had saved it from destruction and obliteration in the floods. He had ensoulded it and resurrected it to its ancient glory.

The massive outpouring of spiritual energy however had begun to take a surreptitious toll of his health. He poured so much energy into these festivals, celebrations and mass mobilisation. Very intense and concentrated meditation inverts the Human Energy Field. This seems to throw out of gear, the normal biological process. That is why, the ancient yogis sometimes insisted on developing a perfect physical instrument first, before they undertook deep meditation. Hatha yoga was used to develop such perfect physical instrument, that could withstand the eruption of psychic energies and the turbulence generated in the Energy Fields and in the human physiological organisms. But in those days, the life spans were long and the relationship with the ecosphere was friendly and symbiotic. Man did not live in opposition and disharmony with nature. He was in synchronity with its rhythms and ecocycles. Today the human life spans are short and one can hardly afford to wait till one has perfected a suitable physical instrument and also inculcated the rigorous self-discipline and inner control that will regulate the outflow of the hormonal output and the inner energies aroused by the paradoxical process of deep meditation and inner quietude. Such deeply meditative experiences of tranquility cause the experience of the "Biological rebound", that unleashes a veritable revolution in the psyche. An organism pushed to one extreme of ergotropic arousal will swing to the very opposite. From extreme inactivity, from hypo-arousal it rebounds to hyper-activity and extreme arousal.

Swami Pranvananda Saraswati had a magnificent physique and a leonine mein. Despite this asset, prolonged years of intense meditation, followed by tremendous expenditure of spiritual energy in these festival, took a severe toll of his health.

In 1985, there was a strange incident. Crowds had started converging on Patne. It was like the mouth of a spiritual volcano from which streams of psychic energy were pouring out into the firmament-in an eruption of "Satwa". Streams of people converged onto the shrine, ostensibly to pray to the diety, but even more, to see the great sage who lived in its shadow. It was like a spiritual sunrise-a new, effulgent dawn and people came to witness the arrival of a new born consciousness of revival and renaissance . All sorts of people converged onto the shrine, the good, the pious, the seekers, the bereaved and sometimes, even evil denizens from the ancient parts of this mysterious land.

Four dark-coloured sadhus had came to the Devi Shrine. They were tall, thin and emaciated looking men with broad foreheads, deep sunken eyes and jet black hair swept backwards. Their straggling, black beards streamed over their dark chests. They spoke a strange dialect. Possibly they were from the deep forest tracts of the Godawari river in the state of Andhra Pradesh. They did not speak to anyone. They camped in the forest, apparently aimlessly sauntering in the woodlands. In reality, they were carefully surveying the Ashram and its environs. They walked around its perimeter, surveying the fence, looking for gaps.

It was a dark moonless night. Well after the evening meal time, these four sadhus slinked out of their camp like shadows. Silently, they came to the Ashram fence. They waited for the inmates to finish their last chores and go to sleep. At long last Shivaji took leave of the master and went to the main hut where the boys stayed. Baba was sleeping alone in his hut now. Quietly, these shadowy figures entered from a gap in the fence. They had removed their shoes and tied them behind their backs with cloth belts, so that they would make no noise. Slowly these sinister figures crawled inside and waited. When they were sure that everyone was sound asleep, they quietly crawled upto Baba's hut. They had some wires and tools with the help of which they opened the latch of the door. With beating hearts, they entered the sage's hut. He was sleeping. Once in his room, they were suddenly immobilised. Later, they told the police "Our wits deserted us". Swamiji woke up suddenly. He felt a sinister presence. "Kaun?" Who is it? He called out loudly. "Shivaji?"

Shivaji was a devoted disciple. The moment he heard his name called out, he sprang up from his sleep. Yes, that was Baba's voice. It wasn't a dream. He rushed out to Babas hut. He was surprised to find the door open. He ran inside and flashed on the light. For a moment he froze. He saw the four dark sanyasis standing there. Suddenly, one of them whipped out a knife. The rest of them ran. Shivaji thought only of his master's safety. He yelled and grapelled with the dark sadhu with the knife. The knife slashed across his arm drawing red blood, but Shivaji wouldn't let go. The two men rolled on the floor. The other three sanyasis ran out and vaulted over the fence, and were gone in a flash. A great commotion arose. The other boys got up and ran to Baba's hut. The assailant was quickly overpowered. The villagers were aroused. Someone had tried to attack their beloved Baba? Was he insane? They were livid with rage. That sanyasi was bound, hand and foot, and thrashed soundly. Baba had to intervene to save his life. The people however were thoroughly enraged at this dastardly attack at a being who was himself the embodiment of Ahimsa and had a Christ-like love and compassion for all beings. A search started for the other three assailants but they were no where to be seen. The police was called. By morning, the whole district of Chalisgaon had descended on the Ashram.

Everyone, who heard of the dastardly deed, was shocked. How could some one dare to commit such a sacrilege? How could someone attack their beloved Baba right in their midst, in the safe keeping of his own people? The police had a hard time saving that battered sanyasi from the near hysterical mobs. Their fury had to be see to be believed. The policemen themselves were furious. Who were these assailants? What were they after? In their rage, the policemen tortured the sanyasi remorselessly to find out. He was hung upside down by his feet and beaten black and blue. The man however was stoic. He would scream in pain, but no words would escape his lips. He would say nothing about himself or his friends. Everytime he was beaten, he would only cry out, "My Guru Save me". (He Guru, Bachao) Baba was told of these developments. The gentle being that he was, he was deeply pained and distressed. "I dont care if he was coming to murder me. That man is wearing a saffron robe. That robe must be respected. Please have all this stopped. I don't want him to be harmed". The police and the people however would not stop. They were baying for the assailants blood. Finally, Swamiji himself went to the Police Station.

Swamiji was adamant and the man was taken in a vehicle and left well outside the town. No one saw him or his companion again but people were greatly intrigued. Who were these people? What had they come for? Many theories did the rounds. On the occasion of Palki, Baba used to distribute saffron shawls to the wandering mendicants and Sadhus, to ease the hardship of their path. Possibly these sanyasis were plain thieves and robbers after the wealth that they thought was available in the Ashram.

Brigadier Lidder who had personally seen the assailant and the policeman who had dealt with him, did not think so. This was no ordinary theif. The man had stoically withstood hours of third degree police torture. They had not been able to prise a word from his lips. His faith in his Guru was a little unnerving. Who was the man who inspired such faith, as would enable a man to withstand physical torture? The man was a hardened fanatic who showed no remorse and guilt. He was there on a mission. What was it? When I heard the news, I was deeply alarmed. I rushed at the earliest to Baba's Ashram. "What do you think was the motive of the attack. Was he after money? Or was it something more?"

"I do not think they were after money?, Baba said.

"Then what was it?"

"The Vishnu Shaligram", Baba sighed. "They were standing in front of it, when Shivaji stopped them". "Quite obviously someone had sent them to get the Vishnu Shaligram. It is a stone of great power and is used in Tantric rituals. You remember, the old couple who had given it to me shortly before their death, for safe keeping?"

"Yes". I recalled that episode with alarm. This Vishnu Shaligram had been in the possession of a family of pious Brahmins for generations. They were worried that it might be misused and hence they had handed it over to Baba for safe keeping. That was just a month before their demise.

Someone, quite obviously, knew of this Vishnu Shlaligram. What was worse was, that he knew about its power and its use. The Guru who had sent these sanyasis to get the Shaligram, was no ordinary person. He was a powerful Magus who could inspire deep devotion amongst his disciples. In the years that followed we learnt that he could do more. A series of bizzare occurences followed. These could have been mere coincidences at first glance but in hindsight one could not help discerning a pattern, a distinct linkage. Baba's health deteriorated suddenly. All of his closest disciples (including me) went through harrowing times. Shivaji was involved in a car accident. Myself and Lidder encountered very negative phases and discord in our careers. Strange and unpleasant events occurred.

After this attack, the concern for Baba's security became obsessive. The boys of the Ashram felt very offended that their master had been targeted despite their presence. Opinion in Chalisgaon itself was divided. Many people felt that these sanyasis were just ordinary thieves who had been attracted by the prospect of material gain. The boys obsessive concern for Baba's physical security therefore was misplaced. The attack however, was a fact of life and the boys were indignant. This led to deep misunderstandings between them and Sharad Bhai who felt that the security aspect was being carried too far. Baba himself was hugely amused by all these obsessive concerns. Yet, something had disturbed him about the manner of this attack. He did not say anything, but he seemed to be engaged thereafter in a struggle with a nameless and faceless adversary. Sharad Bhai had been a pillar of support for Baba's Ashram activities in general and the Palki festival in particular. An unfortunate rift now developed between him and the boys. Many of them found the security aspects far more interesting than routine Ashram chores like cleaning the utensils or sweeping away the dead leaves.

Personally, I was much disturbed. Our external

circumstances are a mirror to our deeper selves. I had encountered the highest of harmony and perfection in this Ashram. Why had things changed so suddenly? What was wrong? Where was the chink in our spiritual armour, that had led us to this impasse. Baba laughed it off.

"Well, even the Avataras, Rama and Krishna were attacked in their own times. Who am I then, to complain? Ramana Maharishi's Ashram at Arunachal was similarly attacked by bandits. It is the fault of the times that we are living through".

I was deeply distressed. May be, we should eschew this second phase of the exoteric, mass action. Life was so much simpler in the earlier mystic phase. Could we not return to that simpler phase and leave out the mass contact and mass mobilisation of the local people? There was a great sadness in the passing away of a phase of peace and tranquility. True, he had reached out to millions of ordinary Indians, but in the process we had lost a lot of that original happiness.

It was something that could not be helped, really.

25

Empowerment : The Establishment of Kalimath

The Palki festivals continued to grow and enlarge in scope. The people of a number of districts were now deeply involved in these lyrical celebrations. Baba's health increasingly became a cause for concern. The larger an organisation becomes, the more entropy it encounters. Despite his best efforts, differences did arise amongst his closest disciples. He sighed once. I used to show him my poems. On one occasion, on an impulse, he wrote off a series of Japanese. Haiku type couplets. One of them read :—

"Thermos

I envy you

You keep things

Warm".

In a simple, lyrical way, it expressed his yearnings for the original love and harmony. He radiated love and "maitriya" (The Buddhist term for compassion). It flowed from his being. He had become a living God to the people. Thousands of them patiently lined up in queues each day to touch his feet and feel that deep peace that emanated from him. He was a being of solitude. He had deliberately emerged from the isolation of his Sadhna to spread Sattwa among the common people. But he yearned for the old peace and quiet.

Kali Temple-Entrance

In the hot summer months, the Sun used to shimmer off the cliff faces and Patne would become unbearably hot. He would then go off to some hill station - either to Toranmal in Maharashtra, or Dehradun or to Andretta in Himachal Pradesh for a month or two of peace, quiet and solitude. He would recover from the oppressive crush of the crowds who now swarmed to Patne in their thousands.

Sometimes, I met him in these summer retreats. It was a blissful throwback to those early days of his mystic phase. One yearned for those peaceful and tranquil times of deep meditation and the deepening experience of the peace that oozed from the vegetation. He was deeply averse to the cutting of any trees or plants. He let them grow in a luxurious profusion in his Ashram. Everywehere he went, he created a luxuriant and rich ecospace teeming with trees, plants, bushes and creepers. He was truly a sage of the forest- ill at ease in the crowds. Yet he soldiered on, despite the strain it put on his health. That mass-mobilisation he felt, was his duty to the peasants and the society that had nurtured him for all these years.

His health waned. He was advised rest by the Doctors. Somehow, he had a permonition about the shortness of his stay on this earth. Once, he fell very ill indeed. We were all greatly worried. His blood pressure used to fall inexplicably to very low levels. His health deteriorated so badly that he felt he was going to die. The worry about what would happen to the Ashram children after his passing, now consumed him. At one stage he was so upset, that he sent for Anil Dada Deshmuk and Tekwaniji of Jalgaon "Give me a promise", he beseeched them, that you will look after the children after I am gone. You must promise". When he recovered he grew deeply thoughtful and pensive. He retired for a long retreat to Toranmal. This rest was deeply needed and did him good. It was during this convalescence that he thought long and deeply about the future. In the immediate circle of disciples he did not see a worthy successor who could continue the work after his passing. Would his disciples be able to organise themselves to carry forth the mission? Frankly, we ourselves were quite doubtful on this score.

It was during his phase of convalsence, that he realised that his span on this earth, was coming to an end. The illness and the close encounter with death confronted him with his unfinished task. It brought to the surface- a deeply held desire that had lain buried within him for decades. A man of few words, he could keep secrets. He had never articulated this desire to anyone- yet, it was there in the course of his illness- when he came face to face with his Hara- he realised the unfulfilled nature of his last desire. He was in truth a great devotee of the Mahakali. His upbringing in Bengal had imprinted in him this deep rooted faith in the Goddess who embodies Entropy in her Dark Form. The Mahakali is the Mistress of the destructive and entropic power of Time- the greatest destroyer, that unravels all empires and civilisations, all that we build and create. Time destroys it all- not for the sake of destruction per se- but to facilitate the process of new and continual creation. Creation and destruction, are two facets of the self-same power – Mahakali. As the eternal feminine, she is the greatest creator- she is also the greatest destroyer. She is the Ultimate Paradox of the power of Time.

He wanted to build a temple to her. As a devotee he wanted to create a befitting temple tc his *Ishta*, his *Aradhya Devi* in Maharashtra- his Action field and his Karma Bhoomi, which had been the seat of his deep meditations and spiritual endeavours. As the excellent exemplar that he was, he had initially wanted that his disciples do all this after he was gone. That would be in the true tradition of Rama Krishna Parmahansa. However, his sudden encounter with death had brought home to him, the impracticability of this desire. None of his disciples individually (or collectively) felt equal to this task.

He also wanted to create an Ashram, where those children who had served him with so much devotion and love, would find a secure niche. He dreamt that they would carry forth his spiritual practices. Their minds were pure, simple and unsullied. Many of them were orphans. However, none of them had his spiritual calibre or even a remote fragment of that greatness. That is what worried some of us even in those days. Devotion coupled with spiritual merit is the true touchstone of the disciple. It was this portion of his aesthetic dream that atrophied the fastest after his going. Possibly it stemmed more from his attachment to these children. Attachment can overcome the discrimination of even a great yogi. These children were certainly his blind spot. However, even if they were, it only highlighted the loving and compassionate nature of the sage.

Having come to a decision- he unleashed his spiritual energies in one last blaze, to build the temple that he had yearned all his life to build. His dream was a temple cum Ashram complex of the most perfect sort. The exemplar that he was, his quest for perfection was perennial and unending. In 1988, the search for a suitable piece of land began. I and the older disciples wanted him to remain close to his spiritual seat near the Patne Devi temple. However his logic was clear cut and unnerring. He could not dream of building another temple near the Patne Devi's as it would detract from the glory of the existing shrine. If it was more grand, it would tend to overshadow the ancient shrine, and that was unthinkable. There were also more practical reasons. The land around was forest land. It could be given on lease only for his life time. No permanent assetts could be built upon this land.

He had to migrate elsewhere then in the evening of his life. The simbiotic linkage between the sage and the ancient shrine was about to end, and that saddened me infinitely. The local people were alarmed. It generated considerable controversy. How could he think of going? He had saved the ancient shrine. He had rehabilitated it. He had, by the power of his tapas, opened this shrine to the multitudes. He had brought them here by the hundreds and thousands. He had brought prosperity to this land. Milk had actually flown. Chalisgaon was now a major milk producing town that supplied the milk needs of the metropolis of Mumbai. His decision brought dismay to the forest people of Patne. To me, it brought the sad realisation that nothing ever remains as it was. Frankly, I could not enthusiasticaly participate in his preparations for going but his logic was irrefutable and sound and one had to bow before its clarity, as always.

A huge Mango orchard was located on the outskirts of the Ellora caves- just where the road climbs up the steep Ghat section, from Chalisgaon to Aurangabad. It was in the Marthawada area. He visited the spot and liked the dense grove of trees. The go ahead was given to purchase it. Once again Baba was adamant that the local people get a fair price for it. He did not want to alienate the poor, in whose midst he wanted to settle down. His vision of a temple-cum Ashram was not an exclusivist organisation, from which the local people were driven out to make way for an exotic clientale from abroad, or from other cities in India.

The land was purchased. An extensive tree plantation drive was launched to green it further and create the ecological niche of vegetation. There was a nala upstream that had gone dry. The stream was damed and diverted to flow behind the Ashrama so that its eternal tinkling music, would form the ideal backdrop. He was creating the forest and the ideal ecological environs for a temple cum Ashram- "In a forest, in a cave, near a stream- in such a place, the monk should dwell". Such a mammoth project required huge finances. He prayed fervently to the Devi- if you want a temple built for yourself- you provide me the means. Please do not make me beg. Let the finances come in their own accord. "I do not want to print coupons" was what he told me. He did not have to.

The finances flowed in freely of their own accord. The engineers, the doctors and middle class citizens of Dhulia, Nasik, Jalgaon and Chalisgaon contributed freely. The magnitude of the project had made sharad, the traditional financier blanche in helplessness. He did not have to worry. The money flowed in from all over. Baba was in a hurry- he had little time left for his allotted mission. At this stage, there stepped in a very wealthy gentleman of humble origins but very great means. It was rumored that his wealth was ill begotten. But he had turned a new leaf as it were. Possibly overcome by remorse and guilt, he wanted to make amends. He started frequenting the Ashram of the sage on a regular basis. His devotion had to be seen to be believed. Sharad , the traditional financier had paled at the magnitude of the project. This was where this gentleman slipped in adroitly. He offered to lay his wealth at the feet of the sage for this noble project. Does a sage differentiate between a saint and a sinner? I do not know. But Sharad at that stage made a very insightful observation. My wealth may be limited but it is not from tainted sources. I can show all my income tax returns. However noble the project, should we accept wealth from tainted sources? Others countered this thesis. The offering boxes at the temples and churches do not discriminate about the source of the wealth offered – they are more concerned with the good end-use it will be put to. I was struck by this observation. In his earlier stage, Baba was very particular about from whom he accepted any offering. He had insisted upon the purity of the source, and the right of the Sanyasi to refuse any tainted offering.

In ethical terms therefore, one was surprised that this gentleman was able to thrust his wealth on the sage. His humility and charm had to be seen to be believed. Maybe he had genuine pangs of guilt and remorse and this was his penance for forgiveness from a sage he thought was a living God. Whatever it was- he, along with many other pious people contributed generously for we cause of the Temple cum Ashram- for the construction of Kalimath. Today, only the Kali temple remains, the Ashram has been converted into a school. The lessons are very clear. Only God is beyond the pair of opposites. A temple to the Lord can be the sea which absorbs all kinds of streams- clear, muddy, transparent or turgid. The offering boxes of the temple make no distinction between the riches of the pious and holy or the guilt ridden seeking the expatiation of their sins. An Ashram however, is meant for righteous endeavour. It can only be created from wealth which is pure and untainted.

The temple was a vision of perfection. Baba said he wanted it built in the Vedic tradition of the Sthapathya Veda. All calculations of its designs were in harmonics of Nine- the mystic number of completion. Baba was an engineer himself. He joined the architects in the design effort. The temple that he envisioned looked so much like a Buddhist Pagoda. It had a Pinkish Red series of cupolas that were shaped like chortens. The roof rested on huge blue pillars. The central hall was spacious. The statue of the diety was of exquisite beauty. It was sculpted by a master craftsman of Jaipur. Baba now called colonel Hardev Lidder and asked him to get the water of all the sacred rivers of India, as also the earth of all the sacred Pilgrimage spots, for the Abhishek of the Garbhagriha. This made Hardev essay forth on a unique pilgrimage to various corners of India. It was a lyrical and uplifting experience. The most ecstatic part of it was when he visited the Badrinath Shrine. He was overcome by an experience of sublime ecstasy. He saw the clouds rolling past, gilded with the gold of the setting Sun. Tears of joy welled up in his being as he heard the voice of the great Sikh Guru Nanakdev himself "Mritak hove Nanka.........." "Dead and inert is he, O Nanak, who does not have the Name of the Lord enshrined in his heart". It was a beautiful and uplifting spiritual experience and Baba's grace and benediction for a disciple who was unquestioning and firm in his faith.

Everything thereafter was speeded up. The sage went into meditation and wrought another miracle. The preliminaries over, the construction work commenced at the pace of a blitzkrieg. The work on the temple had started in Sep. 1988. By Mar.1989 it was complete. Like everything else in his life he supervised every detail himself and insisted on perfection and excellence in everything. The temple was constructed in the Maryada of kar sewa or service to the divine. Masses of people from the four neighbouring districts of Maharashtra girded up their lions and plunged into the task with a rare gusto. What came up was marvellous to behold. It was perfection concretised. The synthesis of the Temple and the Math was perfect and sublime. It was designed with the aim of keeping alive the Hindu technique of festivals and mass celebrations, to elicit the participation of the masses. There were sheds for pilgrims and yagyashalas. There were rooms where visiting Sadhus and pious guests could stay overnight. The temple was neat and clean and so exquisitely crafted. There was a place outside for the breaking of coconuts. Inside it was spotlessly clean. In the mornings and evenings traditional Arti used to be performed here with the beating of huge Drums (Nagaras) and conches. Baba would occasionally lead the chants himself. The rythmic chanting of Sanskrit Slokas and Bhajans in Marathi had a powerful effect on the consciousness. Next to the temple, was a cave-like structure where Baba sat and met the guests and visitors. It was in the traditional design, with windows at the floor level. Behind the temple was the Kalimatha, the Ashram. Baba's living quarters were ensconed in a beautiful garden lush with flowers. In its backyard were planted two Kalpa Vrikshas- the Bao bab trees. The disciples stayed in another hut nearby. They were connected by a cemented path along which grew lush green bushes. Trees and bamboo fronds lined the perimeter. Behind the Ashram was another quiet grove of Mango trees where one could sit and meditate in the profound stillness of a mini forest. Behind us flowed the stream that tinkled and sang over the stones. Perfection itself could not have been more perfect.

The most profound transformation however, was social. The boys belonged mainly to the lower castes and tribes. Baba, as a Sanyasi, was beyond the pale of caste and creed. He did something unique. He empowered these tribal boys to wear the sacred thread and officiate as the priests of the temple. This was a staggering social revolution, well ahead of its time. It left the traditional people aghast. Like the Buddha, Baba had shown his complete disdain for caste and creed divisions. He had very deliberately set out to reengineer the highly stratified Hindu society into an egalitarian and casteless mode. Some decades ago, the tribals and subaltern caste people were not even permitted to enter the temples. Gandhiji had opened the temple doors to them. Baba went a bold step furthur – he empowered them to officiate as priests. It sent reverberations and shock-waves all over. It shook the traditionalists and the orthodox to their cores. It elicited a lot of consternation and shock and murmurs of protest. But Baba did not care in the least. His lifes mission was over. He had built his dream temple and established an Ashram. He had struck a blow for transforming Hindu society into a more egalitarian and class-less loder by way of organising the traditional Yatras and organising the Langars of the Sikh tradition, where people of all castes and creeds intermingled freely. He had foreseen what we had not- the coming conflicts of caste- and the Mandalisation of the Indian landscape. These were to create yet another set of divisions, in a highly diverse and fragmented Indian polity. The need of the hour therefore was the re-establishment of cultural unity. The way to an egalitarian Indian Society had been shown by Baba. The exemplar of tradition himself- he had empowered the tribals and down-trodden. It sent shock waves all over. It was well ahead of its time and it generated more than its share of controversy and discord. But he did not care in the least. As he said, his life's work was done, and he was ready to die.

Behind the temple, in the Ashram was an oasis of peace and quiet. When I went there, for the first time I personally felt very relieved. In later years, Patne had become so crowded and so full of people. Here, at last, was an echo of that earlier peace and tranquility of the mystic phase. He encouraged me to come and meditate in the new Ashram Gardens. The trees and shrubs had grown and made the place green- a mini forest in the middle of the Aurangabad Plateau, near the famous Ellora Caves. The mornings were beautiful and divine. I would attend the Arti, then sit down for meditation on a cot under a shady tree. After one to two hours of meditation, I would recline there in solitude and write my books or poems. At around 1030 the boys would serve tea. The very cup of tea would taste like nectar. Every simple act of living was imbued with the sparkle of ecstasy. There was still a deep magic in his presence.

He had empowered the tribals and down-trodden. He had cast aside the barriers of caste and creed. The establishment of Kalimath, was his final act of grace. It had a symbolic meaning and a deeper message. The message of empowerment.

26
The Last Supper

Rama, Krishna and Gautam Buddha, the Enlightened ones, are the revivalist icons of Indian history. In the Indian cultural context, these mighty personalities have become the icons of renewal and revival. They ensouled the concept of an Indian civilisational renaissance. That is why they have been hailed as Incarnations of the Vishnu consciousness.

What is the Vishnu consciousness? It is the collective consciousness of civilisational renewal, regeneration and growth. It is the upsurge of a civilisational renaissance. In the Indian context, historical personages like Rama, Krishna and the Buddha, have served as exemplars that highlighted the validity of the Indian mode of life and the permanence of the value systems of the Indian civilisation - the ageless and eternal Dharma- the true order of things.

When we study the lives of these great beings we find three distinct phases:-

(1) The earlier phase of high mystic accomplishment achieved by long years in forest exile, and mystic endeavour. Thus Rama spent his youth in the Ashram and 14 years in exile in the forest. Krishna was a disciple of the Vedic Atharvan master Ghora Angiras. The Buddha took sanyasa and spent years in the forests.

(2) An Action Phase in which these civilisational icons came out of their forest retreats, and caught the eye of the masses in a big way.

(3) A Phase of decline near the end, when the civilisational icon had exhausted his spiritual powers and often became the centre of controversy. Rama's treatment of Sita after exile was a cause of controversy. Krishna was accused of engineering the Kurukshetra War to further the rise of his Yadava clans and so on. The Buddha in turn was accused of deliberately subverting the traditional Dharma and doctrine.

The actual legends of these great masters were really built up only after their life time. The legend soon became much greater than the historical personage himself.

One can easily discern a similar pattern in Swami Pranvananda's life. An earlier phase of deep meditation and mystic endeavour. Twelve long years in the solitude of the forest. These were really his best and most blissful years. The Action Phase that lasted for a decade (from 1980-1990) in which he brought about a surprising mass mobilisation and engendered an annual mini Kumbha mela, by organising the Palki festivals which were designed to elicit mass participation and the involvement of the multitudes in religious activities. As a sanyasi he was beyond the pale of caste and creed. He was against the caste barriers and startification of Hindu society and wanted to make it more egalitarian. He chose a region dominated by tribals and backward people, as his "Karma bhoomi". He empowered the tribals by making them the priests of the Kali Math temple. He popularised the Sikh concepts of mass langars or community kitchens that would cut across caste and creed barriers. At the same time, Pranvananda, the sage of Patne had himself done deep meditation and was a man of remarkable spiritual accomplishment and experience. He had tremendous insight. His technical education made him uniquely qualified to interpret his spiritual experiences in modern scientific terms. The prime message of his life was ecological—of the need to preserve our plants and trees and the rich biodiversity of this earth. The way he created an enchanting forest, whereever he went, was beautiful. Ecology gives us the experience of ecstasy and harmony. We have to live in deep harmony with nature. This quest for ecological harmony was the hallmark of his life. The other was his relentless personal thrust for perfection in each and everything that he did. The essence of his yoga was simple long priods of meditation lead to the onset of sukha-contentment. The Sukha deepens into 'Shanti' - great peace. The peace in turn turns to ecstasy. That ecstasy is an evolutiavary end in itself.

The last phase was one of exhaustion and controversy. He had poured out his spiritual energies unsparingly to divinise a region. He had tried to reestablish the validity of the ancient tradition of Sanyasa. Even as in Rama's or Krishna's times, his last phase was beset with controversies. His spiritual exhaustion took a severe toll of his health. The briefness of his lifes span caused him to hasten his life's work. He was worried that he had only a short time left to carry out his mission. Accordingly, he speeded up things and rushed his final projects through. A perfectionist till the very end, he wanted to oversee things for himself. In simple but significant ways, he correctly diagonsed the present, and forthcoming ills of Indian society. He foresaw the impending conflicts of caste, and strove for a casteless and egalitarian Hindu Society, well before the Mandal agitation had torn apart the society in this country. His insights were prophetic, his solutions radical. They were bound to generate controversy and they did. Vested interests started circulating baseless rumours of fabulous wealth in the Ashram. They took fullest advantage of the contributions made by that one particular gentelman, whose wealth had been accumulated from dubious sources. Many of us had warned Baba about this particular individual but he was wholly preoccupied with the construction of the Kalimath. He realised it too late.

A simple and trusting human being, he had been taken in by the apparent sincerity of the man, and his desire to serve and acquire merit. Can a saint close his doors to a sinner? He was deeply hurt by some of these inuendoes and malicious rumours. It was almost like his psychological crucification. I could sense his deep and silent pain.

In the year 1990, I had gone to attend a course at Mhow. The Mandal Agitation had broken lose and caste conflict had reared its ugly head in the streets. The schools and colleges were closed. My wife and children joined me at Mhow. Together we went to Baba's Ashram. He was leaving for some place but stopped when he saw us enroute to Kalimath. The children were delighted to see him. I met him alone for a long audience. He was unhappy about the spate of rumors circulated by the vested interests. Then, suddenly he said.

"You must come and meet me during this Diwali".

I was a little surprised. Diwali was a month away and I was heading for a field assignment in a place of active hostilities in J&K. I was keen to spend some time with my family, before I left.

Yet I knew that he never did anything without a deeper purpose. I opened my mouth to speak, but the look on his face caused me to keep silent.

"As you wish, Baba"

Diwali- the festival of lights. The monsoon clouds cover the Sun for two months. The clouds rumble and lightning flashes in the sky. The rains pour incessantly. Then in October the skies clear up. The sun wins the war against the dark clouds of depression. The night skies shine with a cluster of stars-the Divi-Ali- the "divine cluster of lights" celebrates the victory of the forces of light over the forces of darkness and evil. Lidder and I undertook this pilgrimage together. We reached the Ashram on the morning of 'Diwali' - the traditional festival of lights.

In the evening he called us all to his quarters. In the lawn, a cot was spread. Sweetmeats were piled on this cot. He sat next to it. All his disciples sat on the grass around him. Personally he picked up fistfulls of sweets and distributed them to his disciples. We were all oveorcome by a feeling of deep spiritual love that emanated from his being. Joyfully, childishly, he picked up the sweets by the handful and gave them to us. It was a divine scene of a Guru's love for his disciples. All of us, his closest disciples were present at that feast.

I was overcome. Suddenly, a shock transfixed my being. I had a strong premonition. This was the Last Supper. This was the last supper of our Christ-like being- our Buddhic sage.

I was suddenly overcome with unease. As we left for our rooms I confided my feelings to Lidder. He was disturbed.

"Don't say that", he said.

Some how, I had a strong feeling that I was seeing Baba for the last time.

In the earliest phase, he used to admonish me to talk little and meditate more. It had become a habit. In my annual retreats I tried to stay as much in solitude as possible. In my last visit, he had called me once when I was sitting alone. I remember feeling hesitant - I just wanted to be alone, and to savour the peace and happiness that radiated in the Ashram. Talking would dissipate that euphoria and the tranquility. He had sensed my hesitation, and felt a little hurt.

This time he let me savour the silence alone. I felt waves of love and ecstasy. Beautiful poetry welled up in my being. I was reading the "Madhu Brahman" section of the Brihad Aranyaka Upanishad. Suddenly, I felt a deep experience of cosmic connectivity. That Madhu- that honey, that ecstasy and love is the glue that holds together all life forms in this universe. It is only an absence of that "madhu" that causes the forms to disintegrate. I enjoyed the green peace. I soaked in the sunlight and the silence. I experienced deep peace and emotional highs.

Suddenly, I also experienced feelings of panic.

I wanted to talk to him. I desperately wanted to talk to him, and spend time with him. But he did not call me to his chambers for the customary audience. I felt vaguely uneasy and apprehensive. I kept waiting uneasily. Somewhere deep down I had had a deep premonition. This was the last time I was seeing him. He knew it too. That is why he had called us all, his closest disciples to meet him on the auspicious occasion of Diwali. We met him together in his chambers the day we were leaving. It was the last audience, and it was a collective one. The pain felt was almost physical. By the time we left, he was unwell.

I joined my unit at Kargil. A full- scale war was on. It was undeclared and found no mention in the newspapers, but each day the sky was lit up with tracers and exploding shells and mortar bombs burst in the hills angrily. I was now commanding the unit and deeply involved in the battle.

20th of March 1991, I was sitting alone in my bunker, when I suddenly felt the overwhelming sweetness of Baba's presence in the bunker. I almost sat up in my bed. My eyes filled up with tears. Love and deep affection welled up in my heart. I almost reached out and called out aloud "Baba". The deep experience vanished, and for a long time I was left with an impression of indescribable peace and joy. The peace lasted right through the morning and the better part of the next day.

In the evening, I received the message by phone. Baba had passed away. He had gone into his chamber to meditate. He had called Shivaji and told him that he would be no more, after a few hours. He asked him not to cry or weep as it would make his going difficult. But the time had come. He descended into the meditation chamber. He had very deliberately willed himself to death in the classical way. He had left his mortal coil on his own will and volition.

I burst into heart-rending sobs. The whole universe dissolved in pain. I was left with a haunting feeling of deep anguish and great personal loss. "Please I want to talk with you just once. Just one more time". I wept till I looked terrible. I could not even ask for leave to go for his funeral. There was a war on. Shells were crashing and men were dying. I was denied even a last vision. Silently he had prepared me for the parting. He had told me to do without physical communication and rely upon a mode of contact that would possibly last from life to life. Such a contact only comes from the purity of love and deep compassion- the love that is Madhu- the Honey- the glue that binds together all forms in the universe. The love that helps us to recognise the locales of our earlier lives and our loved ones even when we see them in different forms in a different life.

I cried because I wanted to cry. In the end they had crucified him. The very people he loved and did so much for. Deeply hurt by the rumors and baseless inuendoes he decided to depart at the time of his own choosing. He met all those he loved. He blessed all his disciples. Then, calmly he called his most faithful disciple Shivaji and told him that he was going to enter into Samadhi, that he would not come out. Shivaji began to weep.

"Do not cry. Please do not make my going more difficult. The time has come for me to depart. My work is done", he said.

He calmly entered into the meditation chamber.

A few hours later, his Atman had shed its coil. The vesture, the lifeless remains, were left behind. With an amazing thoroughness, he had carefully planned every detail of his life and his death. He had left behind instructions for his funeral and the mangement of the Ashram after his departure.

Diffidently, I informed my Brigade Commander of my deep loss.

He was confused and a little hesitant, worried that I would ask for leave in the midst of battle. I could not. There was a shooting war on. "I just wanted you to know", I said and put the phone down sadly. Then I buried my head in my hands and wept for hours till my eyes grew numb.

Many, many months later, I went back to the Ashram at Kalimath. In the Darshan hut they had installed a marble statue of Baba. The likeness was so remarkable that I could not help sobbing uncontrollably. I had been denied even the last Darshan. But that was the way he had wanted it to be. He left me with the most pleasant memories of the Guru feeding his disciples with his own hands, in a Christ-like gesture. The Last Supper was the most enduring image.

I went to Patne to the Devi temple. I sat for hours in the now deserted Forest Ashrama. I walked up to the Pitangalya Caves. Each turn of the path was replete with thousands of memories. Had we experienced it all?

"Sweet Auburn, parent of the blissful hour.
Thy glades forlorn confess the tyrant's power
where many a year elapsed
have returned to view
once where the cottage stood
the Hawthorn grew
Remembereance with all her
busy train
swells at my breast
and turns the Past to pain".

Today, many years later, I am again at the site of the deserted Forest Ashram. The huts are broken. A few years hence there will be no trace left of the goodness that we had seen. Yes, the huts of the Second Ashram are still extant. The Forest department has converted one of them to a plant nursery. The locals had prevented them from using the sage's living quarters. They have been left as the only shrine to his memory and of his days in the forest. At the Chalisgaon station there is a painting of the Kalimath temple and Ashram. The temple itself is beautiful and a place of pilgrimage. But the crowds, the throngs have gone. A sign board says it all—"Kalimandir". The appelation of the "Math" is gone. Peace prevades once more. And I can feel his presence. "Please talk to me - one last time" I sometimes find myself whispering in my agony. "Are you listening?" Silence is the only answer. The deep silence of the void-of the Suchness of things. Many years ago we had learnt to hold dialogues with the Void. Today he is a part of that self-same void and I am left longing, yearning for a dialogue again, with my beloved master.

Shiva : Caretaker of
Kali Temple

Sadhus and Sanyasis of all shades and orders, congregate at these vast concourses, to preach their doctrines and share their spiritual experiences. The disciples seek out their gurus. The gurus search in turn, for worthy disciples to teach . The vast multitudes that congregate upon these bathing ghats in their millions come with pious thoughts. This civilisational outpouring constitutes another psychological Ganga of the spirit that renews our tiered consciousness and uplifts us. It is a cyclic ritual of renewal and regeneration. Sushanta participated in this ritual of renaissance. The Purna Kumbha Mela of 1966 was a land mark spiritual event in his life. He joyously immersed himself in the surging sea of pious humanity. The cries of Har ! Har ! Gange ! rent the air. He sat on the sandy embankments of this great Indian river and meditated. The Ganga represents the perenial, the eternal stream of the Hindu Consciousness. The Ganga is the soul of the Hindu civilisation and embodies in its flow its immortal spirit of enquiry and spiritual striving. He met a number of Sadhus and Sanyasis. They looked upon him and smiled – as if he was one of their own already. They encouraged him to live the eternal life, to escape from the fetters and bondage of a worldly existence and seek the liberation of a total renunciation. It would come on its own – in its own good time. This Purna Kumbha Mela of 1966 left an indelible stamp upon his consciousness. He realised the ancient method of the Indian sages who had striven to preserve our civilisational heritage and our innate sense of unity as a people through these cyclic rituals of renewal and the celebration of life per se. most of our Hindu festivals are plugged in to the rythms of the seasonal cycle. These are rooted in the relics of our past as a great agricultural civilisation. Each year, the festivals of spring mean the renewal of hope. There are festivals for sowing and harvesting. There is the festival that marks the end of the rains, and the onset of clear skies that are studded with stars.

Festivals and celebrations of life constitute the primal techniques of mass mobilisation in this ancient civilisation. The Kumbha and the Ardha Kumbha were such deliberate cultural events that had been set in motion to keep the faith alive and vibrant. These celebrations, set millions upon millions upon the move- from the North and South and the East and West of this subcontinent. These wove the fabric of our civilisational and cultural unity even in the midst of a striking and bewildering diversity. The Kumbha concourse, thus forms a seminal land mark event in his life. He had made it a point to attend all the Ardha kumbha and Purna kumbha melas that occurred in his life time. The Kumbha symbolism is deeply mystical. It signifies the pot of nectar that emerged from the churning of the ocean of Samsara by the Gods and the Titans. The nectar in the Kumbha signifies our immortality. Both the Gods and the Titans battled for it. One legend has that one of the Gods (Jayanta) assumed the form of a rook and stole it. He flew for 12 days from place to place. Drops of Nectar fell at Prayag, Hardwar, Nasik and Ujaini and sanctified these places with immortality. Millions of Hindus converge at these sites for the vast concourses of the melas of the Ardha Kumbha and the Purna Kumbha (at Prayag). In fact the movement of these pious millions is a reaffirmation of the living vibrancy of the Hindu faith and its power to move masses of men (if not mountains). It is a very ancient tradition. The Chinese traveller Hiuen Tsang, recorded his impressions of the Kumbha Mela in the time of Harshavardhan, as far back as the Seventh Century AD. He wrote of the congregation of almost half a million people on the Banks of the Prayag. It was in the Ninth Century that the Great Adi Shankracharya, gave the present form to this massive concourse of the Hindu civilisation. He had established the four well known monastries in the four cardinal directions of the Indian subcontinent (Jyotir math in the North, Sringeri math in the South, Goverdhan math

Sushanta came back home. A deep silence seemed to have engulfed him. He felt himself in touch with the collective unconscious of the Hindu race. He wanted to live and breathe its traditions and myths. Then tragedy befell. In 1963 Baro Ma fell sick and was soon on her death bed. Sushanta was distraught. This was the deepest emotional attachment of his lonely life. She was the well spring and embodiment of all love and affection. She was deeply concerned about him.

Tradition decrees that before renouncing the world, a Sanyasin is required to take the permission of only two people- his mother (if he is unmarried) and his wife, if he is a house holder. If they withhold permission, the way of renunciation is barred. It is only with their willing consent that success can be achieved in Sanyasa. When he realised that Baro Ma was about to pass away from this earth, he went to her alone as she lay on her deathbed. Even in her last days there was a kind of a spiritual glow and radiance that emanated from her being. She looked up at him with deep concern and love as he sat besides her and held her hand. He hesitated.

"Baro Ma, Ever since I grew old enough to understand things - I have felt this deep seated inner conviction and urge. I have to take Sanyasa - I have to renounce life. That is my destiny. Your permission and blessings are essential for this". He breathed deeply. "Will you please give me the permission to renounce life after you are gone?" He held his breath for what seemed an eternity.

The stately old lady said nothing. Only tears rolled down her cheeks. Sushanta felt terribly distressed.

But she smiled through her tears.

" I had always known it son. I knew it was your destiny. That is why I took so much care to ensure that you would never stray from the path of moral purtiy", She looked at him with deep affection. "You have my permission son. May the Devi bless you with success in this noble endeavour". She closed her eyes. On her face was an expression of indescribeable peace and tranquility. Sushanta squeezed her hand gently. A few days later she passed away. With her went the last bonds that tied him to the worldly life. Before going however, she had said to him "Sanyasa, my son is not an escape from life. It is not the refuge of the weak. It is for the conqueror. It is for the hero. Before you renounce, you must prove that you have mastered this life. It is not that one has been driven by defeat and despair to flee into an escape. It is that one has achieved and having achieved, renounced it all as a token of his mastery. You must prove that to the world before you renounce this life."

He had heard her with rapt attention. Then solomenly he had nodded and touched her feet.

"It will be as you wish mother".

He completed his engineering studies in 1963 with flying colours. At the campus interviews itself he was picked up by a multinational company. Jessops and Company were good employers. They liked this sincere and diligent young man and he rapidly moved up in the hierarchy. He had a good academic career and now he had an excellent and well paying job. He travelled a lot. Once each year he would go to this favourite pilgrimage spot at Badrinath- the ancient Dham- one of the most sacred shrines of Hinduism. He kept a track of the major Hindu festivals. He visited the Aradha Kumbhas and then he was even able to attend a Purna Kumbha Mela in 1966. The Kumbha Mela is one of the unique Institutions of Hinduism. Every 12 years it seeks to bring together a mighty conclave of the pious and the faithful to the banks of the sacred rivers of India. Millions upon millions bear down to the banks of the Ganga, to renew themselves spiritually in the stream of the eternal Hindu consciousness.

19

Dialogues with the Sea

Testing the Connectivity

The year 1966 was drawing to a close. One day, his father sent for Sushanta. He entered his study to find him bent over his table. It was covered with sheets of paper. He had been casting a horoscope. His mathematical calculations and charts were scrawled all over the pages. He was poring over the charts - his brows knit in deep thought.

"Yes, father?" Sushanta said gently to announce his presence.

The elder Brahmin whirled around "Ah there you are" he looked at his son fondly. How he had grown. How the years had passed. How much of his mother he had in his visage. His eyes misted over.

But there was work at hand. He cleared his throat and took one final look at the charts in front of him.

"Sushanta, are you dissatisfied with your job? Are you contemplating a change?"

"No Baba, but why do you ask?"

"I don't know. I have been going over your natal chart. It speaks of a change- a major change in the direction of your life. And the time is almost upon us. That is why I asked."

Sushanta was awed by the accuracy of the man's mathematical predictions. He was also afraid that his face may betray his deeply hidden intention of seeking renunciation.

"Do you want a change of job?"

"Not really - not for just now at least".

His father gazed at his face quizzicaly. "Curious that the stars should say so. "Are you happy? Are you well?"

"Yes, Baba"

"Oh", he seemed to be at a loss for words. Somehow there were deep barriers of silence between him and his son. Like his mother, he was so quiet and uncommunicative. But, his eyes said it all.

For some reason the elder Mukerjee was troubled by the way Sushanta averted his gaze, "Very well then. I thought, I must ask".

The audience was at an end.

Sushanta was sleeping regularly on the floor now. This audience with his father reminded him how close at hand was the time of ultimate reckoning. Did he really believe in his destiny? Did he really have the will, the nerve to just walk out one day and never, never give a backward glance? And what lay ahead? What was the future, to be? He thought of his youngest uncle, Surendra. "Madness? Death? "He shivered. Surendra's fault had been that he did not trust the void. Did Sushanta? He used to be deeply troubled. He would take long walks sometimes on the shores of the sea. Sometimes along the banks of the Green-brown Ganga Sometimes he would take long walks, late in the nights, when the streets were empty and bare, when the crowds had gone and the street lamps cast lonely pools of light in the sadness of the dark. He often thought of Baro Ma. He thought of the serenity on her face, and then the tears in her eyes. He looked at the decaying ancestral Mansion. Decay! That was the first thought that came to him - the first gestalt- the chief impression that he had whenever he looked at his ancestral house.

in the East and Sharda math in the West.). The great Shankracharya thought in civilisational terms. Hence the establishment of these four cardinal monastries and their manning by saints from the other parts of the country. He divided the Sadhus and Sanyasis into 10 orders (Dashnamis- Saraswati, Puri, Bano, Tirtha, Giri, Parvata, Bharti, Aranya, Ashram and Sagara). These orders were exhorted to assemble regularly at the Kumbha Melas with the two fold purpose of maintaning contact with the sadhus of the other dominations, and fortifying the faith of the lay aspirants. The Kumbha is therefore, a great living tradition of the Hindu civilisation and Sushanta was greatly moved by its power and piety. The Kumbha Mela over he returned home. But the images of the pious and surging masses of humanity and the bearded faces of the Seers and Sanyasis continued to haunt his dreams for months afterwards.

And even while he lived in this world and progressed materially he was all the time deeply conscious of his resolve and firm commitment to the ideal of Sanyasa. He never, for an instant forgot his destiny. He never had any doubt - it was a calm certainty.

He had kept his intention a close secret. Only Baro Ma had known about it, and now she was gone. In his ancestral home, in his well furnished room with a huge mehagony bed and soft mattresses, he used to lock the door and then quietly sleep on the floor. He was toughening himself. Preparing himself for the austere life of renunciation. He was strengthening himself to face upto hardship. At the dinner table he would deliberately eat very little, so that he would accustom himself to the pangs of hunger. So that he would not be overcome- like his uncle Surendra had been, and return home, a picture of abject defeat and betrayal.

He clearly remembered the last words of Baro Ma "Seek perfection in all that you do; Perfection in all your actions.

Never settle for anything that is less than perfect". He had nodded silently. He was a last of the "Mohicans", the last of the Mukerjee clan. Perfection would not just be his perennial quest but his spiritual emblem in later life. His entire life and works, represented this perennial and never ending quest for excellence.

before. That was all he had that day. Some days passed. He was lost in the rush of work. He was working to discharge all his worldly responsibilities now. To pay off his debts. To write all the unwritten letters. To meet the people he had said he would meet, and in the process the certitude seemed to desert him once more. In the busy bustle of life in Calcutta, how remote and far away a life of renunciation seemed. How distant and unreal. Was he sure the coconut could be nothing but a mere coincidence? A pure accident. Was he reading too much meaning into unrelated cues? Was he looking for meaning where none, in fact, existed? This was too simple a test. He had to make very sure. The sheer enormity of the step itself frightened him. It often gave him cold feet. He had a comfortable home, a secure job. Renunciation in this day and age? Would they not call him a drop out? Failure? One who had fled from his responsibilities? Responsibilities!

It was the year 1967. In the Calcutta office he was now the number four in the hierarchy, just promoted from the junior-most rungs of managerial trainees. The two men above him were middle-aged and miles his senior. The boss of the office was an irascible old man, and a hard task master. One day Sushanta was sitting in the Dakshineshwar temple. The doubts had resurfaced. Was he reading too much into a simple coincidence? To make very sure, he must set the void an impossible task. One that could not be fulfilled by a mere accident or happpenstance. A test that would give him a positive and certain indication. He thought long and hard. "Before I go, I want to be the head of this office" - he said to himself. 'So make me.' This was infact impossible. No mere accident could cause it. Only a military coup. He smiled as he thought of his hard driving boss – a typical and a traditional authoritarian. The Jessops, however, were a construction company, not a military organisation. There was simply no scope for such a coup. "This was a difficult test" he smiled grimly to the diety."Give me a sign, O Cosmic mother, If that indeed is my destiny - give me a clear and unmistakable sign through this test. Make me - if you can - the head of this office before I leave".

Sushanta Mukerjee was just 26.

A few days later, a strange series of happenings took place at the Jessops firms branch office in Calcutta. Sushants irate and irascible boss, was denied his next promotion. In a fit of pique, the old man put in his resignation. Not for a day, not a single day, would he serve under his juniors. The company accepted his resignation. The decision had been anticipated. What had not been foreseen was the violent personality clash that look place between the number two and three. There was some confusion about their inter se seniority. They belonged to different branches and simply could not see eye to eye with one another. The number two was appointed the officiating boss. Promptly the number three put in his resignation. This was more than the management had bargained for. They were at their wit's end. The new boss was being posted in from another city and he could not come for a few months still. A representative of the Management came over to resolve the tussle and smoothen the ruffled feathers. He hit upon an original idea. Young Sushanta Mukerjee, the number four would officiate in a purely symbolic manner. He would sign the papers and be the nominal head till the inter se seniority between his superiors could be sorted out.

Sushanta was so junior and such an amiable person, that number two and three readily agreed to this arrangement as a temporary, face-saving formula. Sushanta was truly astonished to find himself officiating as the head of the Jessops branch office at 26 years. He shivered slightly when he got the news. With this episode, his mind was well and truly made up. He felt elated and happy. It was not a void that he had been talking to. It was a warm and comforting

Had he died already to this life? Was he just clinging to the empty shell like a spirit - like a ghost haunting a derelict and decaying mansion? His path lay elsewhere. His destiny was different. It was beckoning now with an urgency that was intense and overwhelming. And yet when we come to the actual point of decision we are overcome with so many doubts and nagging thoughts of confusion. Are you sure that is what you want? Was that right? Was that really his destiny? Or was that just a childish impulse? That vision - was it just a figment of his imagination?

The sheer overwhelming reality of it all. It lingered with him to this day. Could it be really untrue?

"Sushanta, your food is getting cold".

At the dinner table he was remote and far, far away. That was the way he used to be those days. Pensive, indrawn, lost in deep thought. Struggling with a resolution. Wrestling with a decision. Teetering on the threshold. Peering into the brink, suddenly afraid of himself and his intention.

He remembered those dismal scenes. His youngest uncle being brought back home, a wreck, emaciated, hungry and with that desperate, hunted look in his eyes. Betrayed by the void. Led to madness by voices he chose to trust.

And yet, when he had gone to the Kumbha mela, he had met those sadhus and bearded sages. They had accosted him lovingly as one of their own. He felt happy in their company. His destiny lay there with them. He felt so sure in Haridwar, in Badrinath, in any of the confluences of the streams with such musical and feminine names - the Alaknanda, the Mandakini, the Bhagirathi. Their waters flowed with such certainity. With such focus and longing towards a predetermined goal - the Sea. Did they ever, for a moment entertain even the shadow of a doubt? The destiny of the rivers lies in the Sea. They make their own way. They cut their own gorges, they fashion their own flood plains, and in their deltas they seek their final deliverance.

One day, he went to the sea shore. It was near sunset. The vast expanse of the sea stretched away till the horizon. The waves rose and fell. He sat on the shore. The wind flew through his silken mop of hair. He looked up at the Blue void of the sky. "Are you there?" he whispered to himself. "Will you protect me?" Sometimes, he felt like a Parachutist who is framed in the doorway of an aeroplane, a few thousand feet up in the sky-waiting tensely to jump. He jumps on one simple faith - that his parachute will open. That it will blossom like a white orchid and gently sway him down with the breeze, like cotton seed. But, what if it does not open? Would he become a "Roman candle"? Would he crash to the ground like a rock, and be smashed to smithreens on the hard and unrelenting surface of reality? He got up in great agitation. "Are you there?", he looked up at the sky once again. "Will you take care of me - O Cosmic mother?" Or will you forsake me? He started walking towards the sea into the raging waters.

Suddenly, deep within him, everything felt very silent. He did not hear the tumult of the sea any more. He did not hear the breakers crashing upon the shore. He did not see the boiling, frothing foam as it swept past his feet and back, sucking away the grains of sand. He heard himself asking from a great distance. "Give me a sign. Tell me you are there". For some strange reason, he articulated silently a prayer. "Give me a sign. If you will take care of me - Give me- give me a coconut just now". He looked up at the emptiness of the blue sky. He was standing knee deep in the sea waters. He felt something coarse and wet and round. He looked down with a start. It was a coconut that had been washed ashore.

Reverently, he had picked up the coconut and brought it home. He felt a great feeling of peace and calm confidence. A quiet happiness deep within himself. He ate the milk white flesh of the fruit. It tasted like nothing he had ever eaten the earth, the Sun, and the infinities of space. Vedic Metaphysics recognises only two primal forces- the forces of Soma- that attract, cohere, bring together and gravitate. They are the *Sneha tattwa* of the cosmos. And the forces of Agni. These are the forces of entropy, that burn, tear apart, rend asunder and spread out all that there is.

At long last Sushantas doubts were laid to rest. The "vikshepa" the tossing of the mind ceased to torment him. He had come to a noble and pious resolve: to live up to his destiny. He would be a Sanyasi – a recluse and a hermit. In the post-modern age, he would proclaim, by his living example, the validity of the ancient Indian tradition and the classical way of life. He would be an exemplar. He would strive for utmost perfection. He would strive to live the divine life. His actions would speak far louder than his words. He was all set now to prepare himself for the life of the recluse.

And as the Rig Veda proclaims so clearly- every pious resolve is met by an outflow of that euphoric stream of encouragement from within. It wells up in our being. It overcomes our fears and doubts. It fills our life with positivity, hope and optimism. It dispels the dark clouds of fear, foreboding and gloom. We learn to trust. We set aside our reason and open ourselves to the promptings of new, trans-human faculties that usually lie dormant in most men. Faculties that take us beyond the time warp- of the past, the present and the future. Faculties that take us beyond the eternal experience of entropy, to the underlying universal sources of creative order, organisation and bliss. We sink inwards to the levels of the implicate order, we encounter the wholeness of the cosmos-its underlying order, harmony and joy. It is not a mere conjecture. It is an experience of life itself. Beyond the realm of entropy, we encounter a higher ecology, far higher than the confines of this earth - it stretches into eternity, and ineffable ecstasy - it comes from the experience of the Madhu Brahman- the Honey of the ultimate integral experience of cosmic connectivity.

The remarkable experiences of the strange synchronity of events, come in the wake of such core experiences of inner ecstasy. These in turn stem from an enlargement and deepening of the floor levels of our consciousness. That is the secret of meditation. Sushanta felt euphoric and happy. He had now placed complete trust in the void. Meticulously, thought-fully, he now went about his life - methodically closing this chapter, recounting all left over obligations and promises; freeing himself of all lingering karmic debts; the promised visit, the promised call, the last letter, were all carefully carried out. He was leaving and like all things in his life he wanted his going to be as perfect.

19th of August 1967. He completed all his work in his office and then asked for long leave to visit his "friend". He handed over charge, took one last look around his office and then left for ever—there wasn't a single paper pending on his desk. This thoroughness and ceaseless quest for perfection was the hallmark of all that he did in life.

He came back home, carrying that atmosphere of peace and euphoria with him, like a personalised cloud of joy - an aura of bliss. He moved about as if in a dream. He walked through every room of the ancient ancestral house, with its overpowering sense of entropy and decay. In the evening he went to his room. All he took was a painting of the Mahakali, in her blue, four armed form. This had been his surrogate mother. From Baro Ma he had taken the permission. There was no need to ask anyone else. The scriptures sanctioned that path. He left behind a small note.

"I am going to meet a friend".

"I did not tell a lie", he told me. "Isn't God our greatest friend- our dearest companion? I had left home to meet - the eternal Sakha- the eternal friend, witness and companion", he said innocently.

presence- it lived within you and it lived without. It knew your innermost thoughts and needs and wants. It was everywhere - most near and most far. It was connected at once, with all points of the Cosmos. It was a web of connectivity. It plugged in your desires to the sources of their fulfillment, but only and only if you placed implicit trust in its innate goodness. *Only if you relinquished your own obtrusive little ego- your island of separateness from the sea of infinity. The infinity of consciousness in which we all live for ever, only then did it come forth to nurture, to protect, to feed and clothe and guide, as the eternal companion* – the one, at once most near and most far.

He undertook his last pilgrimage as a lay person in Oct 1966. It was late in the season. A winter chill had set in the air. People advised him against venturing to the mountain shrine so late in the season. But he want all the same. It was a beautiful experience – so serene, sublime and divine. Blissful hymns coursed through his being. With each step that he took upon the way, he became more certain that he had taken the right decision. It had begun to snow at Joshimath. The shops were closed and shuttered. Yet, he felt no apprehension. It was as if he was part of a beautiful dream of perfection. A pious lady saw him and asked him home. The old couple covered him with blankets as he lay shivering in the night. The next day he had a beautiful darshan at the Badrinath Shrine. The tall, gaunt peaks of Nar and Narayan loomed into the glorious blue sky. The clouds had cleared up – the Sun shone through in a euphoric stream of light and bliss and benediction. He met the Sadhus. They took one look at his rapture suffused face and embraced him as one of their own. They seemed to sense intuitively what was going on within him. They did not say a word, but the happiness in their eyes, endorsed his decision.

20
Dialogues on the Ganga

A verse from the Rig Veda says "Soma flows towards all virtuous thoughts and blesses them with bliss. It becomes the soul force of all righteous thoughts and actions". (Rig Veda 9.6.8)

All righteous resolves and actions attract the flow of that Soma of bliss, along the numberless channels of cosmic connectivity; the channells that tie us to the web of cosmic life. *Every yearning finds an echo in eternity. Every anguished cry for redemption, comes back to us, charged from the sources of eternal ecstasy and happiness.*

Whenever we make a pious resolve and then act upon it with conviction, we seem to plug into those streams of cosmic consciousness that underlie, the visible universe. In this entropic, decaying universe there is a core of aliveness, order and creativity that is eternal. That for ever renews our spirits and refashions the order and harmony, we have lost in struggles for survival against the forces of entropy. These indeed are the two mega trends of the cosmos. The trend towards entropy, disorder and dissolution. And the equally evident trend towards wholeness, order and integration. This order manifests from the underlying substratum of cosmic creativity, that expresses itself as ecstasy, as opposed to the entropic forces of death and dissolution. Ecstasy celebrates the eternal life and is its chief leitmotif. The Madhu Brahman, is the expression of the underlying sweetness and ecstasy of

Psychotropic plants engender a new order of reality. LSD radically restructures our perception "We see sounds and hear colours". These are chemical routes to restructuring our perception of reality. These are dangerous and revolutionary routes that can do severe damage to our biological apparatus. At the very least, they can leave us hopeless addicts of these psychotropic chemicals that insidiously destroy our bodies and brains and even damage our psychic structures.

The Rig Vedic Route to a Separate Reality

More than 5000 years ago, the Indian civilisation had stumbled upon a deep secret. The ancient Rig Vedic seers and the Atharvans, the sages of the forest had stumbled upon the secret of altering our perception of time; and thereby unlearning our consensus reality. They had learnt to decondition our minds of the consensus realtiy that is imposed upon us from birth. It is structured into our linear-sequential perception of time. If we can subtly alter our perception of time - we can alter our reality, we can experience different and higher orders of reality than are known to our every-day experience. What is the benefit or utilitarain spin off of experiencing this separate realtiy? The experience engenders an ineffable ecstasy. It entrains an experience of deep happiness and joy (Ananda)-the highest tacticle rewards known to man that surpasses the orgiastic rewards of reproductive activity. What was the secret by which we can alter our perception of time? It was simple, said the seers. Focus on the bio-resonater of your own breathing. Hear the sameness of the sound. One breath is no different from another. Breathing is not divided into a yesterday, today and tomorrow. There lies the secret to unlock a great wealth of happiness.

What is the aim of life? What do men strive for? They seek happiness and shun sorrow and pain. The altered experience of time brings great happiness, tranquiltiy and joy. It also brings a deeper understanding of Reality. It expands the boundaries of our everday conciousness. That is why, this core experience of a super orgiastic bliss, was defined as Sat-Chit-Ananda (Reality-Conciousness-Ecstasy). In utilitarian terms however, its greatest spinoff, was in the way it radically enhanced human creativity. Time perception and creativity are both localised in the frontal lobe of the human brain (in the region above the eyebrows). An alteration of our time perception, entrains a response of astonishing creativity and connectivity.

The Rig Vedic and Atharvanic Indian civilisation was a First Wave or Agricultural Civilisation. Its general pace was serene and tranquil. Pastoral life was slow paced and not as stressful as our fast paced, frantic and frenzied Industrial reality of today. Life in the ancient agricultural civilisations of India and China was "Green" and eco-friendly. Yet, even in those ancient times, there were seers and sages who felt it was not "green" enough.

So, they retired to the forests to live a "greener" and more ecological existence in harmony with the Gaia. Their main task was to decondition their minds, of the linear and sequential modes of the perception of time. By their tranquil and meditative life style, they slowly unlearnt their classical view of time. They slipped into niches of, "timelessness and tranquiltiy". They left behind the fast and furious pace, the hurry and bustle of civilisation, and slowly slipped into moods of great inner peace, tranquility and harmony. Over a period of years, they unlearnt the consensus reality and the imposed mode of perceiving time. From a linear-sequential (left-brain-lobe-ordered) perception of time, they transisted to a more ecological experience of time that was Right-Brain- lobe-ordered, that was hooked on to the harmonious rhythms of nature-to the cycles of dawn, midday and dusk. There was little to distinguish one day from the next. Each day became a joyous exercise in the experience of the ecstasy that lies at the basis of all life in nature. The trees and plants and flowers spread their leaves and petals to the invisible rain of sunshine and soak in the ecstasy of life. They turn it into sap and grow gradually towards the light and a quiet happiness. The plants convert light to life. We humans are required to convert life to love and compassion.

Flexi Time: The Electronic Civilisation has started recognising the stress imposed by our linear sequential views of time. We are, for ever, rushing through the rush hours and traffic jams, frantically trying to beat deadlines. All we get for our frenzied pace, are ill health and ulcers. The Electronic civilisation that is replacing the old Industrial civilisation, is now recognising the home as a work place once more. Where is the need to commute through early morning traffic jams and rush hours, when we can tele commute? Concepts of flexi-time are slowly coming in. The home is becoming a work place once more. The normal, linear-sequential view of time, is an enemy of the creative process. The ancient Rig Vedic seers and the Atharvans had understood this process 5000 years ago. Hence their decision to retire to tranquil forest retreats. Hence, their adoption of peaceful life styles that DECONDITIONED their minds, of the linear-sequential modes of the perception of time. An alteration of their time perception modes, opened their minds to radically different experience of a "Unified Reality". A reality in which everything was connected to everything else in the Universe. The experience of this supreme connectivity, engendered great happiness and ecstasy. It overcame the psychological dread of isolation and loneliness. Above all, it made the sages supremely creative. From the harvest of silence, the world obtained the wisdom of the Vedas, the Upanishads, the Brahmans, the Aranyaks, the Ramayana, the Mahabharata, the Gita and the Puranas. All of them were composed in forest retreats, where a pristine poetry enshrined them in meters and rhythms and rhymes that enabled their memorisation and transmission from generation to generation. The Rig Vedic and Atharvanic civilisation saw a tremendous flowering of the Indian genius and intellect and set the pace and tone for a forest civilisation in sharp contrast to the civilisation of the desertic regions. Its secret lay in the secret of the sameness of one breath and another.

Kala Agni The quest for the secret power of time, goes far beyond the need to simply decondition our minds of the learnt reality based upon the normal sequential mode of the perception of time. Wired in the frontal lobes of our brains, is a deep secret. It is a reservoir of a strange binding energy—the creative energy of time. Neurophysiologically, this brain region is concurrently the seat of our creativity and time perception. The process of meditation entrains a strange alchemy in this region. The dormant, "energy of time", is some how kinetised and activated. This energy of time seems to bind our beings together as it were. Let me explain. Biological organisms are like whirl pools (or vortices) in a river of space-time. The water in them keeps flowing ceaselessly. It is ever-changing. However, the form of the whirl pool nevertheless, remains a constant. So also, every minute, the molecules in our biological organisms, are changing continually. The matter in our biological beings, is in a constant flux or change. Yet, our biological forms remain constant (even as the form of a whirl pool remains constant). It is the energy, the fire of time (the Kala-Agni) which seems to bind, or freeze the flow of form, into a state of constancy. When the Kala Agni or the energy of time is kinetised, it is forced to change its direction of flow. The normal direction of its flow is from the past, to the present and into an unknowable future. This is reversed. The arrow of time is dramatically reversed. Something strange happens in the biologic and energic components of our being. The biological organism is now no longer pushed by the precedents of the past. It is no longer a prisoner of the digital bits of information encoded in its genes. The probabilities lurking in the future, push back quantum mechanically, to guide the unfoldment of our biological forms in the present. The organism becomes a prophetic life form. It is no longer driven by the past. It is now pulled by its own future. The reversal of the arrow of time, creates a silent revolution in our psyches. Nature wants us to consciously seek and initiate this process of evolution. It rewards our efforts with the gifts of ecstasy. The ecstasy of Soma descends on our beings, once the flow of time is reversed. Not only do we become prophetic life forms that are focused on the future probabilities and potential, we became recepients of the gifts of ecstasy, the remarkable inflow of order and coherence, that comes in the form of an eruption of Enkephalins and Endorphins in our brains. The Kala Agni—the Fire of time rises and the Soma (with its train of ecstasy) descends.

The Atharvan masters who composed the most marvellous poetry of the Vedas were the seers who had unravelled the secrets of time. The Vedas speak of the "Kala Agni"- the Fire or the Energy of Time. The Kala Agni rises- the Kundalini is kinetised and the Soma descends in streams of truth and ecstasy. The rise of the Kala Agni- the reversal of the arrow of time, entrains the experience of the Ritasyadharas (the streams of truth) and the Madhudharas (the streams of Honey). What the Atharvanic seers and Angirases were trying to verbalises was the transcendental experience that lay beyond Time. It was the experience of the ecstasy of Soma- the sparkling experience of cosmic connectivity, the sparkling of the endorphins and enkephalins in the spaces between our neurons. Nirvana was an experience of the ecstasy of our enkephalins. The most marvellous and mystic poetry in the world is dedicated to Soma- the experience of that beautitude. The Kala Agni rises, the Soma comes down; it descends in waves of bliss like an eternal river of happiness, like streams of Honey and Truth. That harvest of immortal Vedic poetry, in fact, represents the first flowering of the genius of the ancient Indian civilisation.

The Second Flowering : The Way of the Buddha

The second flowering of the genius of the ancient Indian civilisation was witnessed in the times of the Buddha. Pastoral village life had given way to sophisticated city states. The arts and sciences had flourished. So had trade and commerce and merchants had become rich and opulent. Ships carried merchandise to and from distant shores. The city states became centres of capital accumulation. Ware houses overflowed with goods. People drank in gambling houses. Courtesans danced in the palaces and Assembly Halls of Vaishali and Kampil and other city states. Ajatashatru raised sophisticated armies comprising horses, chariots, elephant corps and foot soldiers. The armies laid waste the countryside. The Lichhavis, struggled to maintain their independence. Stress multiplied as the ancient Indian civilisation grew increasingly sophisticated and complex. Armies of artisans laboured to build magnificent palaces, and chariot shaped temples. The pace of life grew maniflod in the cities and metropolises. In such sophisticated times, was the Buddha born. Once again he offered an alternative lifestyle, that offered a retreat from the onrushing, linear view of time. He created monastries and viharas where the saffron robed Buddhist monks retired from city life, into caves and forest retreats, to lead peaceful, contemplative and meditative life styles. The Gates of Eternal peace and tranquility were opened to them in these forest retreats. Quietly, over the months and years, the monks slipped into meditative states that transformed their perception of time from a linear to a cyclic mode; from a grossly materialistic to a spiritual orientation. The secret lay in recognising the sameness of one breath and the other. Mindfullness of one's breathing was a basic meditative technique of Buddhism.

The enlightened one, departed from this earth. His message was taken up by emperor Ashoka and an army of saffron-robed monks who spread to every nook and corner of this subcontinent and then all over East, South East and Central Asia, in the world's first attempt at globalisation. China, Japan, Tibet, Mongolia, Combodia, Thailand, Siam, Java, Sumatra, Bali, Boroneo, Burma and Cylone, all came under the sway of the Buddhist ideology from India.

The Buddha offered a way out of the ills of materialism and consumerism of those times by offering alternative life styles of contemplation and meditation. If the aim of life is to seek happiness and overcome sorrow and suffering, the Buddha taught an alternate life style to his monks and nuns and Bhikshus. The Sangha, enabled the adoption of meditative lifestyles-that deconditioned the minds of the monks. From a linear-sequential perception of time, they slipped gently into a CYCLIC perception of time, based on ecological lifestyles, in perfect harmony with nature. This flexing of the concepts of linear time, unleashed incredible creativity. The Rock edicts and cave temples, the chaityas and viharas and stupas; the exquisite and sensuous sculptures of the Gandhara school of Art, the delicate and faded frescoes of Ajanta and Pitangalya bear mute testimony to this tremendous upsurge of creativity in ancient India that occurred six centuries before the birth of Chirst. The Armies of Alexander came and went. The Mauryan Empire took India to peaks of civilisational glory and passed away into the limbo of time. The Satvahanas came and went-so did the Rashtrakutas. Some works of art that they carved in the Basalt rocks and stones of the Sayhadries however, defy the ravages of time. The rock medium is sculpted into the message of those times. Creativity is inspired by altered perceptions of time and reality. Contemplative and ecological life styles offer us an alternative. We can unlearn our linear view of time with all its stress, unhappiness and pressures. We can slip into cyclic modes of time perception, if we renounce and retire to the forests, to live in harmony with nature, in step with the ecological rhythms of the earth. That is the essential difference between a materialistic and linear outlook and a cyclic and harmonious mode of life that is associated with spiritualtiy. It is not other-worldly, it engenders happiness and creativity. The Sat-chitannanda experience of the Rig Vedic and Upnishadic seers, was replaced by the Buddhistic experience of the great Void-or the Shunyata. David Bhom, in our times, has spoken to us of the "Implicate order" and "wholeness".

The Relevance of Renunciation Today : Today, the philosophy of materialism has reached an apogee in the Industrial civilisation. Never, in all mankind's history, had the pace of the passage of time become so swift, so rigidly linear and so utterly stressful. The collective sickness of the Industrial civilisation has bred the two world wars in the space of a single century. In all the bloody conflicts of the 20th century, over 96 million people were killed and over 300 million wounded or maimed. Is this not indicative of a psychological sickness? A deep-rooted malaise of materialism has drained us of our spiritual and ecological outlook. Does this mean that we have to turn our backs on the Industrial civilisation and material progress? Do we have to join Margaret Meads search for the noble savage? The modern civilisation with its holocausts of ethnic cleansing, is savage enough. What we need, is a new outlook- a new outlook that was the hall mark of the Rig Vedic,Atharvanic and Buddhist civilisations. All of them offered an alternate view of time, not linear and sequential but cyclic and harmonious. They were based, not on a left brain lobe generated linear sequential perception of mathematical and digital reality, but the right brain lobe generated cyclic outlooks that deal with patterns and form and holistic perceptions; not with digital bits and zeros and ones, but with completed Gestalten. We need to focus again, on the bio- resonaters of our breath, to realise the essential sameness of one breath and another. That alone can free us of the tyranny of time.

In our Industrial times, Swami Pranvananda Sarswati, the sage of Patne, lived a model life to demonstrate the relevance of the ideal of retreat and renunciation. A modern-day educated engineer and scholar, he retired into the forest, much as the Atharvanic and Upanishadic sages, and then the Buddhist monks had done, thousands of years ago, to live a simple and meditative life style that was characterised by its ecological outlook and cyclic view of time. Such an outlook and such an altered sense of time perception brings the experience of peace, tranquility, bliss and harmony. An ecological existence engenders the experience of ineffable ecstasy. Swami Pranvananda, taught us to focus on the secret bio rythms of our own breathing, to unleash this ecstasy.

Swami Pranvananda Saraswati, did not tell us this - he showed us, by living the lifestyle of an Atharvan sage or a Buddhist monk. He showed us the relevance of renunciation and retreat. A retreat into the forest, enables us to leave behind our exploitative, manipulative and materialistic outlooks based upon a linear, sequential and logical view of life—a view that is generated by the dominance of our left brain hemispheres. It breeds tremendous stress and unhappiness. The outlook of our Right Brain Hemispheres, however, generates views that are holistic, ecological organic and harmonious. They make us aware of the supreme connectivity of all life and existence; of the cosmic web of interconnections, that weave together this hologramic universe. The sickness of our times, stems from the fragmented and intensly separate experiences of reality and a stressful and linear view of time. The ancient Indian civilisation stressed alternative life styles that permitted the Right Brain hemispherical generated outlooks of "wholeness", to emerge naturally and simply. Meditative and contemplative life styles, usher in cyclic concepts of Flexi time that unleash creativity.

The Harmonics of History

Strange are the harmonics of history. It repeats itself in cyclic order. In 1968 Swami Pranvananda Saraswati chose for his retreat the same forest which the Buddhist monks of Pitangalya (pittalkhora)Vihara and the Chaitya Caves of Ellora had selected over 2000 years ago. In the reign of the Satvahanas, in the Second century BC, a flourishing community of Buddhist monks used to live and meditate just above Patne. Their saffron robes glinted in the Sun. The forest streams cooled their habitat. The sound of running water, had a strange and soothing effect upon the conciousness. "In a forest, in a cave, near a stream, in such a place the monks should dwell". There is no recorded history of the Atharvans, the forest sages who had composed the Atharva Veda and of their stay in these forest tracts. I have a deep conviction. There was a connection somewhere.

Some of us have been blessed enough, to live in the modern day Ashram of Pranvananda Saraswati, the sage of Patne. Baba was regarded by many as the reincarnation of Bhaskaracharya-the great mathematician sage who had left behind his immortal treatises on Mathematics, way back in the 12th century AD. Bhaskaracharyas Ashram had stood exactly where 'Baba' (Pranvananda) had built his first forest Ashram. Possibly, Baba had come back to his own incarnational haunt of the 12th century-impelled by strong karmic connections. Perhaps even earlier on; in the 2nd century BC he had been a Buddhist monk, possibly the abbot of the Vihara at Pitangalya Caves. He looked so much like a classical Buddhist monk. And even earlier than the advent of Buddhism, I am certain he had been an Atharvan- a sage of the deep forest.

We can travel through time with the help of art. The Pallava sculptors of Ellora and Patne, have left behind their message and the quintessence of their life experience in the indelible medium of Basalt rocks of the Sayhadri hills. Today, thousands of years later, we can still experience what they experienced then, through the immortality of their plastic art forms. Archeologists like Madhu Krishna Joshi, sometimes experience powerful feelings of Déjà vu when they gaze at these exquisite statues of the Dwarpalas with enormous ear rings and the voluptuous yakshis with elaborate hairdos and ornaments.

You can travel through space by various means, in rockets, planes, trains and cars. You can however travel through time in messages carved in stone or printed in a book. The treatises of the Rig Vedic and Atharvanic seers, the Upanishadic sages, the Buddhist monks and the mathematical works of Bhaskarcharya have come to us across the centuries in the form of their books. Books encode our messages so that they can survive the passage of time.We can encounter what we wrote or sculpted centuries ago, in another-incarnation and another time. When we suddenly come face to face with our own message, that we had transmitted thousands of years ago, at another point in space and time-the experience of Déjà vu can be intense and overwhelming.

To encounter a Rig Vedic, an Atharvanic or Buddhist Ashram in this day and age was, for most of us, an overwhelming experience. It brought us face to face with a time wrap. We encountered directly, the India of over 2500 years ago. We saw its ideals of renunciation and retreat personified in the being of Baba. Swami Pranvananda Saraswati's message was one of Revival-of the relevance of ancient ideals and life styles in this modern day and age.

The Indian forest civilisation stressed ecological and harmonious life styles. It offered a coutner-point to a linear sequential mode of modern reality by stressing a cyclic mode of time.

On Modernisation What is modernisation? Is modernisation concomitant with Westernisation? Do we have to lose our Indian identity in the process of Industrialisation? Do we have to shed the basic ecological outlook, and visions of supreme synthesis, that is central to the Indian Forest Civilisation? In modernising, must we adopt -the fragmented views of reality that afflict the Western world? Today, when the cultural Blitz of CNN appears poised to swamp our information channels and clothe us in ubiqitous denim jeans and standardised business suits, it is worth while to pause and ponder. The Rig Vedic seers and Buddhist monks propogated an alternative and ecological life style that promised peace, tranquility, happiness and a spontaneous upsurge of creativity. It was a model of development that was sustainable. Creativity is the key resource, that brings about the rise of great civilisations.

Swami Pranvananda Saraswati, the modern sage of Patne, lived an exemplary life of renunciation. His life itself was his message. In his Ashram, we encountered a wonderful synthesis of the ancient and the modern. He did not permit one tree to be cut. He loved the lush growth of vegetation. His Ashram huts looked like the ancient hermitages of the Vedic seers. Yet they had electricity for light. The well had an electric pump set to draw the water- a wire fencing kept out the wild animals- in short, a most harmonious synthesis of the ancient and the modern.

Why did you renounce life? People asked the sage. "To demonstrate that such a life style is still relevant in this day and age". That was his solemn reply. In pursuance of this resolve, he lived the ecological lifestyle that he was talking about. He taught us to decondition our minds of the "learnt realities", and flip into "cyclic modes of time perception". Only if you alter your perception of time, can you experience different orders of reality, and deepen and expand the field of your conciousness. That was the central theme of his life and teachings. The way to achieve this is by focussing on the bio-resonator of our own breathing. Listen to the secret that each in-going and out-going breath whispers to your being. It is all the same. There is no yesterday, today, and tomorrow in our breathing. There is only the sameness of eternity – the existentialism of a never-ending isness. The calm knowledge that there is no separation between Life and Death. Everything is consciousness. That is the key to Happiness.

Summation

The keynote of Swami Pranvananda's teachings can therefore be summed up as under :

* **Depth Ecology of Concioussness** Everything in the universe is conscious. There is no such thing as sentient or insentient, (as Jada or Chetan). The whole cosmos per se, is a vast continuum of conciousness. Conciousness therefore is the primal stuff of this universe. This gives us a kinship with the earth, the oceans, the animals, birds and plants and all living things.
* **How to Experience the Supreme Connectivity of Conciousness** The way to experience the ultimate reality of conciousness (Brahman) is to outgrow our linear, one-way view of Time. Time is a basic force that seems to bind our beings into a form and structure. To free ourselves, we must meditate upon the sound of our own breathing. In our breathing, we have a powerful bio-resonater that can help to decondition our minds of the imposed reality of a

rigidly, one-way view of linear and speeding time, that flows from the past to the present and into a future, we do not known. Meditation helps us to dramatically reverse the arrow of time.

* **Ecological Life Style** To experience the happiness or ecstasy that stems from a depth experience of our own consciousness, we need to adopt life styles that are ecological and harmonious. We need to periodically go into forest retreats. The plants give us peace. The plants convert light to life. They are in fact, the basis of life on this planet. To that end, we must preserve this environment. We must plant and protect trees.
* **Sukha-Contentment** Prolonged spells of meditation and retreat give us a feeling of peace and contentment.
* **Bliss and Euphoria** This peace blossoms into an experience of Euphoria or Bliss. These euphoric moods are great spurs to creativity.
* **Ecstasy** Extended episodes of Euphoria, lead to the onset of Ecstasy. This is an unforgettable peak experience extolled in the Vedas as the flow of Soma- or the onrush of the Ritasyadharas or Madhuharas, the experience of the streams of Truth and Honey.
* **Exteriorization of Conciousness** Spells of ecstasy, could well be the precursors to experiences of an exterorization of the conciousness, to out-of-body experiences that can lead to the phenomena of Anamolous Cognition.
* **Nirvana** The Buddhist experience of Nirvana leads to the experience of the great Shunyata or the great Void.
* This could culminate in the Brahmanical experience of Sat-Chit Annanda or Maha Samadhi, a super

nova of ecstacy that is accompanied by a great widening of consciousness in an oceanic experience of supreme joy. It entails both, ecstasy and enlargement of consciousness, and gives us that happiness which is the ultimate aim of all our striving.

Baba's Samadhi